FLYING THE WAVES

FIRST EDITION

published in 2002
by
WOODFIELD PUBLISHING
West Sussex PO21 5EL, England.
website: www.woodfieldpublishing.com
email: info@woodfieldpublishing.com

ISBN 1 903953-09-X

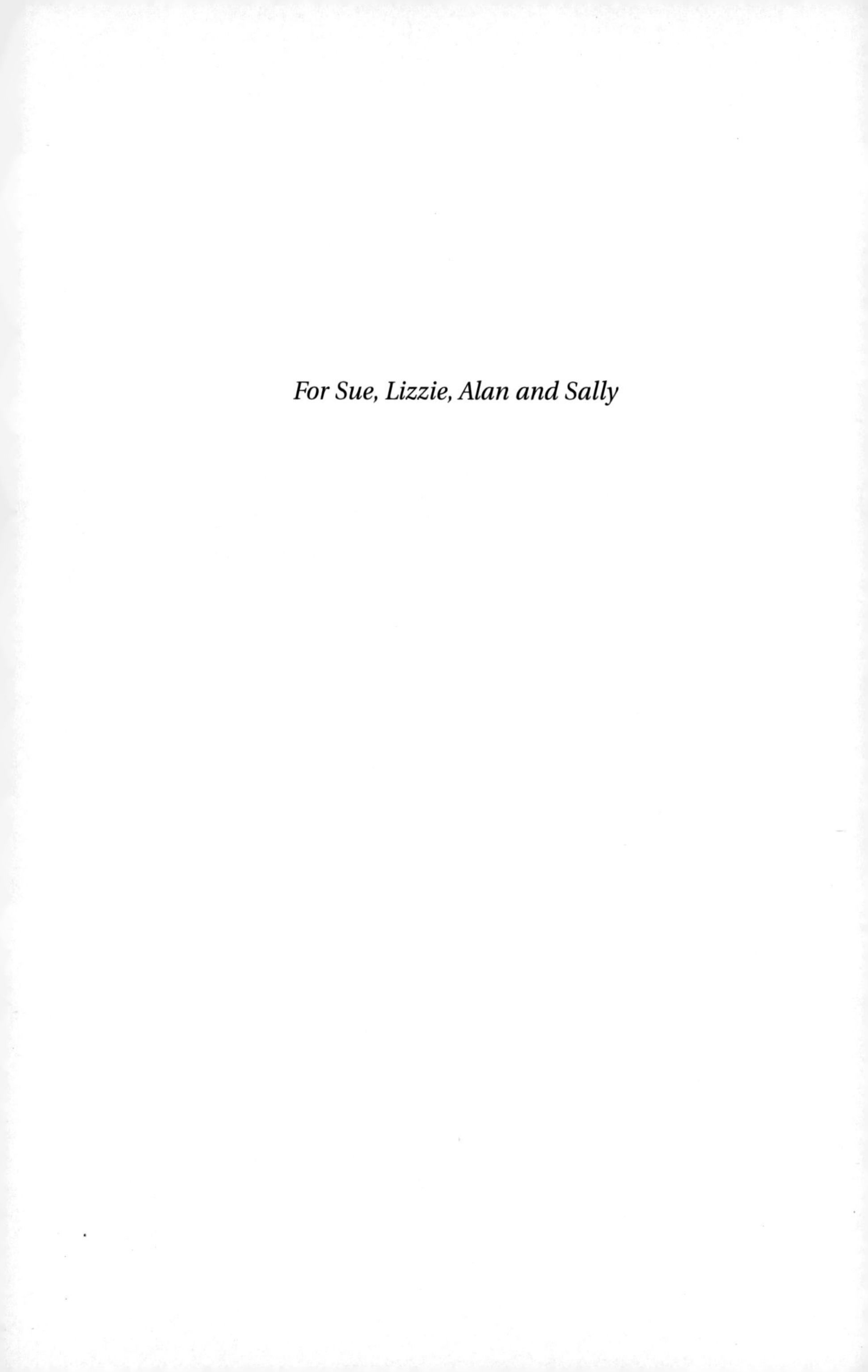

For Sue, Lizzie, Alan and Sally

Flying the Waves

Richard Pike

Woodfield Publishing
~ WEST SUSSEX • ENGLAND ~

Acknowledgements

The author would like to acknowledge the following:

Captain M.L. Soper

HMSO – Public Inquiry into the Piper Alpha Disaster – Cullen Report (Crown copyright material is reproduced with the permission of the Controller of Her Majesty's Stationery Office)

Lieutenant General Sir H.W.R. Pike KCB DSO MBE

Mr R.D. Smith ABIPP

Mr K. Murray

Mr T. Mooney

Mr K. Gannon

Contents

Introduction

"You've never had it so good," we were assured by Prime Minister Harold Macmillan in the 1950s. A sceptical nation, however, seemed less than convinced. By the following decade, the UK appeared to be entangled in a state of perpetual pecuniary doom. Some twenty years after the surrender of the Axis powers in 1945, the economic after-effects of World War Two had combined with other factors to bring the country to its budgetary knees.

Then came North Sea Oil. The national psyche seemed to modify almost overnight. The amazing prospects suddenly altered attitudes; at last there was hope; Black Gold would save the nation from bankruptcy.

An aspect of this macro-economic opportunity not often mentioned was the vital part played by the helicopter. Occasional attempts to provide a seaborne crew-change service were convincingly opposed by unhappy oil-rig workers. As they emerged green-faced and sea-sick after hours wasted on a North Sea passenger vessel, it was quite apparent that the men needed another form of travel. Although most oil-rig workers probably did not enjoy helicopter flying, this mode of transport offered the most practical solution. Without helicopters, the story of North Sea Oil would have been very different.

Those helicopters were flown by gallant lads,
With ups, and downs, and not-too-bads.
This tale relates just a few of the joys,
Faced by those intrepid chopper boys.

CHAPTER 1

Kosovo

THE BALKANS, SUMMER 1999

"Give her some money."

There was an embarrassed silence.

I leant across the table and gave the small child a 10 Dinar note. It was probably more than she expected, but even so, it was still worth only 10 pence. Her mother, half hidden in the evening shadows, nodded; the child moved on to the next table.

"They'll be back every night now," someone grumbled. But he was wrong. In Macedonia, and I suspected in other Balkan countries, they seemed to have their own code. There was poverty, grinding and pathetic, but there was pride too.

Earlier, during the day, I had walked over the old foot-bridge, towards the market area of Skopje, Macedonia's capital city. The bridge itself had been lined with street traders, and a young woman with a tiny blond-haired child had sat listlessly on a piece of tatty cardboard. The woman had stared intently at me, and at other passers-by. As soon as a coin was placed, her gaze was averted; the shame of her situation had been under-scored.

It was July 1999, "the last year of the millennium," we were reminded incessantly. The President of Serbia, Slobodan Milosevic, who was alleged to have instigated a campaign of ethnic cleansing against the Albanian population of Kosovo, had just conceded defeat, following NATO attacks. There were around one million refugees, mainly ethnic Albanians, who had fled Kosovo in terror. They had sought refuge from the Serb attacks on them, and they had sought safety from the NATO bombing. The refugee camps in Macedonia, and other countries, had offered a relative haven.

With the ending of the war, Kosovans had started to drift back to their own country. The UN World Food Programme had contracted our Company (Bristow Helicopters), initially for one month, to supply emergency food-aid by helicopter to needy people as they returned to their damaged homes and villages in Kosovo. It was a far cry from our normal task of flying to North Sea Oil installations from Aberdeen, in Scotland.

As some of the helicopter pilots and engineers sat outside their Hotel in central Skopje, they chatted after a day's flying. They observed the passing pedestrians, a mixture of traditional and modern; the people reflected the general Balkan miscellany. In the distance, the outline of mountains marked the border area with Kosovo. There was a heady atmosphere in the evening heat of mid-summer.

"Another long day tomorrow," commented one of the pilots, John. He had just finished his training, and he was a quick learner. He had fitted in well with the unusual situation. "Man, you should have seen those kids swarming around our aircraft today. I thought we'd never get rid of them."

"Should be used to the long days by now," said Al. Tall and rather plodding, he was a young Captain who saw life as clear-cut, black and white. On the surface he was pleasant enough, but an unattractive bitter streak showed occasionally. "And I don't think we should allow these kids on board. We're supposed to be delivering food, not acting as entertainers," he said.

"Hope the 'Pink Elephant's' a bit better organised tomorrow," Guy referred to the World Food Programme representative. Guy was an ex-Navy pilot with a wealth of experience. "As for the entertainment part," said Guy, "where's the harm? For goodness sake, these people have had enough to cope with. If we can offer a bit of light relief for a few minutes, then go for it, I say."

The pilots and engineers crewed two Sikorsky S61 helicopters, which were based at a camp area near Skopje. Each morning, just after 7am, taxis arrived at the Hotel, and took the crews to the helicopter base. The fifteen minute drive was an education in itself. We passed massive convoys of lorries, a mixture of 'K4' military traffic, Red Cross, and other civilian trucks. The Macedonian/ Kosovan border was about ten miles north of Skopje, and the convoys were snaking their way up to the border crossing.

At the base camp, we had been apportioned one half of a mobile hut for flight planning and engineering management. We had telephones and a FAX machine, and received flight information, radio frequencies, information about land mines and other hazards, and daily weather forecasts.

Once the scrupulous planning and paper-work had been completed, the allocated crew (two pilots, and a third pilot who acted as 'crewman'), walked out to their S61, and went through the walk-round checks, and start-up procedures. Heavily laden with around two tons of flour and HDR (Humanitarian Daily Rations: cardboard boxes laden with high calorific foods), the first helicopter took-off in a whirlwind of dust and debris.

The S61 then began its twenty minute flight north to the United Nation's helicopter landing site at Pristina, the capital city of Kosovo. Meanwhile, the second helicopter went through the start-up routine, to follow ten minutes or so behind the leader.

As the helicopters began their flight northwards, the Kosovan border quickly came into view, easily spotted because of the huge traffic queues. At the border crossing place, a cement factory had been the casualty of NATO bombing, and a layer of cement dust covered surrounding houses. When the S61s entered Kosovo itself, sporadic damage to buildings soon became evident.

"Look at that!" said John one time. He pointed to what was once a country village, in superb surrounding. "It's just a mess." The houses looked so ugly and charred.

"And see the cross-roads?" I asked. "That Inn was probably friendly and welcoming at one time, now it's in ruins." Burnt rafters stood out of damaged masonry, and piles of rubble. "I guess the tanks had a go at that one."

As we flew further north towards Pristina, a railway line, abandoned apart from occasional 'K4' military trains, showed evidence of damaged rolling stock on various side-lines. Smoke rose from villages in the middle distance; sometimes just an innocent bonfire, but sometimes the sinister sign of another revenge house burning.

"There's Pristina appearing in the distance," said John eventually. At first glance, Pristina looked like a normal city, with some high-rise blocks, and the city itself stretched along an attractive valley. However, as we flew closer, John said: "Look at that vicious and random damage. And can you see the ominous-looking smoke in the centre of the city?"

Just south of Pristina, a field had been allocated to the United Nations, and we landed the helicopters there to re-supply with flour and HDR. Later in the month, we flew supplies of plastic sheeting for emergency roof repairs.

"There's Leo," said John. Leo was the interpreter we took on our flights. In his mid-thirties, Leo was an ethnic Albanian who had owned his own printing works before the Serbs began their campaign against the Albanians. Leo's business had been destroyed by the Serbs.

"I'm lucky to get this job with the UN," Leo had said. "Many people are in a worse position than me." He was a tall, good-looking man; his dark eyes, sunken and weary, somehow betrayed the horrors his kinfolk had endured.

For the day's first flight, we were usually allocated a 'box' on a map. We flew to the area, and then circled around, discussing possible landing sites with Leo. We had to consider the mined areas, which were not reliably marked on the maps, and often we agonised over which village to choose; so many of them were damaged, and in some cases, devastated.

When an area had been selected, the helicopters approached the site cautiously, ready to over-shoot if there was a sign of trouble. Eventually, however, a 'critical point' was reached, beyond which taking-off again with a heavy load of flour was not possible. At that point, therefore, the crew were committed to landing at the chosen site.

After landing, the interpreter left the S61 to speak to local people who invariably appeared 'out of the wood-work', sometimes in large numbers. There was a feeling of excitement as the noisy helicopters sat on the ground with the engines and rotors running. Usually there were harrowing tales told to Leo; often there were tears. As he spoke to the local folk, Leo tried to assess how many flights should be made to a particular place, using one kilogram per person as a rough guide. The flour just needed to be mixed with water and salt, and it was ready for baking.

Strong-looking lads were beckoned into the helicopter to help unload. The flour bags were soon piled up outside the aircraft, each bag a 'Gift from Japan', for example, or a 'Gift from the USA': 'NOT FOR RE-SALE'. When the flour had been unloaded, children occasionally were given an opportunity to look around the helicopter. It was then time to return to the Pristina base for re-loading; the helicopters were two tons or so lighter, and therefore had no difficulty lifting into the hover.

After several flights to a chosen village, it was usually mid-afternoon, and the July temperatures peaked at the high thirties degrees centigrade, occasionally even the low forties. The helicopter performance was reduced as the rotor blades became less efficient in the high temperatures. Weary crews were also affected by the heat, but usually kept working until 5 or 6 pm, by which point they would have logged seven or so hours of flying time.

"OK guys," said Leo eventually. "Let's call it a day for today!"

At that stage, we took Leo back to Pristina, before heading south for the Macedonian border. The Air Traffic Control at Pristina airfield was manned by the Royal Air Force, and we 'signed off' with them for the day.

"Look at those traffic queues," said John as we crossed the border back into our 'home' country of Macedonia. We gazed at the motionless lines of vehicles herded around the inadequate border crossing set-up, and we felt profoundly grateful for our ability to queue-jump. John then called our base on the radio: "Two minutes to landing." The engineers were alerted, and prepared for the next few hours which were spent servicing the aircraft, as well as washing the outside, and vacuuming the flour-dusted inside.

In the primitive conditions, all hands helped in any practical way. The professionalism of the engineers, operating under such conditions, engendered an atmosphere of respect between them and the aircrew.

Discussions often turned to the troubles back home; the downturn in the North Sea Oil Industry was leading to down-sizing which was likely to affect some of us. "We could well be on our 'swan song'," said a few of the old hands.

"It's about time we cleared out some of the dead-wood," growled young Alan, glancing away from the hurt looks of several deadwooders.

"And so say all of us," chipped in Porky perkily. A bumptious co-pilot from the Shetland Search and Rescue unit, Porky was not renowned for his diplomacy. There was an awkward silence; several minds began to calculate the best way of dealing with the terrible twins. Folk were tired and cagey, yet they fancied an opportunity to deflate the graceless pair. One of the engineers had revealed his thoughts quite recently about the twin's unhappy blend of personal ambition and bad manners. The pair certainly had stretched a few nerves over the days.

"You may be in the same position yourselves one day," at length Guy had his say. "And this Company's not exactly world famous for its high standard of caring management." A further delicate silence ensued.

Eventually, as the crews continued with their tasks, the uncomfortable issue was quietly put aside. Folk understood that the stressful situation – exacerbated by unusually high temperatures – encouraged underlying attitudes, however unfortunate, to boil over.

In spite of this predicament, the crews nevertheless generally pulled together well, and morale remained high. The urgency of the moment, and the pressing priorities of the task, over-rode other problems.

However, it was perhaps inevitable that during a telephone call to my wife Sue one time I should comment: "I can't help the feeling that my days as a pilot are about to end sooner than we'd hoped."

"You reach the forty year milestone soon, don't you?" she asked.

"I learnt to fly in 1959, when I was sixteen," I replied. "I guess the forty year milestone is reached this month."

"You've had some great flying – military and civil," she said. "You've been lucky; even your flying in the civil world has been exceptionally interesting."

"Civil flying is meant to be dull," I retorted.

"In the airlines, maybe, but it's different on the helicopters," Sue correctly pointed out.

"It's certainly different on helicopters," I agreed.

There was a hesitation in Sue's voice then. Despite the crackly telephone link, and her husband's outwardly nonchalant manner, she knew that he felt more cut up than he was prepared to admit. "You've been flying helicopters, what, twenty years?" at length she asked in a tentative tone.

"Just over," I replied.

"You've had a good run then," Sue spoke quietly, in a sympathetic way. After a pause, her voice appeared to brighten: "Maybe we should think about a special holiday somewhere," said Sue, attempting to divert my feeling of despondency. "At least it'll give you something to look forward to. Where shall we go?"

My mind raced. "I don't know. There are so many places to explore." I paused for a moment, and then continued: "Let's go somewhere outlandish. How about going along with my cousin's idea to visit Kathmandu?"

"Kosovo. Kathmandu. Well they both begin with 'K', I suppose," replied my wife.

"Just a suggestion," I added defensively.

Later on though, some time after our telephone call, I thought to myself: "Kosovo to Kathmandu; there *is* something kind of neat about them beginning with 'K'." My mental processes must have been affected by the heat; I shook my head abruptly. Then after a few moments: "Just maybe… " I thought, "just maybe; both seem equally unlikely places for a North Sea helicopter pilot. However, let's face it: most North Sea pilots are dab hands at dealing with the most unexpected situations, in the most unexpected parts of the world."

CHAPTER 2

A Nepalese Trek

NINE MONTHS LATER... NEPAL, APRIL 2000

Poor Chandri; she even found it hard to cry. It was not her fault – both her parents had died when Chandri was a small child. There was no-one else to teach her even the simple things. Life was tough for an orphan; life was especially tough for an orphan in Nepal. The tears came at length, though, as nature took its course. It was painful to witness. The aura of the moment, sad and highly charged, attempted to say so many things. The situation was extreme; maybe it needed such circumstances to draw out the hidden feelings. Whatever the reasons, eventually – tragically – Chandri's placid face buckled. Perhaps unused to being allowed to show her emotions, the young woman seemed overcome by the situation.

"You have been so kind to us. You are a lovely person," said my wife and daughter, Sue and Lizzie, to Chandri. Sue and Lizzie were themselves in a state of high emotion. In their wildest dreams, they had not expected the dramatic events which were unfolding.

To mark the new millennium, my cousin 'Z' (his nickname had stuck from childhood) had suggested a family trekking holiday in the Milke Dande region in eastern Nepal. The idea, first mooted when I was in Kosovo, had appealed to several family members. As an ex-Gurkha Colonel, 'Z' had long experience (and language fluency) in eastern Nepal, the area where the British army recruited its legendary Gurkha soldiers. An opportunity to learn about this would be of special interest to me, having worked with the Gurkhas on various occasions during my flying career. As feared, my professional flying had indeed ended the previous year; the spell in Kosovo had truly turned out to be a swan song. For this special holiday, I was to be joined by my wife and elder daughter. It would be our own private swan song; it would be an adventure to help mark the end of an intrepid life in aviation.

The thirteen 'trekkers', most of them from various branches of the family, were a disparate team, but nevertheless seemed to get along well. The group had spent two nights in Kathmandu before being flown east for the start of the trekking. From the local airport at Biratnagar, we had driven in Landrovers for some three hours before being dropped off. A few of us had already noticed the beginnings of 'Delhi Belly'. After the Landrover drive, having settled into the first camp-site, I had gone straight to bed. The night was long and restless for me; I was gripped by some bacteriological foe.

The following morning, a number of our group had become affected by the same foe. Nevertheless, we had all managed to keep trekking. The going had been tough, but we were determined to make the best of things.

We were surprised and charmed by the friendliness of the local folk. Remote villages had provided a fascinating insight to the harsh lives led by the Nepalese people. In the villages, a few basic shops lined the muddy streets. There was rarely evidence of any customers; the shop-keepers would sit lethargically, waiting. Goats and dogs, and the occasional cow, would mooch around in the same torpid fashion. Children would watch and follow us. Their small faces would display a mix of curiosity and disbelief. Some of the children spoke basic English; they usually pressed for money with persistence. Invariably, there was a smoky smell as food was cooked. Any activity appeared slow and prolonged; the folk seemed to have time a-plenty. Poverty was rife, but there was no evidence of starvation. If we held both hands together, fingers pointing up, and said the word *'Namaste'* (meaning good-day), even the most crusty local face was inclined to break into an alluring smile.

Beyond the villages, we had admired the unspoilt territory, and sweeping views. There were tracks created by human steps, but roads were non-existent where we walked. Fairly regularly, we passed Nepalese folk, usually carrying ponderous loads on their backs.

Occasionally, we came across yakcows (a cross between yak and cow), the hollow clang from bells attached to their necks warning of their approach.

"This is all rather different from your life flying aircraft," my cousin Prudie had said to me one time. With an attractive smile, and open nature, her enquiring mind had been enthralled when I told her some adventures about flying. "You really must tell me about more of your flying experiences," said Prudie, "I had no idea before now." She then told me, in return, tales about the machinations in her life as a Tour Guide.

The progress of our group was slow, partly caused by the illness, and partly because people wanted to enjoy the local scene. Looking down steep valleys, we would admire rhododendron shrubs with their brilliant red zygomorphic flowers. Occasional magnolia trees, with beautiful foliage and white flowers, would provide a contrast. Sometimes we stopped to admire the intricate blooms of orchids attached to the branches of trees.

After several days of trekking, it was clear that the illness was becoming overwhelming for some. My daughter, Lizzie, was especially badly affected. She had managed to keep walking, with Chandri as her constant aide. Chandri, with her gentle approach, was ubiquitous; she had a profoundly kind and sympathetic nature. Chandri had held Lizzie's hand, and assisted her with every step, especially over obstacles and rough ground. However, Lizzie had reached the stage where she could no longer accept food or drink, and she was growing steadily weaker. It was decided to spend two nights in a camp at Lampokhari, at an altitude of just over 9,000 feet, in the hope that a full rest day would allow Lizzie to recover.

During the rest day at Lampokhari, a group of us opted to climb a nearby hill in the afternoon. Prayer flags marked the top of the hill, along with religious offerings placed in small bowls. The assortment of rice and vegetables, however pathetic looking, nevertheless had been placed lovingly; they were somehow typical of Nepal with its mix of Hindu and Buddhist traditions. The fragile flags fluttered perilously on the hill top; it was a matter of time before they fell victim to the next gale. Just below the summit, we came across a small area used for animal sacrifice. "A goat has been slaughtered here quite recently," said Binod our guide.

When our group had returned to the camp site, the news had not been good. 'Z', as leader of the party, had taken me aside. "The main trouble is that Lizzie cannot accept any nutrition," said 'Z'. "We've held on as long as possible, but I've just spoken to Binod, and we feel it's reached the stage where her health is now in jeopardy. We've therefore come to the decision that there is no choice but to evacuate her as quickly as possible by helicopter." My cousin, the retired Colonel, looked at me sternly. The Colonel had spoken; his orders were paramount; this was not up for debate. It took a few moments for the information to sink in.

"But she's been looking forward to this trek for months," I said. 'Z' shrugged.

"I feel as disappointed as anyone," he said. "But I'm afraid it's reached the point where she needs hospital treatment fast. Which gives rise to another problem." 'Z' coughed. I looked at my cousin.

"Well?" I asked.

"Well," sighed 'Z', "the nearest telephone is 2 hours' trekking away. We're sending two of our fastest porters. They should reach the telephone just before dark. If that telephone is not working, which is quite possible bearing in mind the Nepali system, the next telephone is a further two hours' trek away." My mind raced as it tried to assimilate the implications. At the earliest, we could expect to have Lizzie airlifted by mid-morning the next day.

To support the camp site, we had nearly fifty porters. Thin and wiry-looking, most of the porters appeared incapable of carrying the loads. However, their looks belied the reality. Even the strongest of the trekkers in our group struggled just to lift some of the loads, let alone carry them for miles. The porters, though, had outlandish strength; we often wondered at their abilities, and their footwear: normally flip-flops. For their efforts, the porters were paid the equivalent of £2 per day, which was above the going rate. Out of this amount, they had to pay for their own food.

"The two porters we're sending are really good guys," said 'Z'. "If anyone can make it, they can." I kicked at the dry soil gloomily. A lump of yakcow dung shot from under my foot, and hit the side of a tent.

"Sorry," I said as Spencer's head appeared from inside the tent.

"Any time," said Spencer. An antique dealer from Norfolk, Spencer and his wife Ruth had been struck too by the current wave of illness.

I looked around the camp site. The rows of tents had been placed neatly side-by-side. The porters and cooks bustled around the kitchen area as they prepared the evening meal. Sylvia, 'Z's' wife, held a small class for yoga enthusiasts. Other trekkers sat in chairs reading or sketching, some lay in their tents.

"There'll be room in the helicopter for one person to accompany Lizzie," said 'Z' at length. "It's up to you, of course, but I would suggest her Mum as the most appropriate. Apart from anything else, Sue herself has been quite unwell, and would benefit from hospital treatment."

The following night was long and difficult. Sleep came fitfully for most of the trekkers; all were upset by the way events had turned out. When Chandri came round the tents the following day at 5.30 am, most folk welcomed the early-morning chant, by now familiar: "Good morning. It's Chandri. Would you like some tea, please?"

The camp went through its routine before breakfast; hot water was provided for washing and shaving; trekkers drank tea and ate biscuits; folk got dressed, and packed their belongings ready for the porters to lug to the next camp site. Breakfast was taken as usual at 7.30 am, a sociable event as the trekkers sat outside and discussed the plans of the day. On that particular day, Sunday April the ninth, the atmosphere was more down-beat. Sue and Lizzie were popular members of the party; the group would miss them.

It was decided to wait until 10 am for the helicopter to arrive. After that, the main party would depart in order to reach the next camp site before dark. A rear-party of half a dozen porters, with tents and cooking facilities, would remain with Sue and Lizzie until the helicopter arrived. The two runners sent to the telephone the night before had not returned yet. We could only guess at the likely timing of the helicopter.

After breakfast, the trekkers sat around anxiously. Watches were checked at over-regular intervals. The sky was scanned; ears listened for the clattering noise of the helicopter; an 'H' was marked in white flour by Binod at a landing place I had suggested; the porters prepared flags and smoky fires for when the helicopter was spotted. Eventually, as the time approached 10 am, it was clear to all that Sue and Lizzie were to be abandoned. "We understand completely," they said. "You mustn't worry. We'll be OK. It's important that you get to the next camp in time." The good-byes were awkward and sad. The farewell to Chandri was somehow especially intense.

The first part of the trek that day was steeply down-hill. As we glanced over our shoulders for a final farewell, the two figures, isolated and vulnerable, waved back. They disappeared suddenly as the slope took us downwards.

The slope that morning turned out to be challenging. It was fortunate in a way; it gave the trekkers and porters something positive on which to concentrate. Eventually, at around one o'clock, the group stopped for lunch. The Nepali chef worked his well-versed magic; under the most basic circumstances he produced freshly made – and delicious – cheese pasties, with fried potatoes and salad. That was followed by fruit, and tea or coffee. During the repast, we suddenly became aware of the clatter of a helicopter. "Rescue at last," said 'Z'. "They should get to the hospital by tea-time."

It was the following day before we reached a telephone. Binod then made a call to find out the news of Sue and Lizzie. He discovered that the helicopter used for their rescue had been on charter to a wealthy Japanese couple. The machine had been diverted to pick up Sue and Lizzie, evidently rather to the annoyance of the Japanese couple. The two hour flight through the mountains had been bumpy and rough. An ambulance had met the helicopter at Kathmandu, which had ameliorated the Japanese couple's attitude when they had realised that the matter was serious. At the hospital, six bottles of fluid had been applied to Lizzie intravenously as treatment for the bacterial dysentery which the Doctor had diagnosed.

For the following few days, the remaining eleven trekkers continued their walk, occasionally uphill, but mainly downwards.

They passed through more villages, including the larger one at Chainpur where the group watched the production of local metalwork. The shops lining the main street in Chainpur were manned by individuals lovingly beating and filing various metal artefacts. Hours of labour went into the manufacture of each item. It was highly labour-intensive, but labour was cheap. Items were bought by many in our group; each purchase appeared to involve lengthy haggling before a bargain was sealed. Spencer was in his element; the antique dealer knew what he was after.

In the open country, the trekkers passed through Castanopsis forests, Cardamom orchards, and rice plantations. A small paper-making factory was spotted in an unlikely place on a remote hill-side. The visitors admired the birdlife, which included Steppe Eagles, Darjeeling Woodpeckers, Long Tailed Shrikes, and Indian Cuckoos with their distinctive song. "Look at that beauty," our ornithological zealot, Ben, would cry from time to time; there would follow a frantic focusing of field glasses.

'Z' explained the system for recruiting Gurkhas. "Soldiers who are currently serving," he said, "will act as scouts. They'll tour the villages in this and other valleys from time to time. Suitable candidates will be given the chance to go to a recruitment centre where they'll be assessed further. It's considered an honour to be selected, and there's no shortage of volunteers." 'Z' went on to emphasise that Gurkha soldiers, with their renowned toughness, were held in universal esteem, almost awe. I had worked with the Gurkhas in the Falklands, and in Kosovo, as well as other areas, and knew from personal experience that 'Z' was correct.

Five nights after abandoning Sue and Lizzie, the group eventually reached the final camp site at Dovan, next to the Arun River. In the afternoon, some swam in the river; Prudie even managed a mud bath. That evening, after supper, the guides and porters entertained the trekkers to a traditional final night 'nautch' party with singing, dancing, and drum beating.

The following morning, the trekkers shook hands with each of the porters individually. Again, they were struck by the apparent frailty of the porters who carried such monumental loads. The trekkers then walked for two hours to the airstrip at Tumlingtar, from where they were flown back to Kathmandu.

"Hello! How are you? Great to see you again!" As the bus reached our hotel in Kathmandu, we were relieved to be reunited with Sue and Lizzie. Both had recovered strength, but were still partly affected by the dysentery. Nevertheless, Lizzie had decided to continue with the jungle camp planned for the following week in the Royal Chitwan National Park in southern Nepal; Sue would return home, as planned, the day after next.

At the hotel, Lizzie and I, along with a family of three from Leeds, were briefed on the plans for the coming week. The journey south would take two days, most of which would be spent white water rafting down the Trisuli River. We would then spend three nights in lodges at the Temple Tiger Jungle Camp. On the agenda would be elephant-back riding, jeep rides, rafting, and bird-watching tours.

"Goodbye. Good luck! Keep in touch." The five 'jungle party' bade farewell to their companions as the original group of thirteen broke up. The five, plus William (a day-tripper) were then driven south through the perilous streets of Kathmandu, with horns blaring. Begging was evident in every corner; the entire population seemed to be in the grip of poverty. Skinny animals languished in the general squalor alongside the humanity. Cows wandered across the busy highway; some just lay down in the centre of the road with impunity. The incessant blasting of vehicle horns was directed at everyone and everything, apart from the cows. "If a cow is killed by a vehicle," Binod had told us, "it is considered as serious an offence as killing a human. It can land a driver in jail for twenty years, even if he is not to blame. The cow is a sacred animal here."

Some two hours' drive later, the party got out of their cars for the start of the white water rafting. We were each issued with a life jacket and helmet before walking down to the bank of the Trisuli River. The life jackets were crude. Nevertheless, they were sufficient to help save several lives later that afternoon.

At the river bank, we were introduced to 'Som', who was to be our guide, and the raft 'driver'. "This is the front of the boat," said Som. "This is the back. When I say 'forward', then paddle forward. When I say 'forward faster', then paddle faster. Any questions?" Som's lacklustre briefing to his inexperienced crew was partly the cause of the near-tragedy about to hit us.

We were soon underway, and the rafts drifted peacefully as they were carried down-stream by the river current. As well as our boat, with seven people including Som, there were several other rafts; we all floated in convoy. The river lay in a deep ravine; the sides of the high ground towered over us. Eagles and vultures circled above. The gentle drifting of the rafts provided an ideal chance to quietly observe the surrounding wildlife.

"Forward!" Som's instruction brought dreamy minds back to reality. We gripped our paddles, and started to row as we sat on the side of the raft. Just ahead, we could see the initial ripples from the start of some rapids. As we approached, the noise of the rushing water became gradually more audible.

"Stop!" Som no doubt had his reasons for timing our rowing efforts. After a short pause, however, he again called: "Forward." Our paddles dug into the water as instructed, and the noise from the rapids became quite loud as the first ripples of white water lapped against the hull of our craft. The gentle movement of the raft was gradually changing; as we moved further towards the area of rapids, the raft began to twist and rock. We continued to paddle steadily, and the placid nature of the water proceeded to alter more rapidly. The volume of roar from the river's surface also increased.

Just as we spotted the dramatic swirl which Som had no doubt anticipated, around the bend in the river's course, he suddenly called: "Forward faster." We thrust deeply and vigorously with our oars as the raft's movement became more violent. The rubber boat pitched and heaved as it approached the heart of the rapid. "Forward faster," yelled Som again. We worked our oars even harder as the raft floundered across the turbulent water.

Then the vigour of the boat's movement across the rapid began to decline as speedily as it had built up. "Stop," shouted Som as we returned to calm waters. The rowers ceased their efforts, and laid the oars on the side of the raft. "That one was quite gentle," sniffed Som as he glanced back. The boat soon returned to its drifting mode. We looked behind at other rafts as they negotiated the rapids. Soon all of the boats were drifting calmly again.

The occupants of the other craft were mainly groups of British soldiers with their families. There was banter and splashing between rafts, which Som encouraged. A young lad, Som enjoyed the horse-play. Perhaps he found his passengers staid, and wished he was leading one of the other boats.

The convoy of rafts continued their journey, passing over further rapids from time to time. Some of the rapids seemed stronger than others; they were graded accordingly, and a few had local names such as the 'Twister' and the 'S-bend'. Eventually, it was nearly time to stop for a picnic. However, before reaching the picnic area, we suddenly became aware of another section of white water appearing around a corner.

"Forward," shouted Som. The paddles penetrated the water again, and the raft occupants looked ahead, straining to assess the severity of the approaching rapid. One of the family from Leeds, Malcolm, was asthmatic, and it had become apparent that he was unhappy with the proceedings. He looked ahead anxiously as the ripples on the water's surface revealed that the approaching rapid was a big one.

"Stop!" The instruction from Som was unexpected, and just after he had made it, Som turned to see behind him. One of the other rafts was close to ours, and someone was trying to pass something. Som had turned for just a moment, but when he looked ahead again, he immediately called: "Forward." An uncharacteristic frown marked Som's forehead at that second. "Forward faster!" It was unusual for Som to demand this so soon. Furthermore, a note of doubt had crept into his voice. Som's team of rowers attempted to follow his command, but the momentum was lacking. In a startling action, the raft rocked violently. Unlike some of the rapids, with a build-up of movement, this one was marked by a powerful current at an early stage. Som had mismanaged his team; the raft had insufficient impetus. The efforts of the paddles became puny compared to the strength of the eddy. The rowing team faltered at a critical moment. Just as Som was about to bark a further order, the thrust of the current turned the rubber raft forcefully. Some of the rowers attempted to continue working their paddles, but the might of the rapid mocked the human exertion. Suddenly, a further jerk of the raft caught Som wrong-footed. There was a last second scramble for the safety rope, but it was too late: we were powerless to stop the over-riding force which flung Som from the raft.

I glanced at Malcolm. Rarely had I seen a face reflect such fear. His angular features appeared set in a nightmarish gasp. His asthmatic condition was clearly affecting him; his pallor was grey and washed out. The swirl of the water continued to turn the raft which began to tip alarmingly; the boat was out of control. As the raft's turning and bucking intensified, Malcolm and his family stood up in alarm. Swiftly, they too lost their footing. As Malcolm was tossed from the raft by the puissance of the rapids, Helen and David – wife and son – soon followed.

Three people remained in the raft, all convinced no doubt of the inevitability of their fate. The raft had filled with water by then. It continued to be held in the grip of the current; the craft was whirled around like some fair-ground plaything. I attempted to lunge at the water with my paddle, but the effort was worthless. Lizzie also thrust her paddle at the rapid; her expression was contorted with apprehension. At that second, in an off-beat and offensive surge, the raft gave a vehement movement. William and I managed to grasp the safety rope, but our efforts to save Lizzie from being thrown from the raft were useless.

In tormented seconds, I attempted to do several things at once. There was no sign of Lizzie. Should I dive in after her? In the foul and turbulent water, her position was unclear. I shouted her name, but the roar of the rapids was overwhelming. I searched, and searched again, and for the moment persevered with the struggle to stay in the raft. My heart sank at the appalling prospect confronting us. I continued to search and to call out with growing urgency. Still there was no sign of her. There was an agonised feeling of foreboding in the pit of my stomach.

At length, with William at the front of the flooded boat, and me at the aft, we managed to place our paddles with some small effect. We both sensed that the craft was being pushed away from the centre of the rapid in a gradual process. The craft wobbled and twisted, but we managed to hold our position on board. Some of the earlier casualties were just emerging from the vigorous down-currents. Perhaps there was hope.

Suddenly, in a swirl, Lizzie's head popped up not far from the raft. Her countenance was twisted; she was sobbing. "*Lizzie... Lizzie...* " I bellowed her name continuously above the water's roar. Slowly, surreally, her head turned towards me. As she spotted me, a fragment of smile touched her expression; in that instant we both knew that rescue was a possibility. William and I continued to exert some control over our flooded raft. "Swim towards me if you can," my outstretched hand beckoned at Lizzie. Gradually she drew closer to the boat, until eventually I was able, in a grab, to hold onto her hand. At that second, deftly and rapidly, Lizzie was lifted back into the boat.

"I really thought that my time had come," Malcolm said later.

We sat outside in a specially constructed viewing area in the Temple Tiger camp at the Royal Chitwan National Park. We were surrounded by the noise of jungle wildlife. Bee-catcher birds flew close by, with their brilliant-coloured feathers flashing in the afternoon sun. The viewing area had been constructed on tall stilts, and in the swampy area beneath, storks shuffled and squabbled around their make-shift nests. Further afield, in another swamp near some trees, a rhinoceros lumbered in the undergrowth.

"It seemed to take so long for you to surface after you'd fallen in," I replied to Malcolm as we continued to discuss the events of the white water rafting. Malcolm and his family, together with Som, had been rescued eventually by the soldiers on another raft.

"The inadequate briefing put us all in danger from square one," said Malcolm. He was a senior lawyer; I could see the way his mind was working. "The whole thing was thoroughly badly done; a disgrace," continued Malcolm.

After a pause, Malcolm asked: "How are you feeling now, anyway, Lizzie?"

"Not that great," replied Lizzie, "which is hardly surprising considering how much putrid river water I swallowed." Malcolm continued to mutter his dissatisfaction.

At that point, we were joined by 'Geetoo', a local guide. "Just to remind everybody," said Geetoo, "the afternoon elephant ride starts in half an hour, at four o'clock." We had already experienced a two-hour early morning elephant ride, but during that time had failed to spot the *pièce de resistance,* the Bengal Tiger. However, we had seen different types of feral monkey, prolific bird-life, wild boar, and some plodding rhinoceros.

"Count me in," said Lizzie. The rest of the group also agreed to join the evening elephant ride.

The hum of jungle sounds continued around us as we walked to the platform which had been specially constructed for mounting the elephants. There were two elephants that evening; the first one was backed up to the platform, ready to receive its three passengers: Malcolm and his family. In turn, the second elephant then backed into position for its four passengers: Lizzie and me, Sheila (a solo traveller from Manchester), and Geetoo, who sat on top of the back rail of the box-body secured to the elephant's back. In front of us sat the driver, with a hook and a whip. The driver was not secured; he sat on top of a thin blanket, and held a rope which had been placed around the elephant's neck. The driver had bare feet, which he used to press against the sensitive area behind the elephant's ears. This directed the elephant to turn, or to move straight ahead, or back.

Soon, the elephant train set off towards the heart of the jungle. The atmosphere was relaxed as the bulky beasts trudged along. Geetoo and the driver occasionally conversed, and Geetoo pointed out birds and wildlife to his passengers. We followed behind the other elephant initially, but at length, having descended a steep slope, the convoy split as we entered an area of high grasses. The driver seemed at one with his beast; man and giant were in harmony. As we went past trees, the driver would obligingly hold back branches which threatened to interfere with the passengers. At one stage, Geetoo excitedly pointed at paw marks recently made in soft soil: "They're tiger tracks," he said. But we failed to spot the elusive tiger itself.

Although we had split from the others, we caught occasional glimpses of them through the high vegetation. Geetoo continued to point out fly-catcher birds – with their fluttering white tails – drongos, and other species. The mood was tranquil in the calm evening air. At length, the two elephants were being directed by their drivers back towards the mounting platform. The elephants drew closer together again. The terrain was flat, and still covered in undergrowth; the beasts had no difficulty pushing aside the tall grasses.

Suddenly, in the distance, we became aware of something unexpected. It seemed that a high wind was approaching. Birds started to swoop and cry in alarm. Initially, we were unaffected, and the immediate area remained still. However, we could see the strange localised effect on trees and shrubs as the strong wind approached. When the wind hit us, it was with abruptness, and accompanied by clouds of choking dust.

For a minute, our elephant faltered, and appeared to lower her head slightly. Then she attempted to increase her pace, and the driver began to shout instructions. The driver also applied his whip. "She's trying to run," yelled Geetoo. For the moment, the driver succeeded in controlling the beast, which continued to make towards a forested area. Meanwhile, passengers and driver were affected by the driven dust particles, which dashed against skin painfully, and which made eyes feel sore.

As the intensity of the storm increased, we lowered hats and held up arms to protect our faces. "Put on your sun-glasses," called Lizzie, "it helps the eyes." She had to raise her voice to be heard above the increasing noise of the gale. Our elephant, still unsettled by the sudden arrival of the storm, shook her head and trunk nervously from side to side. The driver continued to shout at the beast, and to whip the top of her head. But the driver's exhortations were not to last long. The animal suddenly stopped. She agitated her head in a violent movement. The driver yelled and beat harder with his stick, but his efforts were no match for the ultimate brute force of the beast. In a dramatic second, the driver was thrown to the ground. At that point, the elephant made a few rapid steps. The beast knew it was then free to break into a run.

At first, the four passengers still on the elephant were silent. It seemed to take time to absorb the danger of their predicament. Eventually, though, in a shocked voice, Sheila cried: "Oh no. Oh bloody hell!"

The dust storm continued to rage all around us, stinging and burning our faces, as the elephant made determined strides towards the tree-line. "Just hold tight everyone. Try to stay calm," said Geetoo, as he held his position on the back rail of the box-body. Our driver, mercifully unhurt after his fall, ran after us. He bellowed instructions at the elephant, but without effect. "The elephant knows she will be punished," said Geetoo. "There's no way she will allow the driver to re-mount." I picked up the rope around the elephant's neck, and pulled at the harness in an attempt to steady the animal. The effort was fruitless; the elephant continued its forward charge.

At that point we reached the forested area, and the beast rampaged towards the trees. As overhanging branches rushed past, the passengers crouched low trying to avoid being struck. The box-body wobbled and shook as the frightened beast trampled through the thick undergrowth. Our driver had been left some distance behind by that stage, but soon we became aware of the urgent tones of another voice.

We looked behind, and spotted the other elephant lumbering after us. As the driver of that elephant screamed instructions at ours, the beast hesitated. This gave the other animal a chance to draw closer. It also gave relief from the vegetation dashing past us, scratching and pushing against limbs and body. At length, the insistent tones of the other driver brought a measure of control to our elephant. The beast began to slow down, and eventually was persuaded to follow behind its mate. "They'll lead us now to the elephant feeding and accommodation area," said Geetoo. "It's the safest place to go."

The lead elephant followed tracks for a period, but at one point the path disappeared beneath a swamp. The animals tramped through the water, but we soon reached a place where the way divided. The lead elephant continued ahead, but ours promptly decided to take a different course, turning to the right. Immediately the driver of the other beast commenced a torrent of urgent instructions. But it was too late; the water had already started to lap against the bottom of the box-body as our animal entered an area where the water was dangerously deep. The other driver continued his fluent scream of orders. Our elephant was clearly doubtful; the animal reluctantly halted in the middle of the deep water. We were unsure whether it was deliberate, or caused by the uneven surface beneath, but our beast suddenly lurched sideways. The passengers grimly held on to the side of the box-body. It felt as if the whole structure was about to slide into the infested water. "Oh no. Oh bloody hell!" repeated Sheila. Her shocked face had drained of colour.

At length, slowly, painfully, as the other driver continued his exhortations, our elephant turned back towards the leader. Steadily the animal made progress away from the deep waters. The two beasts then climbed a slope, and soon we had left the swamp behind.

Eventually, the track became wider as we drew close to the elephant feeding area. Our animal appeared to recognise the familiar territory. As we entered the feeding area itself, a number of elephant handlers quickly appeared. They shouted instructions, and applied whips, and our elephant was persuaded to bend its four legs, in a form of crouch. The passengers then climbed down the tail of the animal.

Little was said at that stage between the four passengers. Nevertheless, the atmosphere of relief was perceptible; we had spent over thirty minutes on the back of the out-of-control beast. As we walked away from the area, we noticed that the elephant remained in its crouched position. We had been told that elephants were short sighted. It was probably only in our imagination, therefore, that the animal's eyes appeared to stare at us.

When we glanced back, we saw that the handlers had started to lash at the elephant with whips. Even in its crouched position, the giant beast swayed slightly, and frisked its trunk as vigorous punishment for its misdemeanour was applied with ruthless energy.

❖ ❖ ❖

"Rafting disasters, runaway elephants, not to mention helicopter evacuation. I thought this was meant to have been a 'special holiday'," my son Alan said to me on the telephone. I mumbled a retort. "To me, it sounds as hair-raising as flying helicopters over the North Sea," he continued.

"Not so sure about that," I said.

"Maybe the North Sea flying tended to make other things seem..." he faltered. "Oh, I don't know, seem a bit tame, perhaps."

"It had its moments."

Alan pondered this for a while, then said: "You should put pen to paper about the North Sea flying; tell the world what went on." He paused for a second before adding: "At least the wild elephant ride might not seem so bad after all."

"The adrenaline flow is the same when things start going wrong," I said, "whether you're sitting in a helicopter, or sitting on the back of an elephant."

"I guess so," replied Alan.

After the conversation, however, I gave thought to Alan's idea. Maybe people should be told what went on in the world of North Sea helicopter flying. For much of the time, the work was routine. Occasionally, though, bizarre and extreme situations arose. Awards had been made for acts of great bravery, and for actions well beyond the call of normal duty. Furthermore, the flexibility of helicopters meant that many of the pilots and crews found themselves in corners of the globe far removed from the North Sea. Perhaps the world *should* be told.

CHAPTER 3

The North Sea

"How did you get involved with North Sea helicopter flying in the first place?" Prudie had asked me on one trekking day in Nepal. "Sounds a bit offbeat for an ex-fighter pilot. Why did you end up somewhere like Aberdeen?"

"I've often wondered that myself," I smiled as Prudie glanced at me. "I guess that after twenty years as a military pilot Sue and I were ready for a more settled lifestyle in the civilian world. I had to give up flying fast-jet aircraft due to a medical problem; my sinuses couldn't stand the pace. Consequently, the Air Force re-trained me to fly helicopters. When I was looking for a job as a civilian helicopter pilot in the early 1980s, Aberdeen was a natural choice; North Sea Oil was buoyant then."

"Sounds quite radical," commented Prudie.

"Perhaps," I replied, "but in the summer of 1981 I was really impressed when a civilian company offered me employment so quickly after retirement from the military. In the July of that year, I stepped more or less directly from a service cockpit to a civil one."

"You were lucky," said Prudie.

"I know," I replied.

I had been appointed to fly the US-built Sikorsky S61, known as 'the workhorse of the North Sea'. My training had started in the latter part of July 1981. My instructor at Bristow Helicopters Ltd, Bill, had given the pre-flight briefing.

"What we'll do today," he had said, "is fly up to the Beatrice Alpha platform in the Moray Firth, so you can get a feel for what it's like landing on an offshore oil installation."

After the briefing, Bill and I had walked together to look at the S61 helicopter standing in the dispersal area of the Bristow helipad at Aberdeen Airport. On our way, we called at the engineering 'line hut' to inspect and sign the aircraft log. The aircraft allocated to us that day (the 29th of July 1981) was registration G-BAKA.

The machine looked cavernous compared to the Wessex helicopters I had been used to operating in Germany with the Royal Air Force. The cabin of the S61 was designed to take nineteen passengers comfortably; more could be carried in different configurations which allowed extra seating. Dinghies were placed prominently inside the cabin, and the whole character was different to the military set-up. Inside the Wessex helicopter there had been an earthy, basic quality designed for operating in the field, whereas the interior of the S61 somehow reminded me – bizarrely – of the London Underground.

Instead of the tactical camouflage colouring of the Wessex, the civil helicopters at Aberdeen were painted in bright red, white, and blue colours for conspicuity. As Bill and I walked around the S61, performing external checks, he pointed out various features.

"Underneath you'll notice the Dayglow chevrons," he said. "A machine like this ditched in the sea once and was floating upside-down. The rescue services had difficulty locating it because the paintwork underneath was white. Hence the Dayglow chevrons – in case something similar happens again..."

Bill continued to point out features of the S61 as we walked around the machine. "The main rotor and tail rotor," said Bill, "both have five blades. The main rotor turns at a speed of around 200 revs per minute, the tail rotor turns even faster. The two engines that drive the rotors revolve at about *26,000* revs per minute each. As you can imagine, there's a hell of a gearbox needed to reduce the 26,000 down to 200. The main gearbox that does this is just below the rotor head."

After a moment, Bill had carried on: "That thing above the main rotor," Bill pointed upwards at an inverted saucer-shaped apparatus, "is known as the 'beany'. It's an anti-vibration device that streamlines the airflow over the main rotor head."

Bill pointed to the main body of the helicopter: "The fuselage is made of aluminium alloy, with a boat-shaped hull, so the machine floats on water. The buoyancy is helped as well by the sponsons on either side, which also house the retractable landing gear. And look at this… " Bill tugged at some rope that was tied to the side of the S61. "After another incident, it was decided to put rope around the hull so that in the event of a ditching in water, survivors would have something to hold on to."

We stepped backwards slightly, and Bill pointed at the five main rotor blades. "These are clever technology in their own right," he said. "The blades are all-metal construction. A spar makes up the leading edge, and is designed so that the tip has about six degrees less pitch than the root. That ensures an equal amount of lift along the full length of the blade. A Blade Inspection Method, or BIM for short, indicates that the pressurisation within the blade is correct. If a BIM warning appears in flight, it can mean big trouble." I was to remember this comment in some months' time when I was suddenly presented with a BIM warning in the cockpit, accompanied by severe vibrations.

Bill and I then walked up the steps of the main door leading into the cabin. Bill said: "This airstair door is water tight, and always kept closed in flight. For winching operations, the cargo door at the front is opened. The winch, when fitted, is bolted to the airframe just above the cargo door."

Bill and I walked forward to the cockpit area, and strapped into our respective seats. As a trainee captain, I sat on the right-hand side. We ran through the pre-start checks, and then held up a single finger as a sign to the ground-crew that we were ready to start one of the engines. When that engine had been started, we gave another sign to indicate that we were all set to turn the rotors. The ground crewman checked around the machine before he signalled back; I then released the rotor brake. The rotors turned slowly at first, but as they picked up speed the noise in the cockpit began to increase markedly.

We did more checks before Bill said: "You can start the second engine now. Then we'll get clearance to taxi out." We ran through the remaining drills to start the other engine; after that we waved to the ground crew to indicate removal of the wheel chocks.

As we taxied out of the dispersal area, Bill pointed to high grass banks surrounding the helicopter operating area. "Those banks are meant to offer some form of protection between here and the main terminal if there's an accident in the dispersal area with a helicopter," said Bill. "I guess they're worried that rotor blades might shoot all over the place, causing havoc." (Some fifteen years later, such an accident did occur when a Tiger helicopter turned too sharply, and ended up on its side. The rotors did indeed shoot all over the place causing havoc, but the grass bank proved ineffective: remnants of the rotor blades buried themselves in the main terminal building. It was pure chance that no-one was killed or injured.)

"The number of daily flights here varies," said Bill. "On some occasions, when we're busy at Christmas time for example, we operate around one hundred flights a day from this Company alone."

We approached the main runway, and the Ground Controller asked us to speak to the 'Tower'. I changed to a different radio frequency and called: "Aberdeen Tower, this is 23A ready for take-off."

"Roger, 23A," said the Air Traffic Control Officer, "you are cleared to line up."

I moved forward towards the main runway, while Bill read out the remaining 'pre-take-off' checks. We both looked along the runway approach sector to ensure it was clear, then I taxied on to the runway, and waited for final clearance from Air Traffic Control.

"23A, you're clear to take-off," the Air Traffic Control Officer called after a moment.

"OK," Bill said to me. "Show me the 'ground cushion' type take-off we've just briefed."

As I raised the 'collective lever' with my left hand, Bill pushed the 'Speed Select Levers' fully forward. This ensured that the engines were at the top end of their governed range. As an ex-fighter pilot, I always felt an exhilaration when lifting a helicopter into the hover; it still seemed not quite natural to me, even after some years as a helicopter pilot. The fighter aircraft needed about a mile of runway before they finally screeched airborne. The operation in a helicopter was restrained in comparison. The S61 certainly felt comfortable and stable as I held it in a hover that day.

"Temperatures and pressures all look good," Bill called. "You're clear to go."

It was the signal for me to lower the nose of the S61 by about ten degrees. I held our height of ten feet or so above the ground as the airspeed began to pick up. It felt sedate compared to the fighter-types, with their surge of acceleration. Then Bill called: "Thirty knots." At that point, I raised the nose so it was level with the horizon. The helicopter started to climb. Just as we reached a height of twenty feet above the ground, Bill called: "Rotate." I lowered the nose again; the machine climbed less rapidly, but nevertheless continued to climb steadily as it accelerated away from the runway. "That take-off technique," Bill had briefed earlier, "is designed to give you an effective profile in the event of an engine failure during take-off."

When the airspeed approached 70 knots, I raised the nose slightly in order to maintain the airspeed. The rate of climb increased a little, and soon we approached 1000 feet.

"You can turn left now onto a northerly heading," said Bill. "And level at 1500 feet." I asked him to read out the after take-off checks, which included items such as checking the altimeter sub-scale, and the retraction of the undercarriage. Soon, I levelled the helicopter at 1500 feet.

"Well done," said Bill. "As we fly north towards the Beatrice field, I'll show you a few local features." Bill made a sweeping motion with his hand. "On the left, you can see the high ground of the Bennachie range of hills." The distinctive shape of the hills showed up clearly. "Ahead is the Oldmeldrum TV mast," continued Bill, "and slightly left of the aircraft is the town of Inverurie. Standing out in the distance on our right is the chimney of the Peterhead power station."

We made various calls to Air Traffic Control as our flight took us further north. "23A you are clear to call Lossiemouth now," said the Air Traffic Control Officer at Aberdeen eventually.

When we had checked-in with Lossiemouth, an Air Force base on the Moray Firth coast, they confirmed that we were under their radar cover while we flew out towards the Beatrice platforms.

"On the nose," said Bill after a while, " is the town of Turriff. It marks about the half-way point between Aberdeen Airport and the

Beatrice." Beyond Turriff, we could make out the coastline. As we approached the coast, Bill asked me to use our second radio box to call the Beatrice A platform.

"Beatrice A... Beatrice A," I said on the radio. "This is 23A. Do you read? Over."

After a pause, Beatrice A replied: "23A. 23A. This is Beatrice A. You are loud and clear. Over."

"Roger, Beatrice A. We should be with you in fifteen minutes, for deck landing practice," I said.

"No prob at all Cap," said the obliging radio operator on the Beatrice A. "The deck crew are expecting you. Are you ready to copy the weather?"

"Go ahead," I said.

"Roger. The wind is 240 degrees at 20 knots. The cloud base is estimated at 2000 feet. The temperature is plus 15 centigrade, with a dew point of plus 11. And the pressure is 1008 millibars. All copied?"

"Affirmative," I replied. "All copied."

"Can we offer you anything to eat this afternoon?" asked the Beatrice A.

"Thanks a lot," I replied. "Refreshments for a crew of two will be most welcome."

"Okey, dokey," said the Radio Operator. "I'll have a word with the galley."

We had crossed the coast by that stage, and before long Bill said: "We could descend to 1000 feet now." After clearance from the Lossiemouth controller, I eased down the aircraft collective lever for the short descent from 1500 feet. Around us, the sea looked rough and forbidding. There were a few fishing vessels, otherwise the expanse of the Moray Firth looked forlorn and deserted. The two Beatrice platforms (Alpha and Bravo) showed on our aircraft radar as blips, and in the distance I could just see the outline of the installations.

"With today's south-westerly wind," said Bill, "we should be quite well placed for our deck landing practices." We continued to chat about the flight, and about more general matters. Like me, Bill was an ex-military pilot. He was a cheerful individual, but inclined to a stringent attitude which resulted in unpopularity with a number of the pilots.

As our range from the platforms steadily reduced, the radar picture eventually showed a remaining distance of ten miles to run. At that point, I called Lossiemouth: "Lossie radar, 23A has ten miles to go. If there are no conflictions, we'll change to the Beatrice A's frequency."

"Roger 23A," replied Lossiemouth. "There are no conflictions. You are clear for further descent, and to change frequency. Call me departing the Beatrice for your return to Aberdeen."

Having made the radio calls, I asked Bill to read out the 'approach checks'. *"Undercarriage down... altimeters set... fuel is sufficient... "* while Bill read out the checks, I lowered the collective lever to begin our height reduction from 1000 feet. The S61 shook slightly in the turbulent conditions, but in general the helicopter was stable and pleasant to fly. "Level off at around 400 feet," said Bill during the descent.

Soon our distance to go had reduced to five miles, and the bulky-looking installations stood out clearly, with spindly legs stretching to the sea-bed. It was the first time that I had seen an offshore oil platform at close quarters. "Just fly directly to the platform," said Bill, "and we'll orbit around to give you a general picture."

As our range from the Beatrice A approached two miles, I asked Bill to read out the 'finals checks'. These confirmed, amongst other things, that the undercarriage was selected down. Shortly after that, we reached the over-head position of the platform, and I started a turn to orbit around the area.

The initial impression of the platform was of the crowding of pipes, boxes, and general equipment placed all over the structure. Tall stacks reached upwards; the name Beatrice A was marked clearly on one of these. A long flare emerged from another stack to one side. At the base of the platform, jets of water were directed onto the sea. Life-boats could be seen hanging from various sections of the structure. On the top surface, in one corner, a heli-deck was marked with two yellow circles, with a prominent 'H' in the centre circle. The whole installation appeared almost Mechano-like.

After orbiting round the Beatrice A, I said on the radio: "Beatrice A heli-deck, 23A request deck landing clearance."

"Roger 23A. The Beatrice A heli-deck is clear."

I continued our turn until we headed into the wind. At that juncture, I rolled out of the turn, and aimed the S61 at the heli-deck. The helicopter was buffeted by blustery winds as we flew close to the installation.

"Make your approach angle quite high," said Bill. "Initially aim for a point at the far side of the heli-deck, rather than the deck itself." I was gradually reducing our airspeed as we got closer to the heli-deck. Crewmen could be seen manning fire pumps around the deck edge.

"You're just reaching an airspeed of 35 knots," said Bill. "At this stage we'll call ourselves 'committed'. In other words, if one of the engine fails from this moment, we'll aim to land on the heli-deck instead of over-shooting." We were crossing the edge of the heli-deck by then, and I was gradually bringing the machine to the hover.

"That's the idea," said Bill. "But don't start the hover too soon. Aim to enter the hover at the same time as you reach a spot about ten feet above the yellow circle on the heli-deck. Today there's not a problem because we're light, and there's a good breeze. There'll be times, however, when you'll be heavy, without the benefit of much wind, and you'll be really pushed for power."

By that stage we had arrived at a position above the 'H' in the centre of the yellow circle, and I held the helicopter in a hover for a moment. Surrounding structures looked alarmingly close. The best technique, we had been told, was to concentrate on holding a steady hover by looking directly towards the yellow circle; my peripheral vision would absorb the general vicinity.

Gradually, I lowered the collective lever to reduce height, and we felt the S61 sink gently downwards. Slowly we descended towards the heli-deck, and quite soon we felt the main wheels touch the rope net stretched over the deck. The netting helped the aircraft's tyres to grip the deck's slippery surface.

Once we had landed, I glanced at the surrounding scene. The oil-pipe stacks towered above us. The platform looked even more crowded than from our airborne view, with cartons, ducts, and a general jumble in the cramped space. The jib of a crane was parked to one side. There was a smell of oil in the salty atmosphere, and I was aware too of cooking aromas from the evening meal preparations. "In very windy conditions," said Bill, "it can get quite alarming. We stop flying when the wind speed reaches 60 knots. Even so, I've known occasions when the passengers have had to crawl on their hands and knees, holding on to the deck rope, to get to and from the helicopter."

To one side of the deck, an orange coloured wind-sock had been placed. As it flew in the breezy conditions, somehow the bleak and windswept nature of the whole environment was emphasised. The bright colour of the wind-sock contrasted with the weather-beaten look of the paint-work on the platform. We were in raw, unforgiving territory. Over the next eighteen years, I would be reminded of it frequently.

Bill must have noticed that I appeared a little apprehensive. He glanced across at me. He sensed my meditations, and seemed amused. A gradual smile came across his face. "Welcome to the weird and wonderful world of the North Sea!" said Bill at length.

CHAPTER 4

Mountain Memories

On my drive home after the Beatrice A flight, I headed towards the Bennachie hills silhouetted against the horizon. As Bill had pointed out during the flight, they were a dominant local sight, with the distinctive summit of the Mither Tap as the main feature. The prominent shape provided a striking back-drop.

During the twenty-minute drive that evening, I reflected on the recent change in life-style which had affected my family. Our baby daughter, Sally, was just six months old when we had moved her – together with siblings Lizzie and Alan – in the early summer of 1981. My wife, Sue, and I had found it difficult to choose a home in Aberdeenshire. "It's crazy," said Sue. "There are a few castles, some crofts, and a mass of faceless estates. It's practically impossible to find anything 'normal'."

At length, we had put in an offer for a house in a village called Monymusk, some 15 miles from the airport at Aberdeen. "One of the best things about the Scottish system," we had been told, "is that there's no gazumping." Our experience, however, had proved that if the seller was sufficiently canny (and dishonourable), gazumping was indeed a possibility in Scotland.

Despite the gazumping, we were nevertheless delighted with our new home, and the attractive surrounding environment. The small village itself had a central square, with a grass area enclosing a war memorial. Around the village square stood a hotel, a shop with a Post Office, and a variety of dwellings. The star attraction was the village Church, the main part of which was over a thousand years old. Monymusk Church was reputedly Scotland's oldest Norman Church still in active use.

Near our new home was a ramshackle collection of huts, which had been used to house prisoners-of-war in World War 2. To one side of the main part of the camp had been a water tower. The water tower had been demolished, but the foundations remained. Our house had been built on the foundations of the old tower. "What do you mean you've bought a house on an old prisoner-of-war camp?" asked my mother. "I thought you were looking for something normal, whatever that may mean."

"It's really not a bad pad," I assured her.

"It sounds most un-normal to me," replied my mother.

One of the huts had been turned into a Chapel by the prisoners-of-war, many of whom apparently had few regrets at being held in such an agreeable place, away from the front line. The Chapel had been made into a work of art, with lovingly designed windows, and elaborate woodwork. During our early days in the village, we were aware occasionally of large Mercedes cars driving around the old camp as former inmates returned to inspect their handiwork. In a few years time, the land would be sold to a developer; all the huts would be demolished including – sadly – the Chapel.

We soon made new friends, including the Whiteley family. Mr Whiteley at one time had been the headmaster of the local school. He enjoyed telling stories of his efforts to teach English to the prisoners-of-war. The prisoners usually worked on the surrounding farms, as a result of which they learnt local jargon, including the word 'tatties' for 'potatoes'. During one of his classes, Mr Whiteley held up a potato in his hand. He pointed at it, and carefully mouthed the word 'p-o-t-a-t-o'. His pupils looked at him in amusement. "Nah... nah," they shook their heads "... tatties!"

As I drove up to the house that evening, the family were just preparing for a walk. "Hi Dad," called out seven-year old Lizzie, "we're going to Dameye. Are you coming?"

"Sure," I replied.

"How was the flight?" asked Sue.

"Weird and wonderful," I replied. "I'll tell you about it on the walk."

"What's that for?" asked five-year old Alan as he watched me change out of my flying suit.

"It's specially made for flying over water," I said. "It's water-proof."

"What's that mean?"

"It means that the suit won't let in any water."

"Why?"

At that point, Alan's questions were interrupted as a papoose was placed on my back, and baby Sally was positioned inside. The family then set off for the small loch at Dameye, hidden amongst wide-spread thicket, a mile or so from the village. Some of the trees on the way to Dameye were unusual redwoods, uncommonly tall, handsome timbers. The redwoods had survived some famous gales, including that of 1953 which had caused massive damage around Aberdeenshire.

"These trees were planted by my family nearly three hundred years ago," the neighbourhood Laird had told me soon after our arrival in the village. As he had my attention, he had gone on to describe certain impediments affecting some of the local folk.

"The Aberdeenshire county-set take themselves rather seriously," he told me in a confidential manner. "The trouble is they're an inbred lot."

"Don't you mean in bread?" I ventured.

"Humph," replied the Laird after a lapse of some moments, which allowed him time to assimilate this pearl. "It's not funny you know. Some of them are really odd. It's a big problem, dammit." After a further pause, the Laird's good looks were adjusted when he glared at me. "There's another thing," he went on. "It's to do with their arrow slits."

"What arrow slits?" I blurted out, mildly bemused by the conversation's erratic progression.

"The arrow slits in their castles of course," he replied, still scowling. The Laird's voice lowered as he looked around furtively before continuing: "You see, some of them are double-glazed," said the Laird with a clandestine air. "Odd. Most odd," he concluded, shaking his head.

The redwoods, however, stood above such problems. As we walked between the lofty trees that day, we suddenly noticed that the two youngsters, who had run ahead, had stopped. They were staring at something as we approached. Promptly, there was a rustle of bracken as three deer leapt up, and scampered off. We watched the deer head up the hillside, their ears nervously pointed, their white tails bobbing. Again we noticed the distinctive shape of Bennachie in the background.

"It's a super place this," said Sue, "we were lucky to find it." It seemed far removed from the world of North Sea Oil, which I was attempting to describe after my flight to the Beatrice A.

"The North Sea flying is well regulated," I said. "It's run like an airline, with its own special airway system. Sometimes we're faced with situations which are most un-airline like, though."

"What do you mean?" she asked.

"Well, it's still very new to me, but listening to some of the stories, we get involved in all kinds of unusual work, including search and rescue. We can end up in the most unexpected places and situations."

"Sounds fascinating," said Sue. We ducked to avoid low branches as the Dameye loch came into view. The water was calm, and a tumble of brambles and wild brushwood stretched to the edge of the loch. Over the coming years, we would get to know this local walk well, with its timeless atmosphere.

The children had run ahead again, and were pointing at something. "Come quickly," we heard Lizzie call. We waded through a small dam, which fed water to the Clyan's burn. Once more, we had to stoop to miss low branches. Under foot, gnarled tree roots twisted through the soft soil. We soon saw that the children were pointing at two swans. The birds had paddled up to the youngsters in the hope of some bread.

"We must go home and get them something to eat, Mum," said Alan.

"Maybe tomorrow," replied Sue.

We stood at the water's edge admiring the graceful swans. Occasionally we spotted fish jumping; they left a pattern of ripples on the surface. Crows moved noisily amongst the tree-tops. Pigeons darted about the sky. At the far side of the loch, a tree leant away from the bank; its branches dipped into the water.

"Can we get Sal down?" asked Lizzie. The youngest sibling was lifted from the papoose, and held by her brother and sister. The swans looked at us with curiosity as we stood at the top of a low wall by the water's edge.

"Can we swim?" Alan enquired.

"You'll disturb the swans," we said.

"And that thing," Lizzie pointed to a heron, half hidden in some reeds on the opposite side of the loch. The bird, large and graceful, looked about warily, but stayed put. It did not seem unduly disturbed by the chatter of the children. There was an intrusion on its peace, but only a temporary one. The family fell silent for a moment as they admired the magnificent heron. Sue and I then sat by the water's edge, and watched the three children as the eldest two took their young sister for a short walk along the loch's perimeter path.

In the quiet spell, my mind picked up its reflective mood again, and the graphic changes which had affected us. Civilian life was so different to the military; at times the attitudes contrasted quite strongly. I had been in the Royal Air Force for twenty years, and sometimes I found it strange trying to re-adjust. It was hard to pin down, but unexpected situations occasionally highlighted the disparity.

In the peaceful environment of the loch at Dameye, I found my mind thinking about a world completely removed from the present. We continued to supervise the progress of the children, but as we did so, I momentarily caught another glimpse of the surrounding hills. The shape of Bennachie's outline seemed to trigger something in my memory; suddenly, I found myself thinking about an incident which had occurred some fifteen years ago. I had been a fighter pilot at the time, flying Lightning aircraft.

"We'll take-off in close formation, and then have a look at the local area," the Flight Commander had said. A detachment of Lightning aircraft had arrived recently in Cyprus; we would spend the next few weeks there. It was early in the morning on a spring day in 1966, and we aimed to complete the flying programme by lunch-time. We tried to avoid the heat of the afternoon, which could be potent even in the spring.

I followed the lead aircraft as it taxied towards the runway at Akrotiri, on the southern part of Cyprus. We kept our canopies open; although it was early in the day, we still appreciated the cool breeze as the aircraft moved. Already there was a mirage effect in places as the sun bore down. An oxygen mask was clamped to my face, and I wore an anti-g suit with inflatable pads around my waist, and down each leg. On my head was a white bone dome, and outside my flying suit was a life jacket.

As we approached the main runway, I operated a switch on top of a lever by my left hand. The canopy was lowered by an electric motor, and I then pushed the lever down to mechanically lock the canopy.

"Phoenix 1 and 2 ready for take-off," the lead Lightning called to Air Traffic Control. We belonged to Number 56 Squadron, and a Phoenix was part of our emblem.

"Roger, Phoenix 1 and 2," replied Air Traffic Control, "you're clear to line up and take-off."

The lead aircraft then moved swiftly on to the runway, and the brakes were applied. Within moments, I had taken up station near the leader, slightly swept back in a close echelon position, in preparation for our formation take-off. The leader glanced across at me, then nodded. It was the signal to increase engine power. I eased forward the twin throttles controlling the two massive Rolls Royce engines. The aircraft began to strain against its brakes, and I noticed the lead Lightning lean forward on its nose-wheel. The rising engine noise heightened my sense of excitement and anticipation. The roar of the engines was loud even with the well-padded bone dome protecting my ears.

At that stage I concentrated on watching the leader. Soon, he gave a further nod, and we both released our brakes at the point of reaching full cold power with the throttles. I felt an immediate jab of acceleration in my back. I continued to watch the leader, and made regular small adjustments to maintain my relative position. As we picked up speed, I was waiting for a further nod from the lead pilot. It soon came. As he nodded, I eased my twin throttles outwards, paused momentarily, and then pushed them forward again. A deep thunder was heard as the engine reheats lit. The whole aircraft seemed to be shaken by the sudden surge of extra power provided by the reheat system. I still looked at the lead aircraft, but my peripheral vision picked up a blur from the runway edges as we accelerated. I watched the lead aircraft's nose wheel lift from the ground, closely followed by the main wheels.

As we became airborne, I was aware quite quickly that the lead aircraft was throttling back to control our rapid rate of climb. The pilot gave a further nod, which was the signal to dis-engage the reheats.

"Today's flight," the Flight Commander had said, "is the first since the detachment arrived, so it'll be an opportunity to look at the surrounding area, and become familiar with some of the local flying procedures."

The lead aircraft gave a further signal, which was the sign for me to leave my close formation position, and to move out into a battle formation. Soon, I was several hundred yards distance from the lead Lightning; this gave us operational flexibility, and I had the opportunity to look at the area we over-flew.

Akrotiri airfield was beneath us at that stage. The airfield stood on an area which jutted out from the southern coast of Cyprus. To the west of the airfield was Episkopi Bay, and to the north-east the town of Limassol sprawled along the coastline. Directly north of us, the lowland area at Akrotiri rose gradually towards the high ground of the Troodos mountains, with the peak at Mount Olympus.

The lead aircraft held a heading which took us to the left of the high ground, towards Paphos. After that, we planned to follow the coast to Morphou Bay and then towards Kyrenia on the north side of the Island. Following that, our scenic tour would take us inland to Nicosia, where we intended to practice a Ground Controlled Approach using the radar system at Nicosia airfield.

The two Lightnings maintained a height of around 2,000 feet, and I held the distant battle formation position, staying level with my leader. The cloudless Cyprus sky looked impressive as the sun progressively increased the ambient temperatures. The landscape beneath showed the numerous small villages in the foothills around Troodos. There was an uneasy atmosphere on the Island. Makarios was in power, and the United Nations peace-keeping force had been on the Island for a couple of years. In nine years' time, the Turkish invasion of Cyprus would dramatically divide the Greek and Turkish communities.

"Ninety starboard, go," called the leader; he ordered the formation to turn through ninety degrees to the right. We approached the Morphou Bay area, and the leader wanted to assume a more easterly heading. As we flew across Morphou Bay, ahead could be seen the pan handle of Cyprus, and the northern coastline of the Island. We shortly flew past Kyrenia, still pointing towards the pan handle, when the leader called: "Phoenix 2, echelon starboard, go." It was the signal for me to leave the battle formation position, and to return to close formation, next to the leader's right wing. When he was comfortable with my position, the leader began a right turn in the direction of Nicosia airfield.

"Phoenix changing frequency to Nicosia approach," the leader said to Air Traffic Control. He then called me to change to the new radio frequency.

"Phoenix check-in," the leader called on the Nicosia frequency.

"Phoenix 2," I replied.

As we flew south from Kyrenia, the Five Fingers Mountains stretched beneath. Scattered communities were settled in ramshackle-looking villages; in the distance, occasional flashes of reflected sunlight marked the metropolis of Nicosia. Beyond Nicosia, the Troodos range provided a graphic back-drop. As I concentrated on holding close formation, a radio call suddenly interrupted:

"Phoenix 2 from lead."

"Go ahead," I replied.

"I can see signs of a possible oil leak on the side of your aircraft." I eased away from the close formation position, and glanced in my mirror. However, the angle was too oblique for me to make out the reported oil leak.

When flying in close formation, my concentration had been on the leader. I had been unable to monitor the aircraft instruments thoroughly, apart from occasional glimpses at the fuel gauges. As I looked inside the cockpit now, however, I immediately noticed that one of the instrument needles was in an eccentric position. The instruments were designed so that the needles normally pointed in similar directions. A particular needle, however, showed that one of the hydraulic systems, used to power the flying controls, had low pressure; the needle approached the red 'danger' sector. At any moment, I could expect an audio-warning in my headset. If the pressure fell to zero, I would have to rely on the remaining hydraulic system to operate the flying controls. If that second system failed, control of the aircraft would be lost; I would have to bale out at once, using the Martin Baker ejection seat.

"Phoenix lead from 2, declaring PAN. I have primary hydraulic failure," I called on the radio. The code PAN indicated a priority just below MAYDAY, the international distress signal.

"Copied," replied the leader. "Suggest you land at Nicosia." It was important for me to land as quickly as possible; Nicosia was the nearest suitable airfield.

"Roger," I replied to the leader. Then I called: "PAN, PAN, PAN. Nicosia, Phoenix 2, I have a hydraulic failure, request priority landing at your airfield."

There was a slight pause, then a voice with a Cypriot accent replied: "OK Phoenix 2. State your intentions please."

"I'll make a visual approach, for landing as soon as possible," I said to the Air Traffic Control Officer at Nicosia.

The lead Lightning by now had moved to a loose echelon position on my aircraft as he followed and observed. I had my aircraft TACAN navigation system tuned to the Nicosia frequency; I tracked the needle which indicated range and bearing from Nicosia. A small adjustment to heading was needed to take me directly towards the active runway. I continued to monitor the good hydraulic system anxiously; in the back of my mind was an awareness of the dire consequences if it failed.

"Nicosia, Phoenix 2 visual with the airfield," I called at length.

"Roger, Phoenix 2. Call Nicosia Tower," came the reply. The Air Traffic Control Officer in Nicosia Tower regulated aircraft flying in the local circuit at the airfield. As I called him on the radio, I was aware of tension in his voice. He was perhaps unfamiliar with operating Lightning aircraft; the sudden arrival of one with an emergency situation no doubt made him apprehensive.

"Phoenix 2 from Tower, you have priority. You are clear to land. Emergency services are standing by." I then began a turn onto the runway heading. Nicosia airfield lay ahead; an inviting stretch of tarmac which would spell the end of my immediate problems. I continued to monitor the aircraft instruments, and performed final checks before landing.

The fast speed of the Lightning ensured that the aircraft approached the airfield quite rapidly. I eased back the twin throttles; the aircraft began to lose height, and the speed reduced towards the correct landing speed. I concentrated on accurate flying; an over-shoot from the approach was the last thing I wanted. I glanced across at the other Lightning; he was still in position. On completion of his escort duties, he would over-shoot, and return to Akrotiri.

Once more, I brought back the throttles slightly to decrease power as I approached Nicosia airfield. The Lightning needed the whole runway length; I therefore aimed to land as close as possible to the runway's edge. Soon the airfield perimeter began to rush beneath the aircraft. A few feet from the start of the tarmac, at just the right moment, I eased back the throttles further, and positively manoeuvred the powerful machine the last few feet directly onto the landing surface.

As I placed the main wheels firmly down onto the runway, followed by the nose wheel, I simultaneously brought back the twin throttles to their idle position. Then there was a momentary pause before I operated a switch to release the tail parachute. There was an immediate deceleration as the tail parachute billowed out of its housing; this was enhanced as I progressively applied the brakes. Gradually, I became conscious of a sense of relief as the aircraft slowed down. "Thank goodness... I didn't need Mr Martin-Baker's help, after all... "

❖ ❖ ❖

"Dad! Look!" Lizzie tugged at my jacket. The three children had just returned from their walk.

"What is it?" I asked. My mind switched back to the present in an instant. "What is it Lizzie?"

"The heron!" Lizzie pointed as the bird took flight. Its wings flapped noisily as the bird flew away. Slowly, it gained height; the bird avoided us as it flew above the tree-tops. Soon, it was headed away from Dameye; the heron made towards Bennachie. It struck me for a moment that my retrospection had been triggered by the similar outlines of the Bennachie and Troodos ranges. Then I told myself it was just fantasy; the flash-back must have been prompted by a tired mind. Bennachie… Troodos… it was absurd, there could not possibly be a connection.

"Dad?" Lizzie tugged at my coat again. "Are you OK?" she asked.

"Me? Yes – fine thanks." There was a pause.

"I think she noticed that you seemed, somehow... distant," suggested Sue.

I looked at them. "Oh, sorry," I said at length. "Funnily enough, I was thinking about something that happened years ago in Cyprus, of all places. I guess it's just my past catching up with me."

The heron cleared the tree-tops, and soon disappeared from sight. We continued to search in its direction, hoping for further glimpses. The children ran to a clear area attempting to follow the bird's path. The foliage of the trees, however, interrupted the view, and as our eyes were taken towards the high ground, once more I was aware of an affinity with the Troodos hills. In reality, though, all that remained was the enduring outline of the hills of Bennachie, and tomorrow's prospect of another flight to another oil rig.

CHAPTER 5

Stormy Weather

SHETLAND, FOUR MONTHS LATER

The old Viscount aircraft banked steeply as it turned towards the runway at Sumburgh Airport. It was late autumn in 1981, my S61 training had been completed, and I had been sent to Shetland for a few days of duty. During the flight to Sumburgh, I had noticed that the seats of our Viscount were worn quite thin. The inside of the cabin had a rather melancholy atmosphere. Even so the aircraft had an old-world quality; despite seeming a bit faded, the passengers sensed a certain gentility, a certain... well, Britishness about the Viscount.

My fellow passengers were a mixed group. Most of them had several years experience of the offshore life. Their usual routine was to spend two weeks offshore, followed by two weeks at home. It was a disruptive life, and we heard tales of difficulties it caused with many of the wives. Some of the men found it lonely living offshore, and often they would operate twelve hour shifts; towards the end of their two week spell, faces would look tired and drawn. Alcohol was strictly banned on all the offshore installations; some of the men appeared to make up for their enforced abstinence by smoking heavily.

In spite of the miscellany of pony-tails, ear-rings, and other items which remained unappreciated by the military-trained mind, I had developed a respect for the offshore workers. They had a tough life. Like the Serviceman, folk had to make the effort to get along with others. They were part of a team. Poor discipline in the offshore environment could put their mates at risk.

A sudden change in the Viscount's engine note interrupted my musing. The aircraft, having banked to avoid high ground, had straightened before touch-down. But Captain Peter Goddard was evidently unhappy; he had initiated an overshoot. The Viscount shook as the engines went to full power, and the passengers felt the turbulent flight conditions as the aircraft climbed away.

"Ladies and Gentlemen," at length the Captain's voice came through the aircraft speaker system, "the strong winds today are from an awkward direction. We've decided to attempt our landing on another runway, where we hope the cross-wind effect will not be so fierce. We should be landing in another ten minutes."

Faces peered out of the old-fashioned oval windows of the Viscount. The landscape beneath seemed bleak. Sumburgh Airport itself was placed on the southern end of the Shetland Isles, surrounded by various hills of eccentric shape. A notable characteristic appeared to be the permanent gale, usually from a westerly direction, which discouraged the growth of trees. Peat bogs were a dominant local feature. Scattered villages reflected a mix of small Shetland crofts and modern kit-bungalows. The main road snaked its way through the countryside, pointing north to Lerwick, the capital town of Shetland.

"Bloody dump," growled my neighbouring passenger; he had been napping during the flight, but now looked below gloomily.

I attempted conversation.

"How long have you been working offshore?"

"Five and half years," he replied. "It's crap really, but it pays the bills. How about yourself?"

"I'm a helicopter pilot," I said. "I've been doing North Sea work for nearly six months now."

"What were you doing before?" As I explained my background to the neighbour, a series of thumps shook the Viscount's airframe as we hit further turbulence.

"My God," gasped the neighbour. "I hope this thing doesn't fall apart." We both tightened our seat belts further, and continued to gaze out of the aircraft window. Presently, we saw the waves below as the Viscount crossed the coast, and flew over the sea. The strong wind whipped spume from the top of the water, and the salty froth was then flung into the atmosphere. It became harder to see out as the aircraft windows picked up some of the spray. At length, the aircraft started a gradual descent as the Captain made towards the airport again, and the passengers watched in fascination as the violent sea drew closer. Suddenly, we noticed the coastline had been crossed once more while the Viscount continued its descent to the runway. This time, the Captain persevered with the landing; there was a jolt as he placed the aircraft wheels firmly onto the tarmac.

"What's on the agenda for you now?" my neighbour asked me.

"Probably a couple of offshore flights," I replied. "In these winds, it'll make a long day."

"Rather you than me," he commented.

In the main terminal at Sumburgh Airport there was a melée of people, mainly offshore workers, as folk waited for their flights. The offshore passengers wore brightly coloured orange suits, and mooched around with bored expressions. The atmosphere in the terminal was somehow unlike most airports. Over the loudspeakers, from time to time we heard a woman's lilting voice, with its distinctive Shetland accent, as she made announcements. The dialect was derived from Norse, and the Viking connection with Shetland was strong.

"We were a Norse dependency from the year dot," a local friend told me one time. "Then we were annexed in the middle ages by those Scottish sods. Frankly, most Shetlanders still feel antipathy towards Scotland."

The Norse connection would be emphasised at annual Up-Helly-Aa festivals, when teams of local folk would dress in Viking gear, parade through various locations throughout Shetland, before setting fire to a mock-up of a Viking ship.

"Hello, Richard, how are you doing?" I turned around.

"Oh, Ruben, I'm fine. How about you?" Ruben was the radio operator-cum-operations co-ordinator for the Bristow's set-up at Sumburgh. Usually dressed in drab black clothing, Ruben displayed a rather down-at-heel impression. He was affected by some myopic difficulty, and it was often hard to look him in the eye. Ruben assumed a local accent which came across as faintly pseudo; he strived for recognition as a Shetlander. However, Ruben was of English birth and parentage; to be accepted as a genuine Shetlander, it was necessary to be born in Shetland.

"I'm fine thanks," Ruben replied to my question. "Now then, we've got a busy day lined up for you. No time to waste. Two flights to the Murchison, so I'll drive you over to Bristow's straight away. There'll be difficulties with the strong winds today, I'm afraid." Ruben was brisk; apart from other characteristics, he was a staunch Company man. "We've had a few problems here," continued Ruben. "Some of the ground equipment has been damaged in these gales." Ruben filled me in with other local chatter as we drove away from the terminal.

Soon we parked at the far side of Sumburgh Airport, and walked into the Company hangar. There was a musty atmosphere, and the air was laden with a sea-salt smell. Tall hangar doors rattled incessantly in the windy conditions, adding to the eerie, run-down feeling.

As I joined my co-pilot for the day, Mark, he briefed me on the flight planning which he had started. "The round trip to the Murchison should take about three hours plus the time on-deck," said Mark. "In these north-westerly winds, our best diversion will be Bergen in Norway. Once you're happy with the figures, I'll pass a load to the client." When planning a flight, we calculated fuel reserves to allow us to reach a diversion airfield at any stage. I double-checked Mark's figures and looked at the weather forecasts. Mark and I had further discussions; we wanted to be quite sure we had adequate margins in the strong winds. Safety was paramount. Eventually, we passed our available pay-load to Ruben, and while Ruben talked to the client, Mark and I went to change into flying suits.

"Got your load details," called Ruben once Mark and I had donned our flying clothes. "There are fourteen passengers with bags, and some freight. I've got the exact figures when you're ready." Mark entered the figures onto our load sheet, which became a legal document once I had signed it. I also had to sign the aircraft technical log. When these formalities had been completed, Mark and I were ready to walk to our allotted S61.

At the base of the main hangar doors was a smaller door. Mark pushed open the small door, which was immediately yanked out of this hands by the force of the wind. Fortunately, a stout chain had been fitted which limited the door's aperture. "Bloody hell," yelled Mark, above the wind's howl, "you take your life in your hands just walking to the aircraft in this place." Grimly, we held on to the paperwork, headsets, and other paraphernalia as we strode to the helicopter. On the side of the S61 was a handle which I turned to unlock the main airstair door, allowing us to scramble on board. "Phew," exclaimed Mark as we entered the relative safety inside the cabin.

"You strap in," I said to Mark, "and I'll do the external checks."

As I walked down the steps of the airstair door, I braced myself against the gale once more. Then I checked around the outside of the helicopter, before returning to strap into the Captain's seat on the right-hand side of the cockpit. Soon we had started the engines and rotors; the helicopter was 'burning and turning'.

Mark briefly spoke to Air Traffic Control: "68A request taxi-out for passenger pick-up."

"You are clear to the main terminal, 68A," came the reply. I released the parking brake, and began to move away from the hangar. For the outbound sector, it was normal for the co-pilot to make radio calls and do paper-work, while the Captain concentrated on flying the aircraft. The roles were then reversed for the return flight.

Soon we had taxied across the airport, and came to a halt outside the main terminal. I gave a thumbs-up sign to the leader of the ground handling staff, which was the signal allowing him to bring our passengers on board. The passengers trooped out in a line, their heads bowed against the strong winds. Amongst them, I recognised my neighbour from the fixed-wing flight, but like the others, his eyes squinted earthwards in the rough conditions, without glancing up.

As the passengers settled into their seats, Mark closed the airstair door with a thump before walking through the cabin area to check the seat-belts, which would be essential in the turbulent conditions.

I talked to the passengers through the aircraft loudspeaker system as Mark strapped in to his seat. The proceedings were routine; passengers and crew alike were used to the system. Little could any of us have realised the dramatic danger we were about to face. Little could others, in another part of the North Sea, have realised the even more hazardous situation which would blow up – together with the violent storms – in the night ahead.

"68A request taxi-out for take-off," Mark spoke to Air Traffic Control again. We were duly cleared to taxi to the runway-in-use. I had some difficulty manoeuvring the helicopter in the strong gale, but managed to avoid a more drastic step: raising the machine into the hover, faced into wind, before air-taxying sideways with the helicopter still headed into the wind.

"68A you are clear to take-off," called Air Traffic Control as we lined up on the runway. Mark had read out the before take-off checks, and I had no trouble lifting the helicopter into a hover; we were assisted by the strong head-wind. I lowered the nose of the machine to initiate the familiar take-off profile, and soon we had settled into the climb-out procedure from Sumburgh Airport.

I glanced back at the passengers. A few tried to read newspapers, but the bumpy conditions made it a difficult task. Some stared blankly out of the windows as the helicopter shook and rattled, affected by the turbulent air. Before long, as we flew away from Sumburgh, a stretch of heavy rain some miles ahead began to show up on the aircraft radar. Normally, we would have attempted to avoid a rain belt, but this one was too extensive.

"Looks like trouble ahead," growled Mark.

"Afraid so," I replied. "There's not much we can do about that little lot. We'll just have to plough our way through."

The atmosphere grew darker as we approached the rain belt and a distinctive sound was made by the first drops as they beat against the aircraft's windshield. The visibility reduced; I could barely see the grey waters beneath and I concentrated on the aircraft's flight instruments for orientation. A needle pointed at a Decca navigation map which moved slowly from one roller to another; the system indicated our position. The Decca arrangement generally worked well, unless rough weather was encountered; it then tended to unlock, at which point it became unusable.

"Here we go," sighed Mark. The radar picture showed that we approached the edge of the heaviest part of the rain belt; green areas appeared in vivid patterns on the small radar screen. The picture looked graphic, almost artistic. Suddenly there was a surge of noise as a wall of heavy rain struck the windshield; the aircraft rocked unsteadily in the wild conditions. I worked at the flying controls, and corrected a tendency to lose height.

"This is grim," groaned Mark. He turned round to look at the passengers. Sombre faces stared back. The newspapers had been lowered and there was an anxious air in the cabin.

"Have a word with the passengers, please Mark," I said. "I'm sure your dulcet tones will comfort them." Mark raised his eyes upwards as he stretched for the hand-held microphone to speak through the passenger loudspeaker system. I continued to concentrate on flying the helicopter, and tightened my seat-belt even more. The rain persisted to beat noisily against our windshield. The helicopter was supposedly water-proof, but nevertheless rain began to seep through various cockpit corners. "There's a puddle of water by my feet," complained Mark as he reached up to stow the hand-held microphone. He had spoken to our passengers, and I glanced back at them.

"The passengers still look kind of nervous," I said to Mark. "What did you say to them?"

As Mark was about to reply, the helicopter was buffeted by an abrupt extra gust. The rotor blades made an unusual noise; they clattered alarmingly in objection to the conditions. The swell of water against the windshield was relentless and even though the time was early afternoon, it had become so dark that I turned on the cockpit lighting to help me see the flight instruments. The heavy cloud had also obscured our vision of the sea.

At length, we noticed that the exotic green colouring of the radar returns appeared to be diminishing; the radar picture looked less complex. "We should be the other side of this soon," said Mark. Although the rain seemed unyielding, and the sound was insistent, we noticed that the atmosphere had become less dark. Eventually, the surrounding clouds became even lighter, and the intensity of the rain began to ease.

Meanwhile, Mark was speaking on the aircraft radio to the Area Controller. He passed our estimated timing for various reporting points, and for our arrival at the Murchison. At this stage, the north-westerly winds had veered to a more northerly direction; the head-wind component meant that our outbound flight time would be longer than normal. We measured our ground-speed by setting stop watches, and timing each ten mile leg.

Close to the median line between Norway and the United Kingdom, the Murchison was one of the more northerly of the extensive number of oil installations in the area known as the East Shetland Basin. As we flew towards the Murchison, the flight conditions gradually improved; at length the heavy rain ceased. The region remained cloudy, and we continued to be affected by turbulence, but nevertheless we made steady progress against the head-winds.

Eventually, Mark called the Area Controller: "Viking, 68A request descent to 1000 feet."

"Roger 68A. Confirm you are just west of the Brent Field." Our Decca, which had unlocked during the rain storm, was serviceable again by then, and the needle on the roller map verified our position.

"We are due west of the Brent Delta," replied Mark.

"Copied, 68A. In that case you are clear to descend from 2000 feet to 1000 feet. Call me landing on the Murchison," said the Viking Controller.

By that stage, we were in radio contact with the Murchison, and had noted details of their local weather conditions. I lowered the helicopter's collective lever to initiate our descent; as expected, the tone from the engines and rotors altered slightly. I scanned the flight instruments, and monitored our height reduction on the altimeter.

Suddenly, as the aircraft began to descend, I became aware of unusual feed-back through the flying controls. The cyclic stick, in particular, had picked up an oscillation. This was accompanied by a strange sound from the area of the main rotors. Mark looked across the cockpit at me; he had noticed the peculiar noise.

Abruptly, the Master Caution caption at eye level illuminated; lower down, a light stating 'BIM' glowed. At once I reduced the airspeed, while Mark carried out Immediate Action Drills. The Blade Inspection Method caption warned us that a problem had developed with one of our main rotor blades.

"Put out an emergency call," I said to Mark. "We'll have to land as soon as possible. The nearest suitable place is the Murchison itself."

While Mark made the emergency radio call, the oscillation through the flying controls became more pronounced. The helicopter vibrated ominously. "I reckon we can just about hold it like this," I said eventually, "but if these oscillations get more violent, we'll have to consider ditching in the sea. You'd better warn the passengers." As we glanced back, it was evident that the passengers were already aware of the unusual state of affairs; their looks reflected their apprehension. As Mark spoke to them, I noticed that the passengers had raised the hoods of their immersion suits, and had started to fully zip-up their suits. When told, they would adopt the brace position.

The Murchison appeared as a blip on our radar picture by then, and we anxiously counted down the range as the oil installation grew closer. Mark read out the before landing checks, and went through the emergency check list to ensure that we had completed all the drills.

"Perhaps one of the blades was damaged during that rain storm," commented Mark as the forceful shake of the helicopter persisted.

When we picked up the Murchison visually, the oil platform looked tantalisingly close, but we still had a few miles to cover. At length, Mark read out the finals checks, and confirmed with the Helicopter Landing Officer that we had deck clearance. I ensured that we pointed into the wind for my approach to the heli-deck, and chose a flight path which would allow an escape route. I had to be prepared for the fact that at any stage an offshore landing may have become unsafe; the helicopter still felt perilously unstable.

Eventually, however, we reached a point where we were committed to the heli-deck landing. As we crossed over the edge of the heli-deck itself, I intended to hold the machine for as short a time as possible in the hover. The strong winds were helpful, and I concentrated on looking at the yellow painted circle on the heli-deck. Time seemed to pass with frustrating slowness, but at last we reached safety: the familiar jolt of the wheels touching the surface of the deck was felt. Quickly, we closed down the engines and rotors.

The end of the emergency situation produced a sense of instantaneous relief for passengers and crew alike. Faces still appeared pale and anxious, however, as folk left the helicopter. It was some time later that I realised how unnerving it felt that our potentially calamitous plight had ceased as rapidly as it had begun. For us, the perilous situation brought about by the storms had ended. For others, however, the danger was about to begin.

ABERDEEN, SCOTLAND – 12 HOURS LATER

It took Captain Malcolm Soper some moments. At length, however, he was awakened by the insistent telephone ring. Captain Soper glanced at his clock and frowned; it was 0220. He was exhausted, having arrived home just before midnight. The high winds that had affected all flights the previous day, had caused hours of delay to his particular flight to the TW58 oil rig.

"Malcolm? Are you there?" the Duty Controller at Bristows had heard the lifting of the telephone.

"Apologies. It's Malcolm Soper here." The reply was spoken quietly, after a pause.

"Malcolm. Sorry to disturb you, but an emergency has arisen." Some seconds of silence followed; both men sensed the moment's significance.

"Go on," said Captain Soper eventually. He was still in the process of waking from deep slumber.

"I'm afraid we need you here right away, Malcolm. The TW58 has been dragging its anchors in these gales and heavy seas. They're worried it might break free and collide with other installations." There was a further pause. Captain Soper weighed things up in his mind. He was fatigued, and well out of normal duty hour requirements. But this was an emergency; the rules changed then. And night call-outs were most unusual; matters must be really serious. He was one of a handful of Captains qualified to carry out winching operations on Search and Rescue missions.

Captain Soper thought for a few more seconds before replying: "I'll be in as quickly as I can." The Duty Controller then told him the other members of his crew, and gave some further details.

As Captain Soper drove through the deserted streets of Aberdeen, his car was buffeted by the strong winds. In his mind, the Captain worked out various scenarios, and the best way of planning for them. At least he was happy with his crew. His co-pilot, Bob Bolton-King, was an ex-Air Force Officer with considerable flying experience, although he was new to the Company and to the S61. His two crewmen, Colin Larcombe and Chris Bond, were both experienced aviators. Captain Soper was aware of the weather forecast; winds were expected to exceed 60 knots, the limit at which normal flying operations ceased. This limit was waived, however, for emergency situations; the matter was then officially at the discretion of the Captain. He ruminated that – ironically – in the most dangerous situations the rule books were pretty much discarded; the onus of responsibility lay directly with the aircraft Commander.

Still deep in thought, Captain Soper parked at the Aberdeen Heliport. The floodlit staff car park appeared bleak and empty, apart from a few cars belonging to engineering staff on night shift. Captain Soper strode towards the Company edifice, his head bowed against the blustery winds. On entering the building, he paced up the stairs two at a time. Soon, he passed through the door leading into the operations and flight planning set-up. The room seemed deserted apart from Jim, the Duty Controller who had telephoned earlier.

Presently, however, the other crew members began to appear. Two S61s were required, and crew discussions took place in earnest as more facts were presented. The Captain of the other helicopter, Andy Zgolinski, was an American shortly to leave the Company. His co-pilot, John Follis, was an experienced aviator, although fairly new to the Company. Captain Zgolinski and his co-pilot would not fly with crewmen; their allotted S61 was not winch-equipped.

"I guess this ultimately rests on our shoulders," Captain Zgolinski said to his fellow Captain at one stage. All members of the crew were involved in the planning and in the deliberations, but the eventual judgement to proceed was made by the two Captains. The flight planning was made using Stavangar in Norway as the diversion; from the TW58, this airfield was calculated to be the fastest to reach in the forecast wind direction.

"Malcolm!" Captain Soper looked up as the Duty Controller called him. He also glanced at the clock; the time was 0445. "Important message just coming through, Malcolm," continued the Duty Controller. Captain Soper walked over to the radio room. There was a clatter from the Telex machine as it churned out messages, and screeches from the High Frequency radio could be heard in the background. The Duty Controller was on the telephone; his facial expression reflected the seriousness of the message. Eventually, the Duty Controller put down the telephone, and looked directly at Captain Soper.

"Their fears have come true, Malcolm," said the Duty Controller. "The TW58 has broken free; it's drifting out of control. The final decision is yours, of course, but the rig's just put out another urgent call." The Duty Controller swallowed nervously as he watched Captain Soper's reaction. The Captain pondered for a few seconds, then joined the other crew members.

"If anyone wishes to stand down, that is entirely their prerogative," said Captain Soper to his colleagues. "For my part, I'm prepared to have a shot. But there will be no criticism of any individual who doesn't volunteer to fly in these conditions." The Captain then looked at the five aircrew individually. In turn, each man just nodded impassively; their decision to go was unanimous. "Thank you, gentlemen," said Captain Soper. "Before we walk out to the aircraft, we'll wait for a further update from the TW58."

Over the next half hour, the crews made final checks of equipment. The two crewmen, especially, checked over the serviceability of their flight suits. If rescue from the water became necessary, it was these two men who would cope directly with the mountainous seas.

After receiving more information from the TW58, the crews walked together to their waiting helicopters. It was still dark as the aircrew checked their aircraft. In the blustery winds, the rotor blades had a tendency to 'sail' up and down, which caused difficulty with the start procedures. Nevertheless, just before 0600, both aircraft were airborne.

The two S61s flew together in a loose formation. Captain Soper took the lead position; although it was dark, the navigation lights on his aircraft were seen clearly by the pilots in the other machine. The distance from Aberdeen to the TW58 was over two hundred miles, and normally the flight would have taken more than two hours. With the gales from a north-westerly direction, however, a tail-wind component boosted their ground speed. The crews reckoned to reach the TW58 in less than an hour and a half that morning.

As the helicopters were buffeted in the rough weather, the crews glanced at each other apprehensively. From time to time, the rotor blades produced ominous clattering sounds as the S61s were affected by violent surges of wind. The air was laden with sea salt whipped from wave tops, and the salt accumulated on the helicopter windshields tended to hinder the pilots' vision outside the cockpit. Attempts to use the windshield wipers were counter-productive; the action of the wipers smeared the windshield.

At length, Captain Soper said to his co-pilot: "Try to raise the TW58 on the radio, please Bob." As the co-pilot made repeated attempts on the radio, all the aircrew listened anxiously. But there was no reply; the co-pilot's persistent calls were met with silence.

The aircrew meanwhile busied themselves with other tasks, including regular fuel calculations; their flight planning counted on a refuel at the TW58, or a close-by installation. In order to carry out the rescue procedures, and then reach Norway with safe margins, it was essential that the machines refuelled – a hazardous operation in the turmoil of the storms.

Suddenly, when the helicopters were some thirty miles from the TW58, a faint radio call was heard: "*... this is the TW58. Do you* *read?...* " The intermittent call had been difficult to hear, but nevertheless it was sufficient to raise the spirits of the aircrew. As the co-pilot continued his endeavours to speak to the installation, eventually two-way radio contact was made. The TW58 gave position updates – the oil rig was still drifting out of control – and details of the current weather. The crews of both aircraft looked despondent as wind speeds of up to ninety knots were reported. The movement of the installation was well beyond normal pitch and roll limits. A further item of bad news caused the aircrew even more consternation: the TW58 refuelling equipment had been blown overboard by the gales. "We'll just have to refuel on a nearby rig," said Captain Soper.

As the helicopters approached the TW58, the surface visibility was poor. When the S61s drew adjacent to the installation, the pilots were unable to see it visually. They were therefore forced to overshoot from the approach, before turning back into the wind to re-locate the TW58 on the aircraft radar. Flying directly into the wind, the ground speed of the helicopters was drastically reduced. Instead of the usual one hundred and ten knots, the aircraft sometimes achieved no more than twenty knots. The crews felt frustration at their slow progress; time dragged dreadfully as the helicopters clawed their way back to the TW58. At length, however, the aircrew managed to make visual contact with the installation.

"We'll go in first," Captain Soper said to his crew, and the co-pilot passed this message to the other S61. Then he said to the TW58: "I want the heli-deck cleared of all personnel." The Captain held his S61 in a hover alongside the TW58 heli-deck as he assessed the problems. He was particularly concerned about loose debris flying into the rotor blades. He was also concerned whether the S61 would hold its position after landing; the forceful movement of the heli-deck could cause the machine to slide. Eventually, however, Captain Soper began to position the S61 for the landing. He remained in the hover, but gingerly flew the machine towards the heli-deck. The deck heaved with alarming violence, but on some occasions the movement was less pronounced; the Captain therefore had to time his landing carefully.

"Standby gents," said Captain Soper to his crew, at length. "We're going for it now." The Captain had judged the moment, and with a deliberate movement, he flew the S61 towards the heli-deck, and landed firmly. As the TW58 crew watched the helicopter, they held their positions away from the heli-deck, waiting for the Captain's authorisation to move. Captain Soper felt trepidation about the severe buffeting against the helicopter. It was highly uncomfortable, but at least it seemed that the S61 was not sliding across the deck. Eventually, he said to his co-pilot: "OK, Bob. You can call them in."

Shortly after the co-pilot had relayed this message, the first of the TW58 crew began to appear on the heli-deck. The men wore orange survival suits, fully zipped-up to the neck, and with hoods covering their heads. The aircrew noticed that the strength of the wind prevented the men from walking normally to the helicopter; they had to crawl on hands and knees across the heli-deck, remaining as low as possible. A rope netting covered the surface of the heli-deck; the men grabbed the rope, and dragged themselves hand over hand towards the helicopter. As each man eventually reached the S61's airstair door, he was pulled into the cabin by the two burly helicopter winchmen.

At length, when all the survivors were on board, the winchmen slammed the airstair door shut. The other S61 in the meantime was holding a hover to one side of the TW58. Captain Soper warned the other machine that he was about to lift. He then raised his helicopter into a low hover, and without further ado flew away from the TW58.

Meanwhile, arrangements had been made for Captain Soper's machine to refuel at an installation some twenty miles away. "We need to take up a north-westerly heading," said the co-pilot. "Unfortunately it's directly into the wind, so it'll be a long haul." As the S61 progressed slowly towards the refuelling point, the crew calculated that they needed to top up to the maximum capacity of the fuel tanks. "It means we'll have to leave four passengers behind," said the co-pilot.

At last, having made radio contact with the refuelling crew, Captain Soper drew alongside the installation, holding the S61 in a hover. As with the TW58 before, he appraised the hazards around the heli-deck. Again, he had to time his moment of landing.

After the S61 had landed, the heli-deck crew were faced with the physical problems of performing the refuel. In the raging storm, it was not possible to walk normally around the heli-deck. The refuelling crewmen had to move in pairs, usually on hands and knees. Temporary safety ropes were rigged across the heli-deck; the aircrew witnessed resourcefulness typical of the folk who worked offshore. Eventually, up to three men were needed to drag the refuelling hose across to the helicopter. In spite of the hazards, the S61 received its vital fuel in the end.

At length, having off-loaded four passengers, the aircrew were ready to undertake the flight to Stavangar. Captain Soper had received the message that the other S61 had refuelled elswhere; the two aircraft would operate independently from now on. "You can do the flying for a bit, Bob," Captain Soper said. The co-pilot took control of the helicopter, and having made further assessments, he lifted the machine into a low hover before departing towards Norway. Initially the aircraft was flown at 2000 feet, with a slight tail-wind as forecast. The pilots could see ahead just two miles or so in the murky weather. "Look down now, Malcolm," said the co-pilot at one stage. "Have you ever seen such massive seas?"

As the flight progressed towards Stavangar, the pilots were having difficulty with the aircraft Decca equipment. Captain Soper, as the non-flying pilot, was spending much of his time re-setting the apparatus, which was becoming virtually useless as it continually 'unlocked' in the tempestuous winds. However, the aircrew required the Decca; none of the other navigation aids were providing useful information.

"This Decca's a nightmare," commented the co-pilot. "Whenever you seriously need the bloody thing, it fails to work."

The crew kept a 'dead reckoning' position, which was normal good airmanship practise. However, navigation aids were needed as well, especially in such extreme conditions.

At length, Captain Soper decided to abandon his efforts to make sense of the Decca. Much as they required the equipment, the stage had been reached when the crew had to acknowledge that it would never become available. The pilots were reduced to 'dead reckoning' navigation; they flew estimated compass headings, and operated stop watches to time their progress. The aircrew monitored the surface of the sea in attempts to work out the wind direction. Gradually, they realised that the wind was changing. No longer was the wind behind them, or even abeam; the direction was veering to give a head-wind.

In a day full of angst, the recognition of their situation at that point was probably the worst moment. There was the real possibility that they would run out of fuel before reaching the Norwegian coast. In the gigantic waves, their chances of survival would have been slim indeed. Privately, Captain Soper had a further eerie reflection: twenty-one years ago to the very day – practically to the hour – he had ejected from a Sea Hawk aircraft into the North Sea.

In a desperate attempt to make reasonable headway, Captain Soper took over control of the S61 from his co-pilot, and descended the machine to 300 feet. The Captain flew the helicopter well above the normal limiting airspeed; it was their only chance of making sufficient progress. "Turn round and look cheerful, Bob," said Captain Soper at one point. "Let's at least try to give the impression to the passengers that the flight's progressing well." In truth, the aircrew were uncertain about their ground-speed, their navigation, and whether their fuel reserves would be enough.

Suddenly, a glimmer of hope dawned. One of the radio-positioning beacons showed signs of life. The crew received confirmation that the heading they flew was pretty much on track. The forward visibility was very poor at that stage, partly because of mist, and partly because the flight at 300 feet had caused a build-up of salty deposits on the windshield. When the aircraft at last reached Norway, the crew were unaware until they were virtually overhead the coastline. Because of their low altitude, the pilots had been unable to speak to Stavangar on the radio. Having crossed the coast, however, at length the aircrew were able to make radio contact. "You have priority over other air traffic," said Stavangar Air Traffic Control;

the Controller also confirmed the helicopter's position. By that stage, the 'low fuel warnings' had started to flash inside the S61 cockpit.

The crew monitored the S61 fuel gauges acutely; they reckoned to reach Stavangar within nine minutes. But the gauges tended to flicker around, especially in rough flight conditions; the S61 gauges were unreliable at these very low levels of fuel. The crew were painfully aware that at any moment one, or both, of the helicopter's engines could stop operating. The pilots therefore deliberately ran the fuel supply to one of the engines at a slightly lower level. If the engine with the lower fuel state 'flamed-out', the pilots calculated that the operating engine would have just sufficient fuel for an emergency landing onto the rough terrain below.

There was little conversation in the cockpit by that stage. The pilots had discussed their plan already; all the crew knew exactly what action would be taken if the worst happened. "Keep smiling at the passengers," said Captain Soper to his crew. He again saw no reason to cause the passengers unnecessary alarm. Perhaps the passengers sensed the strained atmosphere anyway. The tension increased as the distance to the airfield shortened. Slowly, agonisingly, the miles to Stavangar reduced one by one. When the pilots eventually saw the airfield appearing out of the mists, the aircrew received a sudden boost to their morale. The aircraft gauges showed the S61 to be down to the last amounts of fuel. But it turned out to be just sufficient; the wheels of the helicopter finally touched down at Stavangar airfield with both engines still functioning.

It took time for each individual to wind down from the stress of the situation. As Captain Soper glanced at each member of his crew, the looks of relief were almost palpable. Despite the hours of trauma and danger, the Captain's crew had remained staunchly supportive. All ex-military, the men had been trained to deal with extreme situations. However, that day had seen their training stretched to the limit. "Exceptional folk," Captain Soper thought to himself. "Exceptional folk… "

The aroma of coffee greeted the aircrew when they eventually reached the crew room. The Norwegians liked their coffee strong. "I'll have it any way it comes," commented one of the crewmen.

"You mean the coffee?" enquired the other crewman.

"That'll do for a start," came the reply. Captain Soper noted the aircrew banter with relief; normality was returning.

The gales still raged outside, but Captain Soper had just heard about the safe landing of the other S61 at Stavangar. He was informed too that most TW58 personnel had been rescued, apart from an emergency skeleton crew left on board. The installation itself had meanwhile cleared potential collision risks, and was riding out the storm. The aircrew settled into the crew-room chairs as they sipped the coffee, and discussed this news. The men chatted as well about their recent flight; it was an opportunity for nervous tension to be released.

"Captain... Captain!" The aircrew ceased their conversation, and looked in surprise at the member of airport staff who ran into the crew-room. Captain Soper stood up, and walked towards the man who pointed outside vigorously.

"Captain... your machine... she is broken!" The member of the airport staff spoke with a pronounced Norwegian accent. He seemed flustered as he continued to signal. Hastily, Captain Soper followed the man; they ran past waiting passengers, and through the security doors. The moment they reached outside, the Captain was abruptly reminded of the strength of the gales still blowing. The two men battled towards the parked helicopters; the Captain noted that the other S61 had been parked next to his machine.

As they drew closer to the helicopters, Captain Soper soon saw the cause of the commotion. One of the front-positioned rotor blades of his aircraft had been fractured by the force of the wind; the tip of the blade rested on the tarmac. Captain Soper stared at the scene for a moment. "Impossible!" he said. The metal blades were designed to withstand the most severe conditions. In theory, the blades just would not break like that, especially as they had been tethered with ropes.

The Captain crouched low for protection from the storm as he continued to observe the spectacle. Suddenly, he noticed something else: the rotors of the S61 parked next door had begun to turn slowly, overcoming the powerful rotor brake. There was a danger that the blades would gather momentum; the helicopter could become unstable and collide with his machine. Quickly, Captain Soper moved towards the S61 next to his. As the blades rotated, they tended to 'sail' up and down alarmingly in the gales. Ducking as low as possible, the Captain chose his moment to rush towards the airstair door at the rear. He rapidly opened the door, stepped inside the machine, and dashed forward to the cockpit. Captain Soper then reset the rotor brake, which successfully stopped the blades from turning. The Captain then sat down in the pilot's seat while he assessed the scenario.

As Captain Soper looked outside the cockpit, he became aware of a new peril. Some four hundred yards ahead, a row of light aircraft had been parked. Fortunately, the light aircraft appeared to be offered some shelter by a nearby building. Even so, Captain Soper felt unnerved as he watched an approaching line squall. He reckoned that the winds within the squall were in excess of a hundred knots. There was the danger that the light aircraft could be blown towards the S61s. "If that happens," the Captain said to himself, "I'll bolt to the rear of the helicopter for protection."

Meanwhile, Captain Soper remained in the cockpit as the line squall drew closer. The howling noise of the wind had increased to a shriek. The helicopter began to shake even more violently, and the rotor blades 'sailed' spectacularly. The flying controls of the S61 were hydraulically locked, but Captain Soper noticed that the force of the winds had begun to overcome the hydraulic lock. The flying controls had started to thrash around with vigour. The Captain grasped the flying controls, but he was unable to prevent the furious motion. Then he noticed that the 'sailing' movement of the rotor blades had increased. The blade immediately in front of the cockpit was bent upwards, almost to the vertical, before it was flung down again with such power that it struck the surface of the tarmac. The blade then bounced up again, distorted and twisted by the overwhelming forces of nature. Once more the rotor blade was arched upwards, reaching a near-vertical position. This cycle was repeated several times, for several seconds, until finally, with a loud crack, the blade fractured.

Captain Soper sat aghast as he observed these sensational gyrations. Never before had he witnessed anything like it. An experienced aviator, he had seen a thing or two in the helicopter world. But this was something extraordinary. The two S61s remained side-by-side, both with fractured rotor blades, as the Captain endured the scene, unable to prevent the damage from taking place.

As the Captain sat in the S61, he eventually noticed that the line squall was moving away. The drastic activity gradually declined as the wind strength eased; the Captain realised – mercifully – that the danger posed by the light aircraft had diminished. Captain Soper was at length able to leave the cockpit. When he spoke to Air Traffic Control, he was told that the wind speed had increased from some ninety knots, to one hundred and forty knots during the squall.

The gale had lessened, but nevertheless was still fierce as the Captain struggled back to the crew-room to rejoin his colleagues. The strong Norwegian coffee tasted even better, and Captain Soper was at last able to ease up as the aircrew of both S61s, by then reunited, talked with each other about their dramatic day.

During the buzz of conversation, as the men exchanged anecdotes, one of the aircrew suddenly glanced at Captain Soper. "Malcolm!" said the aircrewman. The Captain looked up wearily; he was beginning to realise just how exhausted he felt. "We nearly forgot," continued the aircrewman. "Many Happy Returns of the Day, Malcolm."

Some months after this rescue from the TW58, it was announced that the aircrew involved were to be jointly awarded with the AVCO-LYCOMING Helicopter Heroism Award in conjunction with the Aviation and Space Writers of America. The aircrews were invited to collect the award, together with their wives, at the Aviation and Space Writers Convention held in Miami, Florida.

CHAPTER 6

The Falklands

FIVE MONTHS LATER

My children glanced at me with puzzled expressions; it was not easy explaining to them my sentiments about a photograph in that morning's newspaper. "Well, it's just a photo that sends shivers down the spine," I said to the youngsters tersely, before continuing: "Just a couple of years ago, I helped to train some of these marines in helicopter procedures." The men were tough, no-nonsense types. But the photograph was lucid; the men were pictured on their stomachs, lined in a neat row, as Argentinian soldiers conducted a search. Behind them was the roof of Government House in the Falkland Islands. The Argentinian soldiers themselves wore alien-looking uniforms; some had Balaclavers over their faces. "Are they from *Star Wars*?" asked young Alan.

The dramatic goings-on in the South Atlantic were especially poignant for a number of North Sea helicopter pilots. Many of the pilots were ex-military, and had been involved in exercises with these soldiers. In the early part of 1982, our minds became focused on the activities of our erstwhile colleagues. At home, my children asked me to tell them about this issue which suddenly had become so important. As the build up to the possible invasion occupied TV screens, and the world's press, the subject became predominant.

Some years after the war, my Company was awarded a contract to support the British military settlements throughout the Falklands. I would spend three months there helping with this effort. Those of us who were sent to the Falklands would bone up on the main events of the war, particularly from the aviation standpoint. "Learn about the background to the hostilities," we were told. "It'll help you to understand the attitude of the Islanders."

In the Spring of 1982, as diplomatic efforts to find a solution to the tenuous Falklands issue continued, the worst fears suddenly materialised early in the morning of the second of April. Just a handful of marines were available to defend the Falkland Islands from the invasion force. These soldiers had been strategically placed in last minute anticipation. Two of the marines, for example, had been positioned in an area overlooking York Bay, just north of Stanley airfield. "You men represent the entire British defence of this section of the Islands," they had been told. They were armed with a machine gun, and a few rounds of ammunition. The two men were part of an overall contingent of sixty-eight marines, led by Major Norman, who expected to be outnumbered by odds of some twenty to one if the Argentine forces landed.

Just before dawn that morning, one hundred and twenty men of the *Buzo Tactico* – Argentine specialist commandos – landed by helicopter at Mullett Creek. Clad in black, these men were the first invaders to land on the Islands. They headed north initially, in the direction of Sapper Hill, before splitting into two groups. One group headed west towards some barracks, the other group went east, on the way to Government House which was to become the focus of military action.

Inside Government House, the Governor, His Excellency Rex Hunt, had a personal bodyguard (Marine Dorey), who never left his side once it was clear that invasion was inevitable. After a forlorn dinner the previous night, the Governor had packed his wife and son off to the relative safety of another house.

When Major Norman realised that his over-stretched defences had been outflanked, he ordered sections of marines to fall back to Government House before hastening there himself. Moments after arriving at the House, the Major heard shooting. It was still dark outside, and not immediately appreciating what was going on, Major Norman dashed out of the house shouting: "Who fired those guns?". He quickly realised that it was a machine gunner from the *Buzo Tactico*. Government House was under attack.

Behind the House was a ridge from where the *Buzo Tactico* peppered the building with automatic fire, bursting pipes which sent water flooding into the kitchen. "Get down everyone. Get down!" yelled someone. Those inside the building, including the Governor, got down on the floor and took cover. Outside were thirty-three marines defending the House. During the mayhem, the Governor managed to make a telephone call; he tried to tell the local radio station what was going on.

Some half hour after the start of their assault on Government House, the *Buzo Tactico* suddenly stopped firing. If their plan had been to wipe out the marines, and kidnap the Governor, it had failed. Clearly, reinforcements were needed.

Meanwhile, the two marines at York Point jumped onto their motorbikes, and raced across sand dunes towards the airport; they were desperate to pass on the information that they had spotted a large enemy ship headed towards Stanley. However, the men found the airport deserted. "They've baled out of this place completely," they said to one another. "We'd better fall back to Government House pronto." The two marines then re-mounted their motorbikes, and sped along the road to Stanley. The Islanders had been warned to stay indoors, and the two soldiers did not see another soul until they came to the main street, where a Land Rover and some marine colleagues blocked the road. "You'd better join up with us," the two men were told. "We're going to try to reach Government House." As the group of sixteen marines ran towards their objective, however, they were driven back by sniper fire. As dawn arrived, six of the marines made a second attempt to reach Government House. Despite machine-gun fire, these men made it across the town's football pitch to the safety of a hedgerow, and thence to Government House.

Just after 7am, the Governor telephoned the radio station again, to announce that Argentinian forces were progressing towards Government House with armoured personnel carriers fitted with 30mm cannons. "We don't stand a chance against their weapons," said the Governor, "but I'm not surrendering to the bloody Argies." He agreed, however, to talk to the enemy. As a delegation walked line abreast along the road to Government House, steel helmeted men appeared from their place of hiding on the ridge, chanting "Ar-gentina".

When the delegation reached Government House, Admiral Busser, the deputy commander of the invasion force, pointed out that they had come to take back "what is rightfully ours". The Admiral went on to say that they had an overwhelmingly superior force, and there was nothing the marines could do about it except die. "Your men," said the Admiral, "have fought with bravery and skill." Although the figures were not officially confirmed, it was calculated that the marines had killed five invaders, wounded seventeen, and knocked out an Amtrac armoured personnel carrier, without a single casualty on their own side. "But now your men should lay down their arms," continued the Admiral.

The Governor realised that further armed resistance would be an act of immolation. He therefore ordered Major Norman to surrender. By 9.30 in the morning, to the sound of British martial music broadcast on the Falklands radio, the marines at Government House laid down their arms, and that graphic, grim photograph was taken.

Back at home, the first Saturday session of parliament since the Suez crisis of 1956 was called. The Prime Minister, Mrs Margaret Thatcher, was uncharacteristically nervous as she spoke in the three hour emergency debate at the House of Commons. Later, however, she announced: "The government have decided that a large task force will sail to the Falklands as all preparations are complete. *HMS Invincible* will be in the lead and will leave port on Monday."

As the armed services made ready for war, convoys of trucks headed for the south-west Channel coast, carrying men and equipment. The newspapers commented on "scenes reminiscent of the last world war". I was one of a number of North Sea helicopter pilots who had recently left the military; we dusted down our uniforms, convinced that we would be called upon as reservists, although in the end it never happened. For our family, there was a further personal involvement: my cousin and best man, Lieutenant Colonel Hew Pike, was heading south with the task force as the commander of the Third Battalion of the Parachute Regiment – otherwise known as 3 Para.

While the task force of some one hundred ships progressed towards the South Atlantic under the command of Rear-Admiral Sandy Woodward, further diplomatic endeavours were made to resolve the crisis peacefully. We became news-hungry as the unfolding of events occurred.

The news about one particular incident was initially suppressed, but when we eventually heard about it, the incident was much discussed by the North Sea aircrews. It involved the effort to extract SAS men from a glacier in South Georgia; they had run into trouble during the planned recapture of the Island. Three Wessex helicopters had difficulty finding the soldiers in the ferocious weather. At length, however, the men were located and loaded on board. However, one of the Wessex crashed on take-off in the white-out conditions. Astonishingly, there were no casualties, and the soldiers were re-distributed amongst the two remaining helicopters.

During the next attempt at take-off, another Wessex crashed. The one surviving machine continued to its support ship (*HMS Antrim*) to report the appalling information. "Thirteen SAS men, and four helicopter aircrew are still marooned on the glacier, and they'll probably die if we can't rescue them before nightfall," the Captain of *HMS Antrim* was told. When the sole remaining Wessex headed back to the glacier, most onlookers felt that "there was little chance of anyone coming out alive." However, the pilot, Lieutenant Commander Stanley, landed at the glacier once more, but reckoned that approaching nightfall would prevent another flight. The capacity of the helicopter should have been about half-a-dozen men, but incredibly all seventeen men were squeezed on board. With such an overloaded machine, the take-off must have been pretty fraught. However, a combination of strong winds and piloting skill no doubt saw them through; the Wessex made a successful departure from the glacier.

When the Wessex reached *HMS Antrim*, the ship was highly unstable in the colossal seas. Unlike Captain Soper in the TW58 rescue the year before, Lieutenant Commander Stanley was too overloaded to allow him the luxury of assessing deck movement while he held a hover alongside. "I've got just one option," the Lieutenant Commander thought to himself. "Head straight for the heaving deck, and crash land." The manoeuvre was hardly text-book, but it was successful: all passengers and crew survived the landing with nothing worse than cuts and bruises. For his part in this operation, Lieutenant Commander Stanley was one of three airmen later awarded the Distinguished Service Order.

On April the twenty-sixth, Mrs Thatcher spoke in the House of Commons about the "professional skill" with which the re-capture of South Georgia had been carried out. The previous evening, she had emerged from Downing Street with news of the re-capture, and said her famous words: "Just rejoice at that news and congratulate our forces and the marines... rejoice, rejoice."

Early in May, Vulcan V-bombers, brought out of retirement, attacked the runway at Stanley airport. At the same time, helicopters put ashore the first SAS and SBS units on East and West Falkland. Despite these activities, diplomatic peace efforts were pursued by General Haig and others to allow the task force to turn back. However, towards the end of May it became clear that the talks had failed, and the task force thus approached the Falklands ready for action. "D-day is set for Friday the twenty-first of May," the task force troops were told. As the world watched with trepidation, the aviation aspects in particular were observed, and endlessly discussed, by the North Sea aircrew. During the landing operations at San Carlos, the reality of the situation hit us vividly. "Have you heard the news?" we asked one another. "Two Gazelle helicopters have been shot down. Three aircrew have been killed." The Argentine Air Force attacked the British with Skyhawks, Mirages, and Pucaras. They were opposed by the Harriers of HMS *Hermes* and HMS *Invincible.*

The Argentine pilots used incorrect bombing techniques in the first days of the war, and the bombs they used were old ones with faulty wiring, otherwise British casualties might have been considerably worse. Even so, a British frigate, *HMS Ardent,* was sunk on D-day, and other ships were damaged. A Wessex helicopter flew to *HMS Ardent* to offer assistance. Most of the two hundred and thirty crew were at the bow, but they waved and pointed at something off the port quarter. Two men were in the water, and were clearly drowning.

The Captain of the Wessex spotted the drowning men, and felt that his best option was to winch down the doctor on board (Surgeon Commander Jolly) to help rescue them. The pilot (Lieutenant Crabtree) displayed exceptional skills as he manoeuvred the helicopter, at times in thick smoke from the burning ship.

"My winchman is completely untrained," the pilot no doubt thought to himself, "but it's our only hope." Each man was grabbed in turn by the doctor, and lifted to safety, albeit with some struggle.

As the landing force got under way in the early hours of D-day, my cousin Hew led 3 Para ashore. The Regiment had to cruise along the beach looking for a suitable landing site, with a man in front probing for hidden rocks with a pole. Eventually, 3 Para moved towards Port San Carlos where they found to their surprise that some forty Argentinian soldiers had been the previous evening.

"What on earth..?" they looked at one another in amazement. Evidently the Argentinians had departed in haste; they left behind a collection of half-eaten meals.

The landing force, having spent a few days consolidating the bridgehead at San Carlos, looked forward to the arrival of supplies. However, when the news of the sinking of the *Atlantic Conveyor* on May the twenty-fifth was announced, there was an atmosphere of despondency. "Three Chinook helicopters, and six Wessex, have gone down with the ship," they were told. Brigadier Thompson reminded his men that the army boot or LPC (Leather Personnel Carrier) was their most important item of kit. The men would walk to Stanley. In the newspapers, we saw extraordinary photographs of the troops 'yomping' across the Falklands.

Three days after the loss of the *Atlantic Conveyor*, 2 Para were engaged in the battle for Goose Green. Halfway through the battle, the Commanding Officer, Lieutenant Colonel 'H' Jones was killed. He was my cousin's opposite number, and the news for Hew must have been particularly poignant. By the end of the battle, the bloodiest in the Falklands war, two hundred and fifty Argentinian soldiers had died. 2 Para lost eighteen men.

When the fighting at Goose Green had ended, groups of Argentinian prisoners were moving ammunition, when some artillery shells exploded. A British medical orderly dashed into the resulting fire, and dragged clear two seriously wounded Argentinians. A third man lay in the flames, his legs blown off and his stomach gaping. The orderly, unable to reach the man, fired four shots into his head. When Surgeon Commander Jolly was asked later about his opinion of this incident, he replied: "I just hope I've got the courage to do something like that if it happens to me. It's the bravest thing I've ever heard."

The task force had faced a series of set-backs and tragedies, including the sinking of *HMS Sheffield* by an Exocet missile on May the fourth (two days after the demise of the Argentinian ship *Belgrano*), and the destruction of *HMS Coventry* by three bombs on May the twenty fifth. The bombing of the landing ships *Sir Galahad* and *Sir Tristram* at Bluff Cove early in June resulted in the deaths of thirty-three Welsh guardsmen, along with casualties from the support services, including the killing of two medics and a doctor.

However, by mid-June the movement towards Port Stanley approached its acme, as various units drew near to the high ground which stood between the British advance and Stanley. The exploits of 3 Para were of particular interest to our family. For some days, my cousin's men had reconnoitred the ridges and crags of Mount Longdon, five miles west of Stanley. They hoped for a silent and rapid advance. 'A' and 'B' Companies would climb the hill in a pincer movement, while 'C' Company was held in reserve. As Hew said: "That was the plan."

The plan, however, soon ran into difficulties. As 3 Para moved up the 600 foot heights of Mount Longdon in the early pre-dawn hours of Saturday morning, June the twelfth, a corporal stood on an anti-personnel mine some 700 yards from the first of the Argentinian trenches. The enemy immediately opened up with a barrage of machine-gun fire, mortars, and artillery. Despite the Argentinian shooting, 'B' Company gained a foothold on an outcrop of rocks just one hundred feet below the summit of Longdon. It was still dark, and the Paras discovered that the enemy were equipped with effective night-sights; the Argentinian shooting was unexpectedly accurate.

To counter the enemy fire, a Forward Observation Officer with 'B' Company began to direct the British artillery and naval gunfire. This was achieved with almost pin-point precision, the shells sometimes falling a mere fifty yards ahead of our own troops. Hew said later: "Inevitably, in a battle like this, our own soldiers did become endangered from our own fire. I think they were the closest rounds I've ever experienced. Some of them were *extremely* close. But we had no casualties from our own batteries, and that speaks volumes for the skill of our gunners."

Hew moved forward to join 'B' Company during the battle. One enemy bunker harassed our troops with deadly fire from a machine-gun. A platoon advanced to silence it, but the platoon commander was hit. A twenty-nine year old, Sergeant McKay, took over. He rallied the remaining men, and charged the bunker which was fifty yards ahead. One of his corporals was shot, and fell into the bunker still firing. Sergeant McKay worked his way around to a position above and behind the bunker, threw two grenades, then fell dead across the bunker. The Argentinian fire was silenced at last.

Other platoons were engaged in similar actions. The men used anti-tank weapons, grenades, and finally bayonets. "It really demonstrates the highest possible forms of bravery and determination and tactical skill to close with those kinds of positions," said Hew. "Because until one did, the Argentines just went on fighting."

By this stage, 'A' Company began to move up to reinforce 'B' Company. The men found themselves in a narrow pass, unable to outflank the enemy because of Argentinian snipers with night-sights. "The only thing to do was to pass a platoon one at a time, more or less frontally, fighting along it just a bite at a time," said Hew. The men of 3 Para had been in action for some six hours when they eventually reached a position nick-named 'Fly Half'. It would take another four hours before they reached 'Full Back'. By then the fighting had become hand-to-hand. As the misty dawn arrived at about 7am, Hew witnessed the gruesome sight of his men clearing the area. "With their bayonets fixed on their rifles, these young soldiers looking grim and determined, moved forward through the thick mist of dawn," said Hew. "It is a sight I shall never forget. A lot of enemy were killed with those bayonets."

When Mount Longdon was finally taken, twenty-three of Hew's men had been killed, and forty-seven had been wounded. The Argentinians lost over fifty men, many of them bayoneted.

By Monday the fourteenth of June, the Argentine resistance had crumbled. At home, we saw the legendary TV clip of the weary British Officer interrupting his interview for a moment when someone passed a message. The Officer soon turned back to the interviewer: "A white flag has been seen over Stanley," said the Officer. Then his face broke into a smile: "Bloody marvellous," he chuckled.

That Monday evening, Major-General Moore flew to Stanley in a Sea King to meet the Argentinian General Menendez. After the meeting, Major-General Moore read out the following statement: "In Port Stanley at 9pm Falklands time tonight, June 14 1982, Major-General Menendez surrendered to me all Argentine forces in East and West Falkland, together with their impedimenta. Arrangements are in hand to assemble their arms and equipment and to mark and make safe their munitions. The Falkland Islands are once more under the government desired by their inhabitants. God save The Queen."

FOUR YEARS LATER

It seemed wholly surreal peering down from the helicopter as we flew over the top of Mount Longdon. Clive glanced at me. "What do you mean?" he asked. A scrawny individual, with a mop of red hair, Clive had the unfortunate habit of chewing raw garlic. He was the local S61 Training Captain, and as I had arrived recently in the Falklands, we had to fly several sorties together before I was allowed to fly 'in command'.

"Looking down now, it seems so innocuous," I continued. "But just a short time ago, this hill was the scene of so much agony."

"The Argies," grunted Clive, shaking his head. After a moment he added: "They were better equipped than anyone realised." We continued to scrutinise the hilltop as I flew in a circle. At length, Clive returned the conversation to aviation matters. He pointed down the hill. "When you're flying here," he said, "be especially mindful of the volatile local winds which usually come from the direction of that valley down there."

In the cabin of our S61 was Sparky, our aircrewman, some military passengers, and we also carried stores and equipment. Having over-flown Mount Longdon, we took up a heading just south of west towards Darwin and Goose Green. Each day we were presented with a list of destinations by the military tasking agency. That day, after Goose Green, we would cross Falkland Sound towards the Fox Bay settlement in West Falkland. From there, we planned to head north towards Saunders Island, after which we would fly to the settlement at Port Howard. For the last part of our 'round robin trip', we would over-fly San Carlos on our flight back to Stanley Airport.

We flew low over the peat-bog terrain of the Falklands. The bleak surroundings, where the troops had 'yomped', offered little protection from the elements. There were no roads, although tracks between the settlements were occasionally discernible. Apart from the settlements themselves, there was a complete absence of human civilisation; the wild-life roamed uninhibited. A particular aspect of the local topography was the stone runs; tumbles of rocks which covered many of the hills. To the north, I noticed plumes of smoke.

"That smoke's caused by natural peat fires, deep underground," said Clive. "It's really weird. It's thought they were started by lightning strikes and the peat just keeps smouldering. There's no cost-effective way of reaching these infernos to douse them. They reckon that some of them have been burning for ten years or so."

With the absence of civilisation, there were few flying restrictions to worry us. We descended the S61 to 'n-o-e' – nap of the earth; it was a rare opportunity for pilots to fly at ultra-low level. The military passengers seemed unfazed; some appeared to enjoy the sense of exhilaration. Despite its bulky size, the S61 was responsive and satisfying to fly at low level. We flew at an airspeed of one hundred and ten knots, which seemed sensationally fast at 'n-o-e'. The harsh

Falklands landscape became a blur as it rushed beneath the helicopter.

A few of our passengers were Gurkhas. These soldiers, we had been told, flew in helicopters under sufferance, and on the assumption that the machine was about to crash at any moment. Their hypothesis became a reality one time, when a squad was on board a Chinook helicopter which clipped a Falklands hilltop in foggy conditions. When the aircraft broke up, one of the pilots was tragically killed. However, there was a less serious aspect of the accident. As the Gurkha passengers were thrown haphazardly from the Chinook when it disintegrated, one of them ended up head-first in a snow drift. A helicopter crewman eventually noticed this individual, and ran across to help. The crewman immediately began to tug at the man's feet to extract him from the snow drift. The crewman feared the soldier was seriously injured, or worse. However, when the Gurkha was eventually uprooted, and placed the right way up, the man merely shook himself down, adjusted his headgear, and saluted the crewman with the words: "Thank you very much, sir," before jogging over to join his colleagues.

As we progressed towards the settlements at Darwin and Goose Green, the sun bore down through the helicopter cockpit; it was January 1986, mid-summer in the Falklands. At length we approached Goose Green, and we noticed just outside the settlement a cairn with a cross at the top. "That's the 2 Para memorial," Sparky pointed out. In a few weeks, during my allotted time off, I would have the opportunity to stay for a couple of nights at the Goose Green settlement. I lived in the home of Ian and Eileen Jafferys, whose house was requisitioned by the Argentine Air Force for use as an Officers' Mess during the conflict. One afternoon, I walked across the marshes to inspect the 2 Para memorial, which stood in sad isolation. I read through the list of twenty names, eighteen of them members of 2 Para, headed by the name: 'Lt Col Jones H. VC'.

Soon we drew near to the Goose Green helicopter landing site. I made an approach to the white circle with a centrally marked 'H', while Sparky opened the front cargo door, and gave directions. Clive continued to point out local features, including a large hall with a red roof, and a small tower at one end. "That's the Hall where the settlers were detained for a month by the Argies," said Clive. "They had a pretty rough time." Once we had landed, some of the passengers left the helicopter, taking items of freight. When they were at a safe distance, Sparky called out: "You're clear above and behind." I lifted the machine into a hover, before lowering the nose for our take-off in the direction of Falkland Sound.

Crossing the stretch of water between East Island and West Island, Clive told me to keep an eye open for dolphins, whales, and other species. "It's not often that something is spotted," said Clive, " but it's usually quite spectacular when a whale is sighted." On two occasions during my three month spell in the Falklands I saw whales in Falkland Sound.

At length, the settlements at Fox Bay East and Fox Bay West came into sight. The collection of white buildings with corrugated iron instead of roof tiles was typical of Falkland housing. The local population welcomed visitors in their homes; guests were such a rarity. The helicopter crews, therefore, during their time off, sometimes would arrange to be left at a settlement from an opportune flight. An individual would then walk into a settlement, and speak to the first person in sight. Accommodation and hospitality were soon arranged (there were no hotels), and the local folk seemed hungry for conversation with the outside world. Many Falklanders had arrangements with friends back home, who would video-tape TV programmes and send them by post. The news might be months out of date, but it was still watched avidly.

One time, I stayed with Peter Felton at his house called 'Felty Towers' at Fox Bay settlement. Peter explained about the culture of self-dependency. "There are no garages here," he said. "If your car needs a service, or a tyre change, or an engine overhaul, you do it yourself. Same with the plumbing, or the house wiring, or the broken-down washing machine. You have to be a jack-of-all-trades to survive here. If you need to order a book, or a new fridge, or anything, it will be delivered by the supply ship, but may take months to arrive." Peter was the resident school teacher. He had one pupil who attended the classroom, and six pupils he taught by speaking with them over the radio network.

"The most useful form of transport is this thing," Peter told me as he wheeled out his motor-bike. "It's either this, or horse-back," he said. We opted for the motor-bike when he took me to a nearby penguin colony. We parked the machine at some distance, then moved very slowly towards the colony. As we drew closer, we dropped onto our stomachs and crawled the last few feet to avoid disturbing the Gentoo penguins. Peter stretched out a gloved hand which the Gentoos inspected, and pecked at with curiosity. Some weeks later, I applied the same techniques at a colony of magnificent King penguins near Volunteer Point.

As the 'round robin flight' made towards the Fox Bay settlement for landing, some residents stared up at the helicopter when we approached the heli-landing site. "The locals are pretty much used to us by now," commented Clive. "As well as us, and the occasional military helicopter, they're visited frequently by the Islander aircraft of FIGAS (Falkland Island Government Air Service). The Islander delivers mail, takes patients to and from the hospital at Stanley, and that sort of thing. Before going to the hospital, though, the locals normally use the radio network to speak to the medics at Stanley for advice."

Once we had landed, some of our Gurkha passengers disembarked. They were replaced by other Gurkhas, who would stay with us until our flight eventually reached Stanley. "They're tough buggers," Clive nodded grimly towards the Gurkhas. "I wouldn't advise upsetting that lot," he said. I was tempted to make some comment about the garlic. However, we kept the S61 'turning and burning' as the passengers changed over, and at length the airstair door was closed by Sparky as the newcomers strapped into their seats. We were able then to lift the helicopter into a hover, before departing on a northerly heading towards Saunders Island. As we departed Goose Green, Clive pointed out the settlement's new woollen mill. "The high quality wool from this area earns them a lot of money," commented Clive.

The wild, unspoilt territory was marked by unusual hues of green and yellow; the terrain looked rugged and untouched. We flew over some high ground as we approached Chartres, and beyond that the settlement at Hill Cove came into sight. "That's a nice settlement," Clive pointed at Hill Cove. "I recommend staying there if you get the chance." In April, I would follow this advice. Staying with Tim and Sally Blake, they proudly took me to see the only real forest in the Falklands. Tim Blake was the local Justice of the Peace, and he also acted as the postman, and the Air Traffic Controller. During my stay, a FIGAS Islander made a mail delivery. It was Tim's job to raise the wind sock. When the flight had departed, Tim then sorted the mail; I noted that he studied the envelopes with interest. Not many secrets could be conserved in a Falklands settlement.

Hill Cove settlement was on the shoreline; in the waters beyond, we looked at an archipelago where Saunders was the largest island. "What a great view," commented Sparky. Again, unusual tones of colour marked the mature, weather-beaten territory; unlike the northern hemisphere, in this domain any disfigurement of the landscape was not generally caused by man, but by the ruthless forces of nature.

"Watch out for 'Biffo'," said Sparky as we approached the Saunders Island landing site, adding: "we should get fed here."

'Biffo' was the eccentric lady who lived on this tiny settlement. True to form, she soon appeared after the S61 had landed; she brought gifts of cakes and biscuits for the crew. "It ensures we come here frequently," grinned Sparky.

We had now reached the farthest point of our flight around the Falklands. Having dropped stores at Saunders Island, we took-off once more and flew towards prodigious colonies of Rock-hopper and Gentoo penguins at the far side of the Island. "We'll avoid disturbing them if we fly at a good height," said Clive. The penguins stood their ground as we circled round. The wild, rocky landscape was ideal for the colonies. "Those giant rocks near the water-line are not giant rocks at all," said Clive. "They're sea lions. They can be aggressive, so watch out if you ever walk near one." The huge, blubbery beasts shuffled uncomfortably as we flew above them.

At length, we set off on a south-easterly heading towards Port Howard. There was more high ground to negotiate, but eventually we saw the Port Howard settlement tucked around an attractive bay.

During the war, there had been a strong presence of Argentine soldiers based at Port Howard; about one thousand men camped there, on the eastern shores of West Falkland. When I stayed with the settlement manager in early March, the manager and his wife described watching a Harrier when it was shot down by enemy fire.

"The pilot was flying over Falkland Sound, and it was obvious when he had been hit," they said. "It was shocking. The pilot ejected from his aircraft, and we watched the parachute as it descended into the sea. We were dying to race out in boats to assist, but we couldn't do anything. We felt so helpless."

The pilot was picked up by the Argentines.

"He became the only British Prisoner of War," said the manager. "We found out later that they had taken him to Buenos Aires for interrogation. He suffered a nervous breakdown as a result, but he eventually recovered and returned to flying. The pilot came to stay with us after the war, and it was an emotional time for us all. We had to keep the lights on all night for him; it meant special arrangements for the generator, which is programmed usually to switch off at 11 pm automatically."

Port Howard was the venue of another dramatic event in the war. An SAS man, Captain John Hamilton, was hiding with colleagues in a hilltop overlooking the settlement, when the soldiers were discovered by the enemy. Captain Hamilton had been one of the SAS men rescued by Lieutenant Commander Stanley from South Georgia in April. Tragically, Captain Hamilton was unable to escape when the Port Howard hide-out was discovered, but he provided covering fire to allow the other three members of his squad to evade capture by the enemy. However, during the intense fighting, Captain Howard was killed.

"The Argies were so impressed with the bravery and skill of Captain Hamilton," said the Port Howard manager, "that they gave him a full military funeral."

The manager walked with me around the site used by the Argentinian soldiers as their base.

"Most of them were raw recruits," he said. "They hadn't been properly trained and didn't know what they were doing half the time. It was sad really."

We came across items of obsolete webbing, part-used tubes of tooth-paste, old socks and shoes, and cans of food by now rusty and unappetising. The disused camp-site stretched over several acres, and we could almost picture the cadaverous looks of the troops unlucky enough to have been thrown into that profane environment. Just beyond the campsite, large swathes of countryside had been surrounded by barbed wire; every so often a red notice had been placed saying: 'DANGER – MINES'.

Within the Port Howard settlement, a small museum had been established. Inside the building a collection of military hardware had been arranged, including Argentine artillery weapons, machine guns, and mortars. There were various maps, and instructions in Spanish on field craft and first aid. Other miscellaneous articles lay on a table, for example odd medical items such as a kit for taking blood pressure, field utensils, a gas mask, and a pilot's helmet. A section had been set aside showing photographs of Captain Hamilton, including a picture taken at his funeral service. Above the gravestone stood a cross with the SAS plaque placed at the top, and beneath was the simple inscription: *'Capt. John Hamilton – Killed in Action – 10 June 1982'.*

Inside the Port Howard set-up, the manager took me to see the settlement shop.

"We open twice a week," he said, "and are re-supplied by ship every six months. Our stock is valued at around £60,000, and we could probably keep the settlement going for well over a year without re-supply if necessary."

The warehouse appeared well organised; shelves displayed clothes, shoes, stationery, cigarettes, drink, washing-up liquid, and a wide selection of canned and other foods. Fresh vegetables were grown locally under plastic sheeting.

"The plastic doesn't always survive the gales we get here," said the manager. After a pause, he continued in the prosaic manner typical of Falkland folk: "But that's OK. We just build a new shelter when the gale has quietened."

It was impressive to see the rows of tomatoes and other vegetables growing successfully in such a harsh climate.

"You need to watch out for strong local wind effects with all this surrounding high ground," Clive said as we approached the assigned landing place at Port Howard. Then he pointed out a small notice saying: 'Port Howard Airport'. Set at the top of a gradient just above and to the north of the settlement, the 'airport' was well placed to take in the fine panorama all around Port Howard. The sunlight that day accentuated the colours daubed across the slopes overlooking the settlement.

Clive commented on two Land Rovers parked at the side, ready to carry away the equipment we had brought.

"This lot are pretty well organised," remarked Sparky. Two of our Gurkha passengers helped Sparky to off-load the equipment; we were then ready to lift again.

As we took-off, and headed towards Falkland Sound, Clive said: "This is the last leg for today."

We climbed the S61 to clear the high ground beyond Port Howard, and maintained our height as we crossed the Falkland Sound.

"The bay over there is 'Grantham Sound'," Clive indicated as we approached East Falkland.

Flying to the north of Grantham Sound, we soon spotted the settlement at San Carlos.

"You can see the San Carlos war memorial down there," said Clive. The war memorial was a circular wall built around several grave stones, set to one side of the settlement. At one end of the wall, a number of plaques were conspicuous. Beneath the plaques, numerous poppy wreathes had been placed in a neat row. Outside the wall stood a lone flag-stand; at the top, a Union flag looked noble as it flapped in the breeze.

"Time to make for home," said Clive eventually. We descended to low level again, and headed towards Stanley airport. The flat terrain approaching Teal Inlet – the boggy landscape no doubt known in exhaustive detail by the yompers – was bordered to the south by ranges of hills. As we flew beyond Teal Inlet, the high ground before Stanley, including Mount Longdon, soon came into view. We maintained our easterly heading as we passed over Mount Longdon, and then Stanley itself could be seen.

"The total population of the Falkland Islands amounts to some two thousand souls," commented Sparky. "About half of them live in Stanley itself."

We looked across at the capital's prominent buildings which included a cathedral, a Town Hall, the Governor's House, and an impressive new hospital under construction. The bulk of the housing, however, was similar to the 'camp' (the area beyond Stanley) with wooden buildings, and tin roofs painted in a variety of bright colours. Scattered amongst the buildings, we saw rusty oil tanks and other items carelessly cast away. There was also evidence of the Argentine presence, with guns and discarded ammunition boxes left lying around.

"The locals here are untidy blighters," remarked Sparky. A Shetlander, Sparky often noted similarities between his home territory and the Falklands. "Folk just dump things," said Sparky ruefully, "some people just don't seem to give a damn."

"Stanley's got its own small police force," Clive informed us. "They have to attend to cases of larceny, and the odd brawl." Inebriation was evidently a fairly regular problem amongst bored members of the populace. The police sometimes checked for drink-driving instances, and kept an eye on the road network around Stanley.

"Soon they'll have a novel addition," commented Sparky. "The only road system on the Falklands is being supplemented by a carriageway between Stanley and the new airport at Mount Pleasant." From the air, we clearly saw the construction works as the new road snaked its way through the peaty countryside.

"The shops around Stanley hold an astonishing variety of stock for such a small population," said Sparky. "If a particular emporium runs out of some item, the rival stores soon rally round to help out," he added. There was a necessary tradition of self-help and make-do. The distinctive local accent (similar to, but not identical to the New Zealand accent) would be heard as Falkland folk mobilised to help one another in day-to-day life.

"Over there's the Stanley harbour war memorial site," Clive pointed out. Some time later, I went to look at the site. A semi-circular wall bore a variety of plaques and shields. In front of the wall, an obelisk had been built; at the summit stood a figure with one arm held upright. On the face of the obelisk the following simple words had been inscribed: 'In memory of those who liberated us'. It struck many people as curious that, on the British mainland, the first monument in memory of the war's victims was not opened until March 2000. On that occasion, The Queen and Baroness Thatcher attended the opening ceremony of the Falkland Islands Memorial Chapel at Pangbourne College, in Berkshire.

"At the Bank in Stanley, you can get the local pounds," Sparky told me. The Queen's head was engraved on the coinage, and the bank-notes depicted scenes of penguins and seals. In one corner of the pound note was a shield portraying a sheep; below the sheep, an old-world schooner sailed above a banner saying: 'Desire the right'. I often sensed a lack of the real-world in some of the establishments in the Falklands. The Bank, however, was different; for me, that was one place where there was a no-nonsense, business-like atmosphere.

We flew behind the metropolis, which stretched for a mile or so along the water's edge. Beyond the town, towards Cape Pembroke, was Stanley airfield which was our base before the helicopters moved to Mount Pleasant at the end of April. Around Stanley airfield there was a litter of parts from Pucara aircraft, and Huey helicopters. One of our Company pilots, Mark, was a qualified engineer.

"I've worked out a deal with the Falkland Islands Government," he told me. "I'm allowed to recover various items from crashed Argentine aircraft strewn around the Falkland Islands. With these parts, I'm going to rebuild two Pucaras and two Hueys. One of each type will go into a Government museum and I can keep the other machines."

We flew the S61 to our allotted parking spot, and closed down the helicopter (G-BFMY); our round robin flight had lasted for just less than five hours.

"We'll deal with the post-flight paper-work," said Clive, "then head for the coastel. I think they've got a dining-in tonight."

The coastel was an accommodation set-up. Originally designed as a prison ship, the large floating structure had been positioned on the outskirts of Stanley. As we walked the half mile or so distance between the airport and the coastel, Sparky and Clive discussed details of our prison ship life.

"It's not too bad when you get used to it," said Sparky, "though it's a bit of a pain having the military system imposed on us." As part of the contract with the Ministry of Defence, it had been agreed that our engineers and crewmen would live in the Non-Commissioned Officers' Mess. The pilots, though, would be accommodated in the Officers' Mess. This division occasionally caused problems. One or two of our engineers, in particular, seemed to harbour something of a chip-on-the-shoulder attitude. This was exacerbated by our different pseudo-military positions.

Within the maze of corridors and various levels of the coastel, we eventually found the way to our rooms. The metal structure had a gloomy, soulless feel. That evening, as Clive had predicted, a dining-in had been arranged in the Officers' Mess. The dining room staff had laid out Mess silver on the tables, and a special menu had been organised. During the meal, conversation often centred on the events of the war. My neighbours were interested as well in the North Sea flying activities; they grilled me on numerous points of detail.

"Flying the waves," someone said, "sounds intriguing."

At length, the President of the Mess Committee stood up.

"Just before the loyal toast and the speeches," he said, "I think it is timely to remind ourselves that the population of military personnel stationed on the Falkland Islands is now considerably more than the number of local residents. This calls for some tact when we deal with the local folk. They're undoubtedly grateful for what we did in 1982, but nevertheless we're sometimes in danger of swamping them. We perhaps need to bear this in mind rather more."

There was a general muttering and nodding of heads in agreement.

The President of the Mess Committee remained standing as the time for the loyal toast approached. The port decanters continued their journey round the table; the conventions of pouring were carefully observed. There was a respectful atmosphere as the evening reached a traditional part of the proceedings. A minor shuffling of chairs could be heard as the members prepared to stand.

The President of the Mess Committee called: "Mr Vice."

The Vice-President of the Mess Committee rose to his feet, and said firmly: "Ladies and Gentlemen: The Queen."

The assembled officers then stood up, and repeated "The Queen" as they raised their glasses. A few voices could be heard saying quietly: "God bless her," but this addition was generally frowned upon.

At this dining-in, though, we all became aware of an unusual addition. I glanced across at a fellow diner, and noticed a doctor – a local man invited as a guest – who appeared to be immersed in thought. During the meal, there had been some lively discussion about the events at the end of the war, including Major-General Moore's statement that the Falkland Islands were once more under the government desired by their inhabitants.

The doctor stared vaguely at the table as his unexpected words were heard by the assembled guests. He spoke the words in a subdued, but nevertheless in an audible tone. Somehow there was a lonely quality surrounding the doctor as he seemed to reflect intensely on the unwelcome experiences of residents in 1982. Our conversations concerning the loss of life and individual tragedies brought about by the Falkland's War had been quite heated. Perhaps this was focused in the doctor's mind when he repeated the final four words of Major-General Moore's statement.

The doctor said simply: "God save The Queen."

Kosovo, Summer 1999 – the author with a group of ethnic Albanians.

[see Chapter 1]

Kosovo, Summer 1999 – United Nations S61 flying towards Pech.

Summer 1999 – United Nations S61 over Western Kosovo.

[see Chapter 1]

Summer 1999 – United Nations S61 over Central Kosovo.

Spring 2000 – Nepal – A village market.

Spring 2000, Nepal – The author makes friends with two Nepalese children.

Spring 2000, Nepalese trek – taking a meal break [see Chapter 2].

Spring 2000, Nepalese trek – Nepalese villages [see Chapter 2].

Falkland Islands, 1986 – the author's S61 near the river Marlow, East Falklands [see Chapter 6].

Falkland Islands, 1986 – Port Howard Airport.

Falklands 1986 - Pukara and S61 at Stanley airport.

[see Chapter 6]

Falklands 1986 - the author flying over Falkland Sound.

Falklands 1986 – Pukara and Huey reconstructed by Captain Mark Harrisson [Chapter 6].

Falklands 1986 – ammunition and weapons discarded by the Argentinian forces.

Falklands 1986 – the author makes friends with some King penguins at Volunteer Point.

Falklands 1986 – plaque commemorating the liberation of the islands.

North Sea, July 1988 – fire on the Piper 'A' drilling platform (see Chapter 7).

North Sea, April 1990 - S61 over Claymore 'A' and Tharos platforms.

S61 Oscar Charlie winch training on a supply boat. (opposite).

S61 Oscar Charlie on a winching excercise with Lerwick lifeboat (above).

S61 Oscar Charlie winching with a Shetland fishing boat – the MFV 'Evening Star'.

Rescue S61 Oscar Charlie at the hospital landing site – Lerwick, Shetland Islands.

Rescue S61 Oscar Charlie offloading a casualty at the heli-pad, Aberdeen hospital.

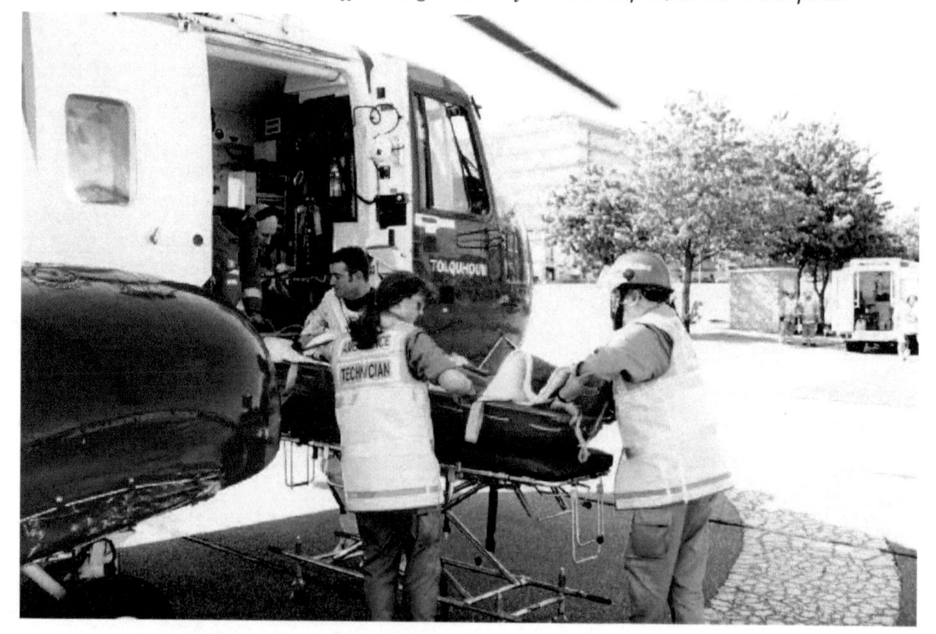

S61 Oscar Charlie on a winching excercise with Lerwick lifeboat.

Sumburgh Airport – Bristow Tiger AS 332 L outbound for the rigs.

Sumburgh Airport – offloading passengers before refuelling.

Rescue S61 Oscar Charlie over a snowy Foula, Shetland Islands.

Rescue S61 Oscar Charlie recovering casualties in the snows of 1995, Shetlands.

Shetland Islands – S61 Oscar Charlie on a winching excercise with the Lerwick Lifeboat.

Rescue S61 Oscar Charlie over the Shetland Islands in the snows of 1995.

S61 helicopters over the rugged Shetlands coastline.

Oscar Charlie flying the waves.

CHAPTER 7

Piper Alpha

JULY 1988

It was a dawn start for me on the morning of July the seventh, 1988. The trees were in full leaf; the landscape was lush. The fine fragrances unique to the beginning of a summer's day, fresh and stimulating, provided at least some reward for my untimely rousing. I had been back from the Falklands for some two years already, and that morning my schedule meant an early flight to the 'Tharos', an accommodation and fire-fighting rig positioned next to the 'Piper Alpha'. As I drove along the empty Aberdeenshire roads, I listened to the radio news. The announcer spoke about a problem during the night on the Piper A platform. "Information is still coming in," said the announcer, "but we have reports of some fatalities following an explosion." I mulled over in my mind the influence this news might have on my flight; other than that, the drive towards Aberdeen Airport continued normally.

As I walked upstairs to the flight planning room, even before reaching the area, I had a perception that something was seriously wrong. On entering the flight planning room, a dramatic and terrible atmosphere was suddenly palpable. Some of the helicopter rescue crews who had been called out in the night, were just returning from the scene of Piper A. Their haggard looks, and distressing tales dominated the room. I walked towards a chum of mine. I nodded 'hello' to my friend as he glanced up. I looked at him anxiously. At length, he spoke quietly. "There was a fast rescue craft in the area," he said. My friend began to shake his head slowly from side to side. "The guys were just... ", my friend's voice became even more subdued, "... well, just liquidated."

It was a long time before all the horrors that took place that evening were finally pieced together. In the Public Inquiry that followed Piper A, Lord Cullen observed that the installation had been inspected by the Department of Energy just the month before the tragedy happened. Lord Cullen stated that the findings were: '... *superficial to the point of being of little use as a test of safety on the platform'.*

The loss of one hundred and sixty-seven souls on that abhorrent night had a far-reaching impact on the North Sea Oil Industry; the catastrophe exposed a complacency which seemed to have crept into North Sea activities. All these activities, including helicopter operations, would be profoundly influenced in the future.

Just before ten o'clock on the evening of July the sixth, there was a frantic series of telephone calls between engineers in a gas compression module, and the two men in the Piper A control room. A sound of buzzers in the control room accompanied the tripping of a pump in C module, several levels down. Night shift personnel were attempting to restart another pump which had been shut down for maintenance. Unknown to them, a pressure safety valve had been removed from that pump by the previous shift; apparently the hand-over procedure had been lax.

In the Piper A cinema, men had their enjoyment of the film 'Carrie' spoilt by noise from the excessive size of the gas flare outside the installation; a deep roaring sound was audible.

Beneath the installation, a diver worked at a depth of fifty feet. The previous diver had just finished his decompression, and had changed before joining other stand-by divers to await instructions from their supervisor. The divers and others watched the gas flare. The flame had grown to enormous proportions, and there was a surprisingly large gap between the 'tulip' at the end of the stack, and the start of the flare itself. At one point, the flame momentarily died, then with a thunder resumed its exceptional vigour.

Within the Piper A accommodation area, a number of folk were listening to the radio, or watching television. Some had just tuned in for news or sports programmes. Some heard the ten o'clock time signal, others said they did not hear the tones. A few claimed to have heard the start of the news. Suddenly, the programme was interrupted by a high pitched screaming noise. Survivors and witnesses described this sound in various ways. Some thought a group of scaffolders were "acting the goat". One man heard a "banshee" sound, which he thought was an air starter on the crane. A group of men in a workshop tea room discussed the "loud screech". One person described the sound as being akin to "somebody strangling a woman".

Positioned just twenty-five metres from the Piper A, with its stern towards the platform, was the vessel *Lowland Cavalier*. The master was actually looking at the Piper A when an explosion occurred. He described it as follows: "Well, I actually saw the explosion; I did not hear it. I actually saw it before I registered anything else. What I saw I can only explain as like the starting of a gas burner, a water heater. It seemed to go along the bottom of the platform; like a very light blue explosion or ignition more than anything else, then contracting again, and then a further explosion coming from a certain point which I believe to be below the crane pedestal and slightly to the left."

The explosion flung the two men in the Piper A control room across the area, causing them injury. The control room itself was devastated by the blast. Equipment and tables were hurled about, and there was a sudden chaos of debris with telephones, computer equipment, and furniture littering the area. Smoke began to drift into the control room; vision was further hampered because the main lighting failed, although the emergency lighting came on initially. The platform communication system had been destroyed; the control room staff were unable to issue instructions or warnings.

The diver working beneath the platform experienced a simultaneous flash and bang. Ten seconds later, he noted a second flash and bang. The immediate efforts to recover the diver were hampered by fires, but he was eventually retrieved. This man survived the conflagration, and went on to help with the rescue of others during the night.

In the accommodation area, personnel were catapulted from their beds. The cinema emptied as folk ran to their cabins to don survival suits. Most people made for the galley, at the top level of the accommodation area, to muster for a head count, and to take instructions; this was the emergency drill they had been taught in training. At first, conditions in the galley area were tolerable.

The Radio Operator was joined by the Offshore Installation Manager (OIM) a few minutes after the initial explosion. The OIM instructed the Radio Operator to send out a Mayday distress call; the OIM then left the radio room. Within a matter of seconds, he came running back, apparently in a state of panic. The OIM told the Radio Operator that the radio room access was on fire, and full of smoke. They discussed abandoning the area via an escape hatch. Before leaving the radio room, the Radio Operator broadcast his third and final message following the explosion: "Mayday... Mayday... we're abandoning the radio room... we're abandoning the radio room... we can't take any more... we're on fire."

The OIM then made his way to the galley area, where it was estimated that around one hundred personnel had congregated. A survivor described how the OIM stood on a table in the centre of the galley, presumably trying to take some kind of command. However, this was virtually impossible due to panic, commotion, and heckling. One man told the OIM that he was supposed to be in command, and to get them out of there. The OIM told the man to calm down. The Offshore Installation Manager was in charge of over two hundred souls that evening. Tragically, the OIM was not numbered amongst the sixty-one who survived.

About twenty minutes after the initial explosion, there was a second major explosion which caused a massive intensification of the fire. The smoke in the galley area began to get much worse, and when the emergency lights went out, general panic set in. Men were forced to crawl along the floor at low level, and to use wet towels as make-shift face masks. The smoke started to incapacitate personnel both physically, and in their thought processes. The men dipped towels into the fish tank, and some poured juice from the fruit machine over their heads. One man shouted: "Is there anyone here from Bawden Drilling?"; he thought he was going to die, and wanted to be near someone he knew. Some personnel were beginning to succumb already.

In spite of the danger, it was clear that a large number of people apparently made no attempt to leave the accommodation area. One survivor, a rigger, gave the following account to the Cullen Inquiry: "I just said to myself 'get yourself off'. I got my pal Francis, and I got him as far as the reception, but he would not go down the stairs because he says: 'We have done our muster job; they'll send choppers in'. I said to Francis 'I've tried to speak to the lead production operator; he cannot talk to me, Francis. We'll have to get off'. Francis would not go, and he just slumped down. Anybody that knows the rig and the reception next to the bond, he slumped down there. That was as far as I could get him."

Various reasons were suggested why so many people apparently made no attempt to leave the accommodation area: lack of leadership; lack of information; lack of ideas about what else to do; belief that helicopter rescue would reach them. Survivors spoke of how "the bedlam inside the galley affected people badly". Whatever their reasons for staying, these personnel faced certain death.

In the absence of organised leadership, small groups of people searched for a safe way to leave the accommodation area. A number of survivors said that it was only their familiarity with the installation which saved them. Some drillers aimed to reach the drill floor, from where they made their way to a point which allowed them to drop into the sea. Two operators on the Piper A wearing breathing apparatus led a group of men down to a clear area. They told the men to hold their breath, and to follow them to the level below. Having led the men to clear air, the operators said they were returning to start fire water-pumps. The two operators then disappeared into the smoke. They were never seen again.

After the second explosion, the Tharos received a VHF radio message from the platform saying: "People majority in galley area. Tharos come. Gangway. Hoses. Getting bad." The Tharos had moved towards the platform, and opened fire monitors to create a cascade of water. Survivors spoke of how the water cascade allowed them to get their body fluids back up; they "lapped the water like dogs". The Tharos helicopter had been launched quickly (about ten minutes after the initial explosion), but the pilot had reported that the heli-deck was obscured by smoke, and he was unable to land.

As survivors dropped into the sea, most were picked up by fast rescue craft. It was estimated that up to eleven fast rescue craft were in use at one stage. One man managed to swim to the Tharos, and climb up a fixed ladder. Several survivors were taken to the standby vessel *Silver Pit,* whose paint-work had been blistered by the explosion. The *Lowland Cavalier* moved away from the platform, and launched her work-boat and one of her lifeboats.

Some fifty minutes after the initial explosion, there was a further violent explosion; the vibration was felt a mile away. Debris was projected about eight hundred meters from the platform. A group of men who had made their way up to the heli-deck were forced to jump off. Some curled themselves up into a ball, and incredibly five men (including the Radio Operator) survived the fall of one hundred and seventy-five feet. One man gave this account: "The explosion was like a massive mushroom effect from the guts of the rig... it just engulfed us with a deafening bang. I felt the searing heat chasing me all the way. I was walking around bewildered as if nothing was left and I felt the fireball come up and hit me in the face. I had my hands up and they got severely burned. I didn't decide anything. I just thought I was burning alive and I took a run and jumped off the heli-deck."

The Fast Rescue Craft from the vessel *Sandhaven* was destroyed; its occupants were killed with the exception of one crewman who miraculously survived. This man – his lifebelt disintegrated, and his hard hat melted on his head – began to swim towards the platform, where he was grabbed by another survivor. One man who had climbed the Piper A flare stack in desperation, was seen no more. To avoid being engulfed themselves, some of the vessels moved away from the platform. One diver described how he was dragged through the water by the *Silver Pit.* As the ship gathered momentum, he was drawn down into the water, and was aquaplaning like a water-skier without skis.

As Search and Rescue helicopters converged on the area, they were joined by Rescue 01, a Nimrod from Kinloss. My colleagues from Sumburgh, flying the Shetland coastguard helicopter (call-sign Rescue 117), were joined by two Sea Kings from Lossiemouth, and a Sea King from Boulmer. One of the Lossiemouth Sea Kings had been recalled from a mountain rescue incident. Other helicopters joined them later. When the aircraft took-off from their various bases, little information had been given to them. The crews had no word about the extent of the incident, or what would be required of them. However, they must have approached that torrid beacon with a sense of dread. The entire area was illuminated by brilliant orange flames, and a pall of thick black smoke provided a noxious navigational aid.

When they reached the scene, some of the helicopters moved injured men from the *Silver Pit* to the Tharos. The *Silver Pit* had been overwhelmed by the disaster. The vessel had taken on board thirty seven survivors, some of whom were seriously injured. Several survivors, despite being badly burned, had to climb up rope netting to board the *Silver Pit*. One survivor, a Frenchman, had had his clothes blown off; shards of skin hung from his badly burned body. Other survivors also suffered terrible burns, and breathing difficulties. When the rescue helicopters arrived, these men were the first to be evacuated. The process of evacuation was slowed because the *Silver Pit* had inadequate stretchers, and these had to be carried around awkward, oil covered stairs. Several survivors were highly critical of the *Silver Pit*; some described vessels such as the *Silver Pit* as "a token gesture" by operators, a "necessary evil" to satisfy the legal requirement for a standby vessel. The Cullen Inquiry, however, agreed with the view that the Master and his crew showed great courage that night. The Inquiry did not place responsibility for the *Silver Pit's* deficiencies on the Master.

The first helicopters also evacuated non-essential personnel from the Tharos to other nearby installations, who provided additional medics in their place. As the helicopters circled the area, the crews observed survivors still clinging to various parts of the Piper A structure. The survivors stared at the helicopters; the crews watched in agonised impotence, tormented by a sense of powerlessness for the rescue which they could not deliver.

The helicopters helped to comb the sea for survivors. At one point the *Silver Pit* called the Boulmer Sea King on the radio: "Helicopter off the starboard bow, we have seriously injured people who need medivac. Can you handle it?"

"*Silver Pit*, this is Rescue 131. Please give details of your injured."

When the details had been given, the pilot said: "Message understood. We'll come to the stern of your vessel and put the winchman on board. 'Fraid we're very short of space." The winchman, when he arrived, talked to the deck crew and pointed out that the Sea King was pretty much bulked out with corpses. "We'll do what we can," he said.

Most of the casualties were taken to Tharos, where an emergency hospital had been set-up. Initially, the rig medics had to cope alone with the influx of appalling injuries, but eventually they were joined by a team of Doctors from the Aberdeen Royal Infirmary. When the first casualties had been stabilised, they were flown from Tharos to the Aberdeen Royal Infirmary accompanied by medics. On reaching the hospital, some of the medics described heart-rending incidents when young wives would approach them for news about their husbands.

After their flight to the hospital, the rescue helicopters returned to the Tharos where a stacking system had been organised. As they orbited to await their turn for landing on the Tharos, the crews observed the morbid scene below. The remains of Piper A, defiled and charred, still burnt furiously even though the bulk of the platform had collapsed into the sea. The flames were fed by pipelines from other installations. In the water, the crews caught glimpses of pathetic flotsam; hard hats, storage bins, broken furniture, life-belts, clothing, boots, books, and pieces of paper.

My flight to the Tharos, planned for that morning, was cancelled. The area was already inundated with helicopter traffic; I was not required. Nearly two weeks later, however, on the nineteenth of July, I was scheduled for another flight to the Tharos. By that stage, 'Red' Adair had been summoned to help extinguish the Piper A fire, which continued to burn out of control. As we reached the area, it was even then overshadowed by clouds of smoke and fumes.

My co-pilot Geoff mentioned the sense of apprehension, almost dread, he felt as we approached the Tharos heli-deck for landing. The Tharos continued to pump powerful water-jets at the remains of Piper A. Fast Rescue Craft zoomed around the locality, still searching. Several other ships were in the vicinity. Even though it was late July, the whole area had a grey, cold feeling.

The prevailing wind blew the sullied smoke from Piper A away from the Tharos heli-deck area, and our approach was made in relatively clear air. After landing, I left my seat to walk through the cabin to open the 'airstair' door. Then I descended the aircraft steps onto the Tharos heli-deck; I had to supervise the unloading of our freight and passengers. The Tharos had a weary, dejected atmosphere. There was an unusual, acrid aroma hanging in the air. The deck crew had work-weary expressions; they set about their duties like automatons. A bridge linking Tharos to the remains of the Piper A had been placed. On the platform remains, I saw a group of three or four men studying the fire. The flames were subdued, but still clearly visible. "That's 'Red' Adair and his team," the Helicopter Landing Officer told me.

My job on the heli-deck proceeded routinely. I checked around the helicopter, and a deck-hand brought a small phial for me to inspect; it had been dipped into a fuel sample. Satisfied with the colour of the phial, I gave him a thumbs-up. The deck crew were then able to proceed with the helicopter refuelling process. After the freight had been off-loaded, it was replaced with shore-bound items. I had to check that the freight had been securely tied down; the deck crew were then clear to bring our home-bound passengers on board.

Soon the whole process, slick and well practised, had been completed. After I had signed for the fuel, I glanced at 'Red' Adair and his team before climbing the steps back into the S61. As we took-off from the Tharos, Geoff and I went through the familiar departure routine. We left behind the smoke and fumes, but even as we drew further from the installation, the feeling of dismal pathos lingered. In some months' time, the remains of Piper A would be consigned to the bottom of the sea. The physical remains of the disaster would be manifest no longer. Folk would be left with just their own distinct memories.

As Geoff and I progressed towards Aberdeen Airport, we spoke about the catastrophe, and the individual tales of sadness which were still surfacing. At one point Air Traffic Control asked: "Confirm you are inbound from the Tharos?" We said that we were. "Is Piper still on fire?" he asked. We said that it was. "Roger," replied the Air Traffic Controller. After a moment he added: "I guess there'll be flames there for ever." It was just a chance remark, but as Geoff and I glanced at each other and nodded, we both knew that he was right.

JULY 2000

The children's voices shrilled with delight around Hazlehead Park, Aberdeen. We had suffered a spell of dull summer weather, and that day was no exception. As the children enjoyed running about, the parents too seemed in good spirits, determined to make the most of their visit despite the lack of sunshine. Many of the children had not been born at the time of the Piper Alpha tragedy. For them, the disaster was something out of the history books.

While we walked slowly towards the section of park which contained the Piper Alpha memorial site, my wife commented on the beauty of the surrounding expanse. Neatly tended flower beds of Begonia extended across the park. Exotic trees and shrubs stood in the grounds. When we entered the area of the memorial itself, we looked at numerous wreathes of flowers, carefully arranged at the base.

As we strolled around the memorial stone, we examined the three carved figures at the summit, and we reflected on some of the individual accounts that had followed the Piper Alpha disaster. "Remember young Mark?" asked Sue. "Wasn't it his first time offshore?" The young man was the son of a fellow pilot, and we had met Mark once or twice. At the age of just nineteen he was the youngest of the one hundred and sixty seven victims. "He never stood a chance," my wife added quietly.

There were other quirks of fate, for example the steward who agreed to a last minute change of shift. Then there was the luck of the duty rota. A high percentage of those who survived were on duty at the time; only twenty-two off-duty personnel survived.

We continued to walk slowly around the memorial stone. All about, rose shrubs shook in the breeze, serene and somehow soothing as they overlooked the venerated site. The symmetry and dignity of the scene contrasted so sharply with the event itself. The names of those lost had been boldly inscribed on the side of the stonework. A lonely figure inspected the memorial at the same time as us; with despondent expression she stared intensely at one of the names.

Many of the wreathes had personal messages written on tags; cellophane wrappers cocooned the fading flowers within. Hands, unknown to us, had laid the wreathes some days ago in remembrance of the disaster's twelfth anniversary. For these folk, Piper Alpha was not merely something out of the history books. For them, Piper Alpha was an on-going ordeal, cruel and – like the fire itself – an all-consuming ogre, which had devoured innocent souls during the improvisation of its monstrous, repugnant rampage.

That ogre had loitered in dark shadows of complacency, an imposter behind the facade of safe surroundings. When its moment eventually came, the ogre ultimately struck with staggering swiftness, ensnaring its victims in a ruthless maelstrom. "... They'll send choppers in... " the plaintive cry highlighted the blind conviction of many folk that eventually they would be saved by the ubiquitous, magical abilities of the helicopter. How tragically was their faith annihilated on the night of the Piper Alpha disaster.

CHAPTER 8

Search & Rescue

Shortly after the Piper A disaster, I was sent to Shetland for a brief spell of duty with the Search and Rescue Unit. The folk at Sumburgh were still discussing the aftermath of Piper A, and the involvement of their specially equipped Coastguard S61. The atmosphere, as in most places, remained subdued and shocked; the terrible events continued to play on peoples' minds.

"When you're flying on Search and Rescue duties, you'll act as co-pilot," I had been told by the operations co-ordinators. "As you haven't done the Search and Rescue Captain's course, you can't act as Captain." Normally the Captain flew the aircraft during winching operations, but if he was unable to do so for some reason, then it was up to the co-pilot to take over.

At the Search and Rescue Unit in Sumburgh, the specifically adapted S61 was safeguarded in the hangar, ready to be towed out at a moment's notice. The unit was positioned on the southern tip of the Shetland Isles, adjacent to the sea shore, and exposed to the ferocity of Shetland's enigmatic weather. The crews stayed in the vicinity, biding their time until needed. The unexciting atmosphere was occasionally interrupted by the scream of the 'scramble' alarm, but most of the day was spent hanging about. A few practise flights were organised from time to time, otherwise we just remained on duty, ready and waiting for an emergency call-out.

Sometimes I would take a 'beeper' and wander along the desolate, lonely sands, prepared to race back if the beeper sounded. I would walk along the pristine beach, accompanied by seagulls swooping and squawking; occasionally I was treated to the sight of a seal sliding through the raw seas. The seal would stop swimming now and again, and a moustachioed head with sad-looking eyes would suddenly appear. The seal would gaze at me with a puzzled expression: "What are you doing here?"

From time to time, I would bend down to pick up unusual, brightly coloured shells from the beach for my daughter to add to her collection. The fresh, pollution-free air felt untouched by the troubles of the world. The tangy mixture of sea-side smells evoked reflective moods, and the lonesome walks were an opportunity to quietly think through some of the conundrums of life.

On occasions I would make for the radio room to strike up conversation with Ruben. Usually dressed in his favourite black clothing, Ruben loved to gossip about rumours and scandals within the Company. He reminded me of Doctor Spock as he sat at a specially constructed desk, answering telephones, and speaking to aircraft on the Company radio system. Ruben's myopically challenged eyes would rove around slyly, on the look-out for any opportunity to bring a spark of action to the monotonous lifestyle.

"Did you hear what happened to Brian yesterday?" asked Ruben between telephone calls. I claimed ignorance. "Only went and landed on the wrong rig," continued Ruben. "Can you believe it? The name was painted on the side, loud and clear, and there's old Brian, the Chief Line Training Captain, went and landed on the wrong one."

"Tut tut," I replied, well aware that I had nearly done the same thing myself. "That's dreadful," I continued.

"Could happen to anybody, I s'pose," added Gary, who had just joined us. A quiet individual with a somewhat dog-eared beard, he was the winch operator on duty; the Search and Rescue aircraft carried a crew of two winchmen in addition to the two pilots.

"Can't understand it myself," said Ruben. "What's the point of painting the name on the side of a rig if you don't bother to read it?"

"Well, sometimes the letters get obscured by oil and general crap," I said. "And in some light conditions, it can be hard to read the name." Ruben's eyes flicked doubtfully from side to side.

"The problem is that the passengers are all as nervy as hell just now," said Ruben. His rotating chair squeaked as he shifted about uneasily.

"You can hardly blame them for that," interjected Paul as he sauntered into the radio room, hands in pockets. Paul was the other winchman on duty. He was an ex-Navy man with a somewhat jaunty air. "It's a bit like when the Chinook went down a couple of years ago," continued Paul. "After that, none of the passengers wanted to fly in helicopters," he added.

"I know," said Gary. "They all totally refused to go in another Chinook. That was the end of Chinook flying in our patch of the North Sea. We haven't seen the bloody thing since." As Gary spoke, Paul sat down on a tatty chair in one corner of the room, and placed his feet on the edge of a desk-top.

"Wasn't Gordon the Captain for the rescue of the two survivors of that Chinook accident?" asked Paul. Gordon was the other pilot currently on duty with us; he was ensconced in an office with a pile of paper-work. As his name had been mentioned, we all peered through glass partitions which separated the various offices. We confirmed that Gordon was at his desk still. A staunch Scotsman with a dark beard, Gordon – unlike most folk – normally wore his Company-issue hat and matching black coat at all times. "Good old McHat/McCoat," commented Paul as we gazed across at Gordon sitting stoutly in his untrendy attire.

"Yeah, you're right about the Chinook rescue," Ruben continued eventually. "McHat/McCoat and crew had just got airborne for a training mission. The Chinook was returning from the Brent Field and was about two miles from here on final approach, when the front and rear blades collided." Ruben shook his head slightly. "I think the machine did a complete loop the loop before plunging into the sea. Forty-two passengers and three crew were killed; only the Chinook Captain, and the passenger sitting immediately behind him, miraculously survived the accident. Those two must have had guardian angels that day. It was pure luck that our machine had just got airborne for a training flight, and got to them very quickly."

"You hear some amazing escape stories," said Paul. "It's the same with this Piper A business." He coughed tersely.

"Terrible thing," said Ruben, continuing to shake his head from side to side slowly. "Mind you, 'Red' Adair always said that rig was an accident waiting to happen." Ruben glanced at us ominously.

"Didn't he help design the Tharos?" asked Gary, who had positioned himself uncomfortably on the side of the desk-top commandeered by Paul's feet.

"Yeah, I think so," said Ruben after a pause. "Again, it was only luck that the Tharos happened to be positioned so close to the Piper A."

"Not that it did that much good," interjected Paul, as he sat upright for a moment. "Everything was just overwhelmed by the size of the explosions."

"I know," sighed Ruben. "Our guys did their best, but it was pretty frustrating for them that they couldn't have done more." At that point, the telephone rang, and Ruben grabbed the receiver greedily, hoping for signs of action.

"Our aircraft did well, under the circumstances," said Gary, while Ruben spoke into the telephone. "The S61 earns its reputation OK as the 'workhorse of the North Sea'."

"You're right there," added Paul, shifting his feet. "It's not often that we're let down by the S61."

We thought about this, and then Gary said: "There was the Scilly Islands' accident in 1983, remember? That S61 belonging to British Airways Helicopters crashed into the sea. I think twenty people were killed. Awful thing, but I guess you can't blame the aircraft itself for that." We nodded in agreement, while Ruben continued to speak secretively into the phone.

"Let's go for a coffee," suggested Paul. We left Ruben to his telephone conversation, and passed the highly polished Coastguard helicopter as we walked towards the coffee bar. Behind us the hangar doors continued their resounding rattle in the ever-present Shetland winds. By the coffee bar itself, we saw Joan the hangar cleaner as she carried an enormous pile of dirty towels to a washing machine. We said "hello" to Joan, who grunted grumpily "helloo," in her strong Shetland accent. Her frowned expression, however, yelled: "lazy aircrew lounging about as usual while I do all the work around here."

Inside the coffee bar, there was a smoky atmosphere as a few engineers sat chatting during one of their regular breaks. Many of the engineers were local Shetlanders, and sometimes it was hard to decipher their vivid dialect. They nodded briefly at us through the fog when we entered. "Any trainin' plar'ned for this a'rfternoon?" asked Peter, one of the engineers.

"No, I don't think so," I said.

"McHat/McCoat is weighed down with paper-work at the moment," Paul added as we made towards the large stainless steel hot-water device for making the coffee; "I don't think he's very keen to fly."

"He's probably plar'ning next year's Up-Helly-Aa," said Peter, an affable local who was an experienced S61 man. "In that case, when you're re'edy we'll do a gro'ond run to check for oil leaks fr'am number one engine. We could have done it on sta'rt-up if there was a trainin' flight, but 'Himself' will sta'rt ra'ntin' if we leave it too long." 'Himself' was the local chief engineer, a vexed Irishman with an abrasive, grating nature much disliked by the other engineers.

"Sure, no problem," I said enthusiastically, "we could do it now, if you like." Peter rose from his chair, and the two of us walked away from the coffee bar fog. "Bloody smokers," muttered Peter. I went to check the technical log, while Peter proceeded to open the hangar doors so that the Coastguard S61 could be taken outside. Peter started the tractor which was already attached to the S61's towing hook. Within moments, he had driven the helicopter outside, and I then opened the 'airstair' door to enter the machine.

The atmosphere inside was unlike most normal 'crew-change' S61s. There was a salty, sea-worn smell which could be sniffed straight away. By the 'airstair' door, a seat had been placed in front of a special TV-type screen. The screen could produce infra-red images which were sometimes useful in locating survivors. One of the crewmen would sit there if required, and relay information to the pilots. Most of the other cabin seating had been removed, and by the cargo door a large water-proof mat had been placed.

Just outside the cargo-door was the helicopter's winch. The duty winch-operator would use a switch to raise or lower the hook at the end of the winch wire. If needed, the pilots had a separate switch to operate the winch. In most rescues, the winchman would be attached to the hook, and would be lowered to the scene by the winch-operator. Usually, the winchman would then place a casualty into a double-strop arrangement, and a survivor would be accompanied by the winchman up into the helicopter cabin.

The Captain also had a guarded switch which, in dire emergency, would activate an explosive bolt to guillotine the winch wire clear of the aircraft. This facility would be used some years in the future at a rescue in November 1997, involving the vessel *Green Lily*, when the crewman tragically lost his life. However, the guillotine system failed on that occasion; the winch-operator had to resort to manual wire-cutters to rid the S61 of its hopelessly entangled hook, which was in danger of dragging down the helicopter. The crew then had no choice but to limp home with their paralysed machine battered by violent storms, agonising in their minds over and over again the fact that one of their number had been left behind.

It was also the winch-operator's job to give detailed directions to the pilot. For example, in a hover, the winch-operator would give a constant commentary, such as: "*Move right two... steady, steady... right a further one... steady, steady. Safe height, no lower... survivor approaching the strop. The winchman has the survivor. Steady... steady. Your sinking... up one. Raising the winchman and survivor to the door. Maintain your position.*" The units "up one" or "right two" were measures judged by an individual crewman, rather than specific distances.

The helicopter winchmen, at the end of the wire, were courageous, highly trained individuals, who were often the first to reach an emergency situation. All the winchmen received extensive medical training, some to paramedic standard. Inside the Coastguard helicopter was specialised medical gear, including heart resuscitation equipment, and Entonox pain relieving gas.

As I moved forward into the cockpit area, several differences between this S61 and the 'norm' were seen at a glance. In particular, a complicated auto-pilot had been installed which gave the pilots a considerable number of options. Approaching a survivor, for example, at the touch of a button, the helicopter would automatically carry out a circuit, and fly the machine into the wind before entering an auto-hover. In some conditions, such as poor visibility at night, the facility was invaluable. In other circumstances, perhaps in very stormy winds, the autopilot could not cope, and the pilots would hover manually without it.

The Coastguard helicopter also had numerous additional lights, and extra radio and navigation systems. As a result of the extra equipment, the helicopter was appreciably heavier than normal, which could present problems if there were large numbers of survivors.

When I sat down in the pilot's seat, I nodded at Peter who had positioned himself by the ground power unit outside. I slid back the small window, and shouted above the whine of the ground power unit: "Number one engine start, and head turn?" Peter gave a thumbs-up sign to confirm what I had read in the technical log. Then I went quickly through various pre-start checks: *battery on, start master on, fuel valve for number one engine on, anti-collision lights on, rotor brake applied.* I made a brief call to Air Traffic Control for clearance. Whilst I proceeded with the checks, I noticed Ruben's bored face staring out of his radio room window. "Poor old Ruben," I thought. "Better go and cheer him up with a dollop of bad news after this."

Soon, I had completed the pre-start checks, and held up one finger to Peter to show my readiness to start number one engine. Peter checked around the vicinity of the helicopter, and then held up one finger to show: "clear to start." I raised my left hand to grip the left-hand speed select lever in the roof area of the cockpit, pressed the small button at the base of the lever, and advanced the lever to 'ground idle' after a pause.

Immediately there was a screech as the number one engine above and behind my head began to fire up. The cockpit dials for that engine sprang into life: compressor revolutions increased, engine temperature increased, and the fuel pressure began to register. As the number one engine picked up speed, I continued to monitor the cockpit gauges. If I was unhappy with any of the readings, I could have brought the speed select lever rapidly back in order to close down the engine.

When the number one engine had stabilised, I glanced outside at Peter. I also noticed Ruben, whose expression revealed a flicker of interest aroused by the noise of the helicopter. Both men stared at the S61 as I raised my finger again, and made a rotating signal. The signal was repeated by Peter, to show that I was clear to release the rotor brake. Just to the side of the speed select levers, I gripped the rotor brake handle, and released it positively; the rotors immediately started to turn, quite slowly at first. Then I nimbly moved my hand back onto the speed select lever, and began to move it progressively forwards. The lever acted like a throttle; it was one input to a computer-controlled system to keep the engine within a defined band. In theory, therefore, the rotor head would also be kept within specific limits.

Carefully, I advanced the speed select lever towards its 'flight' position. The shriek from the number one engine intensified, and the noise of the rotors could be heard as they picked up speed. The engine instruments were joined by the rotor revolutions gauge as it sprang into life. Steadily, the rotor revolutions increased towards one hundred percent.

While the rotor blades gathered momentum, I had to move the cyclic stick fractionally and judiciously to make sure of their correct position. The blades appeared as a 'disc' outside the cockpit window, and it was important to maintain the right gap between the natural horizon in front, and the edge of the disc. If the blades were badly placed, they would castigate the pilot by producing a series of noisy and uncomfortable thumps.

Quite quickly, though, the speed select lever was in its correct 'flight' position, the rotor revolutions gauge had settled at one hundred percent, and the engine dials were reading correctly. At that point, I pressed my stop watch to time the two minutes of 'burning and turning' required. Standing close to the ground power unit, Peter looked on happily, and I noticed that Ruben was using the telephone again. I observed the rather murky weather conditions outside;

moderate winds provided good gliding opportunities for the seagulls along the shoreline.

Soon, the two minutes had elapsed, and I pulled back the speed select lever to the 'ground idle' position, allowing the engine to stabilise before shut down. When the rotor speed had reduced to forty percent, I applied the rotor brake. Then I completed other cockpit checks, before walking back to the 'airstair' door. Peter had already climbed up to the inspection hatch by the engine, and as I walked down the steps of the 'airstair' door, he was peering carefully into the number one engine. He gave me a thumbs-up sign, indicating that he had found no traces of oil leakage.

As I passed the radio room, I heard Ruben's dulcet tones in excited conversation, so I walked across to hear the latest item of tittle-tattle.

"Well, would you believe it?" whistled Ruben, shaking his head as he replaced the telephone receiver. "He's only gone and put up a notice, bold as brass, warning all pilots about the dangers of being careless."

"Oh dear," I said. "That's terrible. What are we talking about, by the way?"

"Old Brian," Ruben scowled slightly at the tone of my silly question. "Arrogant bugger has posted a notice saying that if someone in his position is capable of landing on the wrong rig, then it could happen to anyone."

"Oh dear," I repeated, knowing that I would never dream of doing such a thing. "That really is arrogance for you. Mind you, I suppose he has a point."

"Some folk at Aberdeen are seething," said Ruben gleefully, ignoring my latter comment.

"Oh dear," I said once more. "We can't be having that." Ruben glanced at me; a further scowl fleetingly shadowed his brow. I looked back at Ruben for a moment. A keen Company man, Ruben worked very long hours for little thanks. He was not popular, and he was under-appreciated, but in truth his heart was in the right place.

"Can I get you a cup of coffee, Ruben?" I asked at length. "We missed out just now."

"Yeah, cheers." Ruben brightened slightly. "Two sugars, and a dash of milk please."

Peter was manoeuvring the tractor as he returned the helicopter to its place of safety within the hangar. Walking towards the coffee bar, I passed a row of offices. 'Himself' could be heard with raised voice as he argued with someone during a telephone conversation. McHat/McCoat appeared deep in concentration as he too spoke on the telephone. The pile of papers before him seemed to stand as high as an hour ago.

Just before entering the coffee bar, I glanced back at McHat/McCoat. He was still in earnest conversation, but he raised an eyebrow in half-hearted greeting when he spotted me. McHat/McCoat, hero of the Chinook rescue and Piper A, was undoubtedly a sound character and excellent pilot. Nevertheless, I felt he looked a somewhat sad figure, this staunch Scotsman, as he sat with upright back and gloomy expression, his black hat placed firmly on his head. "Good old McHat/McCoat," I thought to myself, "we really ought to think up another nickname for the poor old fellow."

CHAPTER 9

Calm Before a Storm

The coffee bar remained brimful with smokers' fog. As I entered the room, the same group of engineers still sat in one corner. Paul and Gary stood chatting by the stainless steel urn, in a partitioned area. I made some coffee, and went to sit down in the main part of the room, where the conversation centred on the subject of the weather.

"Them weather forecasts," said Jimmy, a demure local with an ancient blue hat cocked to one side of his head, "always tell on what's har'pening doo'n soo'th. Hardly a bother a mention o' us. That Michael Fish on TV's partic'olar craa'p. Hasn't even he'rrd of Shetland if you asks me."

Whilst most folk merely nodded in approval at this profound and possibly correct statement, I was suddenly struck with an idea. After a number of seconds, I declared boldly: "I went to school with the famous Michael Fish."

A few extra puffs from the smokers was the only acknowledgement of this bomb-shell. Paul had just joined us, though. As he sat down, he asked: "Which school was that then?"

"Eastbourne College," I replied with a feeling of mild awkwardness.

There was an isolated moment of silence which was broken by Martin, the Gentle Giant, asking: "That near Edinburgh?"

Someone snorted, then Paul interjected: "Even further south, I believe."

A further delicate pause was soon broken by Jimmy. "Aye, a right royal sassenach we have here," he said. Someone snorted again.

"And proud of it too, no doubt," said Paul, as he tried to abate the racial direction of our conversation.

"Like it or not," I said determinedly, "in my geography class we had Roach, Pike, and Fish. And I remember that young Fish was pretty dubious when it came to geography." Jimmy gazed at me sceptically. "Mind you, I wasn't much better. Come to think of it, that Roach chap wasn't too sharp either." A few guffaws followed this statement.

"What was the teacher's name, then?" asked Jimmy, narrowing his eyes. "Mr Kipper?" The assembly held shocked silence for an instant. Then an explosion of coughing from Jimmy marked the sudden appreciation of his own remark.

Meanwhile, Joan had entered the room with a pile of freshly laundered towels. She sniffed the smoky air disapprovingly, and moved towards the hot-water urn. She placed the towels in a cupboard, and turned to observe the assembled company.

"I should waa'tch oo't, you lot" she said at length. "The Poisoned Dwarf is on the waa'r-path."

The engineers sat up anxiously, and noticed the movement of the vexed Irishman towards the coffee bar. As 'Himself' walked through the door, there was a prompt change of atmosphere. The engineers said nothing, but their eyes looked around fretfully. 'Himself' quickly made a cup of coffee, before turning to glare at everybody. "Aircraft cleaning time," he announced. These were his only words before he picked up his cup, and smartly left the coffee bar. The engineers glanced at each other, then slowly began to shuffle out of the room to start their duties.

"We could give them a hand when they've got the kit ready," sighed Paul, as he produced some brightly coloured brochures. He laid the brochures carefully side by side on the low table in the centre of the room.

"Planning a holiday, Paul?" I asked.

"You've got to do something to stay sane around here," commented Paul ruefully. "We're thinking of taking the kids to the States. There are some good deals at the moment."

"Yup," I said. "We took our family to California recently. Had a great time. Strongly recommended."

"Did you 'do' Disneyland?" asked Paul. In the hangar, the engineers moved equipment noisily in readiness for the aircraft wash.

"We did indeed," I replied. "The only problem was that my son wasn't well."

"What happened?"

"From the start of the day, he complained of tummy pains," I said, undeterred by the clattering noises outside the coffee bar. "The pains got worse and worse," I continued, "so eventually we took him to the Disney sick-bay. It was a good set-up, but by mid-afternoon the poor wee chap was pretty bad. He was groaning as he lay on his bed, and he looked pale and lacklustre. However, in a flash of inspiration, it struck me quite suddenly what the trouble might be." There was a grunt from Joan, who listened to my story at the same time as she tidied around the coffee-making area. "Struck *me,* mind you, not the medical staff," I added.

I sipped at my cup of coffee. Then I continued: "At length, I got the nurse over and said: 'I think it might be appendicitis.' The nurse looked doubtful at first, and shrugged her shoulders as she examined her patient once more. Suddenly, however, she stood up straight, looked at me firmly, and declared: 'I agree, honey.' Within minutes, they had wheeled Alan out of the sick-bay, and – along with the rest of the family – into the back of a Mickey Mouse ambulance. Literally."

There was a further grunt from Joan, before Paul asked: "Did it work?"

"Yes it did," I replied. There was a crash as one of the engineers dropped a tool. 'Himself' stood to one side, just outside his office, hands on hips as he supervised. "It was fascinating driving through the back-stage of Disney, where the public don't normally go," I went on. "The sparkling smiles had dropped, as had the image of youth and vigour. Most of the staff lounged about, long-faced and exhausted."

"Did you have holiday insurance?" asked Paul.

"The hospital asked the same question as we walked in through the doors," I replied. In the hangar, there was a slight furore as 'Himself' berated the Gentle Giant for his clumsiness. Water hoses were connected up. Long handled brushes were made ready. "Luckily we did have insurance," I continued. "The surgeon operated that night to remove young Alan's appendix. It's quite a thought. Just a few decades earlier, and they couldn't have helped him. The poor lad would have died."

'Himself' had glanced over in our direction, but Paul had become buried in his brochures. "We could give the engineers a hand now," I said at length, "to keep the peace if nothing else." Paul looked up briefly, glimpsed the Poisoned Dwarf's eye, and groaned. Gary, who had been sitting quietly in a corner, stood up. The three of us then walked into the hangar.

A pungent smell of chemicals had entered the atmosphere; a special mixture was being applied to the outside paint-work of the S61. I picked up a long-handled brush, and went to help with the cleaning process.

"I shouldna' bother, laddie," the Gentle Giant said to me. "This stuff is ric'ht shit on your hands. Leave it to me wi' me gloves."

At that point, I caught sight of Ruben, and quickly remembered my promise to take him a cup of coffee. "Thanks, Martin," I said. "I'll be back shortly."

Soon, I had made Ruben's cup of coffee, and I performed a wide berth of 'Himself' as I walked through the hangar towards the radio room. Before entering the radio room, I glanced back at 'Himself'. He remained standing outside his office, with hands on hips still as he observed the goings-on. 'Himself' was undoubtedly an excellent engineer, and had his work cut out in this strange environment. "Shame about the personality hang-ups," I thought to myself.

"Here you are, Ruben," I said, as I entered the radio room. "One cup of coffee with two sugars and a touch of paint-work cleaner."

"Cheers," said Ruben. I could see that he was longing to tell me something. Quietly, I went over to the tatty chair in the corner, and sat down. Ruben hopped excitedly from one foot to the other. I said nothing, but looked at him knowing that he could not resist for long; at any moment his news would be out.

"Even old Smithy's got involved with this one," said Ruben in hushed tones.

Smithy was the Flight Manager at Aberdeen. "The tr'uble with this bl'udy C'umpany," Smithy-from-Manchester said to me one time as he dusted down the Sergeant's stripes on his old military uniform, "is that we're managed by bl'udy NCOs. They ain't got no vision."

At length, I said to Ruben: "Well that sounds interesting, Ruben."

"I know, I know," cut in Ruben joyfully.

"Well what's he had to say about it anyway?" I asked, stifling a mild yawn.

Ruben became clandestine as the tone of his voice lowered. "Well, I'm not absolutely sure to be honest with you," he said. "But there's even a rumour buzzing round that Brian will be told to take down his notice."

"Well that would be a pity," I said. "It must have taken him ages to think it up."

"That's not a fact, mind," said Ruben, oblivious of my comment. "Don't go telling anybody anything yet."

"No. I'll definitely try not to," I confirmed.

At that moment, a voice cut across our conversation as the loudspeaker connected into the Company radio system crackled into life. "Sumburgh, this is 82 Bravo, do you read?"

Ruben reached across for the hand-held microphone, and said: "82 Bravo you're loud and clear. Go ahead."

"82 Bravo, requesting a refuel en-route to Aberdeen. We'll be with you in twenty-five minutes."

"Roger 82 Bravo, no problem. I'll fix it up," replied Ruben, before saying to me as an aside: "Bugger."

Ruben then picked up the telephone to order fuel for the Tiger helicopter. Depending on the head-winds of the day, the helicopters were sometimes unable to fly directly from the oil installations in the East Shetland Basin to Aberdeen. The machines would therefore arrange to refuel at another installation en-route, or they would fly via Sumburgh.

As Ruben made his telephone call, Joan entered the room carrying a Hoover. Soon she had connected up the noisy machine, and began vacuuming the radio room, and the neighbouring crew room. During the consequent lull in conversation, I picked up a sheet of paper with the latest weather reports and forecasts, and studied the prognosis.

A general cloud-base of two thousand feet was anticipated, with visibility of around four miles.

Whilst I studied the weather sheets, McHat/McCoat appeared in the doorway. He shouted above the noise of the vacuum cleaner: "I don't think we'll plan a training flight for this afternoon," he said. "I've got a lot of paper-work, and the weather doesn't look too bright." Ruben and I nodded in acknowledgement as McHat/McCoat added as an aside: "If we do get airborne for real, by the way, it'll be my 199th rescue mission."

"That sounds a lot," I said. "Are you sure you've got that right?"

"Yup. I've been up-dating my log-book today," replied McHat/McCoat. "I've been doing this job rather a lot of years, I'm afraid," he added as he left to retreat to his office.

I noticed that the aircraft cleaning had reached the stage of hosing off the chemicals. I stood up, and left the radio room to help the Gentle Giant as he drenched the machine with water. I used a long-handled brush to clean around awkward recesses on the S61, trying to avoid damage to numerous radio aerials and other equipment. Soon the machine began to gleam following our efforts to combat the destructive salty environment. The Gentle Giant then turned off the hose, and went to open the hangar doors to encourage a through-draught.

"Better go and top-up with some more coffee, I guess," said Paul eventually. He looked at his watch. "Nearly half-past three," he said. "The day's dragging already." He could not have known, of course, that a helicopter was at that moment about to declare a *Mayday* distress call. Paul could not have known that the S61 was about to be gripped by a calamitous fire which would destroy the machine. He could not have known that the nineteen oilmen, and two helicopter pilots on board shortly would need our urgent assistance.

"OK," I said. "More coffee it shall be."

We wandered slowly towards the coffee bar, and Paul continued to question me about holidaying in the States. "What's the best time of year to go?" he asked. "What's the driving like over there?"

Joan had finished her vacuuming session around Ruben's feet, and lugged the Hoover awkwardly across the hangar. McHat/McCoat was at his desk engrossed in another telephone conversation.

As we headed towards the coffee-making machine, Paul volunteered to make the coffee. "I'll do the honours," he said. "How do you like it?" He reached for a mug marked 'Visitor' as he began to make my black coffee.

The steam from the hot-water urn trickled steadily onto the unexceptional brand of instant coffee. There was a distinctive redolence as Paul stirred up the mixture inside the mug. He continued to quiz me on details about America. "Driving there is really not a problem," I said. "Practically all the cars have automatic gearboxes, and the Americans in general seem to be rather polite drivers."

The liquid level had reached only half-way up the mug, when Paul's hand gave a small jerk. Quickly, he turned off the flow of water.

The shrill of the scramble alarm screamed through the atmosphere as Paul hastily put down the mug. The noise was accompanied by Ruben's almost comical figure as he stood outside the radio room, waving his arms vigorously.

CHAPTER 10

Fire in the Air

As I raced towards the radio room, McHat/McCoat simultaneously emerged from his office. His hat had been cast aside, and he struggled to don his flying suit. Paul and Gary ran into the radio room, where one of them picked up a special telephone, linked directly to the Coastguard. In professional tones, they spoke to the Duty Coastguard Controller, and wrote down details on a specifically designed pad.

While I speedily put on my flying suit, snatches of information could be heard as the crewmen spoke. *"S61... G-BEID... British International Helicopters... inbound from the Tern... fire in the air... fifteen miles east of Bressay... "* It was not my job, however, to learn a mass of details yet. My main concern was to run to the helicopter as quickly as possible in order to start the machine. Whilst the crewmen gathered data, McHat/McCoat stood near them to gain an over-view of particular aspects or dangers. The Captain had to be satisfied in his own mind that it was safe to proceed. As the co-pilot, however, I concentrated on getting the S61 'burning and turning', ready for the others to join me.

I ran through the open hangar, and headed directly for the waiting S61. The 'airstair' door was already ajar, and I paced up the steps. Peter had towed the helicopter to an ideal position outside the hangar, and he stood by the ground power unit, which he had just connected up. I dashed forward into the cockpit area, and sat down in the co-pilot's seat on the left side.

With greater urgency than for the recent ground-run, I once more went through the pre-start checks: *main battery on; standby battery on; start master on; fuel valves both on; rotor brake applied.* Quickly, I glanced up and signalled to Peter who gave a thumbs-up, indicating clearance to start the number one engine. I grasped the left-hand speed select lever, and pressed the small button at the base. *"Come on, you bugger...come on..."* My impatience was unnecessary; quite rapidly the screech from behind signalled the progress of number one engine's start cycle.

"Ng stabilised... temps and pressures all good... motorize the DC genny..." Peter was there, ready for my next signal. I grasped the rotor-brake handle, and nimbly released it all the way back. *"Steady... steady,"* I forced myself not to advance the speed select lever too promptly. *"Don't break the machine now, for goodness sake..."* I compelled myself to adopt the professional, unflustered approach, deeply instilled through the years.

Soon the rotor revolutions gauge indicated one hundred percent. I went through further checks, then made another signal to Peter, who cleared me to start the S61's second engine. The commotion from the helicopter 'burning and turning' was promptly augmented as the number two engine began its start cycle. I glimpsed Ruben's face as he stared out from the radio room. He appeared to have wakened up; Ruben and each individual had his or her own specific duty in our overall team effort.

Number two engine was stabilising just as McHat/McCoat arrived. He seemed breathless as he began to strap into the seat next to mine. Just outside the cockpit, Peter was in the process of detaching the ground power unit. As these activities proceeded, I called Air Traffic Control: *"Sumburgh, Rescue 117 shortly scrambling to the north-east."* My terse message was briefly acknowledged by the Duty Controller.

Paul and Gary were hastening to the helicopter at this stage; the crewmen staggered a little in their heavyweight flying suits. Soon they entered the cabin, and slammed the 'airstair' door closed. Gary moved forward towards the cockpit, and plugged in his headset. Paul strapped himself into a seat in the cabin.

"Right, guys," Gary spoke calmly, but he was panting slightly. "Make your initial heading 035 degrees. It looks like the S61 is ditching thirty-five miles from here."

I then gave control of the helicopter to McHat/McCoat, and picked up the check-list card. "OK," said the Captain. "Just run through the before take-off checks quickly."

"Fuel contents... altimeter setting... radar altimeter on... anti-collision lights on... Ts and Ps..." briskly I read out the checks. When these had been completed, McHat/McCoat said, "Get clearance to lift from our present position, please."

The Captain had no wish to waste time taxying onto a runway; the steady wind meant that we had sufficient power for a vertical take-off.

After I had spoken to Air Traffic Control, they replied promptly: "Roger Rescue 117, you are clear to lift from your present position."

McHat/McCoat then called: *"Lifting..."*

With my right hand, I eased forward the speed select levers to ensure both engines were at full power for the take-off. The Captain raised the helicopter's collective lever, momentarily held the machine in a hover, and then raised the lever further to ensure a rapid vertical climb. As soon as we had cleared the roof level of the hangar, with the sea-shore ahead swiftly coming into view, McHat/McCoat applied a forward input to the cyclic stick. The S61 then moved away from the hangar area, and began to pick up forward speed as it continued to climb.

At that point, McHat/McCoat turned the machine left onto the north-easterly heading required.

"Confirm our airborne time, please," he asked me.

"Airborne at three forty; the scramble alarm sounded at three, three, three," I replied.

"Roger," said McHat/McCoat, too absorbed to notice the quirk of timing, "we'll level at one thousand feet. It should keep us clear of the cloud-base, and we'll get a slightly better ground-speed than higher up in these easterly winds." After a moment, the Captain said: "I'll have the after take-off checks when you're ready, please."

"Re-check fuel... altimeters: set QNH... radar on... undercarriage up..." again, I went swiftly through the necessary ritual of the check list. McHat/McCoat was levelling the S61 at one thousand feet, and the airspeed approached the required one hundred and ten knots.

"Sort out that radar ASAP, please," McHat/McCoat said tersely.

I moved my right hand forward, and made adjustments to the radar set in the centre console. The picture showed numerous returns, mainly from fishing and other vessels as they converged on Lerwick harbour. It was impossible at that stage to determine the outline of our target.

"It's a fairly crap picture, I'm afraid," I said.

McHat/McCoat grunted slightly, and replied: "I can see that. Just keep working at it."

At that moment, we flew past the small island of Moussa on our left side, one of over a hundred islands in the Shetland archipelago. The Moussa Broch, well known as perhaps the best remaining example of a Broch in the world, stood proudly in the middle of the isle. Ahead, the misty surroundings painted a dismal picture of grey.

"At least we're well clear of the cloud base," commented the Captain.

In the cabin behind us, Paul unstrapped in order to make equipment preparations. He was the man who would be lowered by winch to deal with the survivors. Paul made adjustments to the special harness he was placing on top of his heavy-duty flying suit. It reminded me of a mountaineer's routine, as he double-checked various clips and springs for serviceability; his life depended upon their security.

At that stage, we were unaware if there were casualties involved. However, the spectre of Piper A the week before was an unspoken thought on most minds. It would be Paul's job to apply First Aid, and to deal with the trauma of injuries. As I glanced back at Paul, it struck me as bizarre that the hands so recently making us cups of coffee, soon would be applied to potentially dire life-saving activities.

On the left side of the helicopter, occasional glimpses of the more easterly islands around Aith Wick and the Bay of Fladdabister appeared. They provided a fleeting but somehow comforting contact with the Mainland of Shetland. As the eccentric domain snaked northwards, its slim, singular shape was mostly hidden by the foggy conditions. While I persisted with attempts to improve our radar picture, we began to pick up the outline of Bressay Island, shaped liked a protective hand around Lerwick harbour. Just to the east of Bressay was the small Isle of Noss.

Suddenly, McHat/McCoat was pointing at the radar picture. "I think that might be them," he said. The Captain's experience in Search and Rescue activities was paying dividends. He maintained our airspeed at one hundred and ten knots, but initiated a slow descent towards the surface of the sea. By then, we had lost sight of the territories on our left side, but the radar picture showed about ten miles remaining before we reached our suspected target.

"Run through the pre-winching checks, please," the Captain said to me.

"Hoist Master to 'Crew'... temperatures and pressures all within limits... fuel contents sufficient..." quite rapidly I had covered the items on the check list. McHat/McCoat continued our slow descent towards the sea, and I concentrated on the radar picture. I began a count-down of the range as we approached our objective.

"Target on the nose, range six miles," I said. As I made the call, all eyes made concerted attempts to see ahead, but the poor visibility thwarted our efforts.

"Target still on the nose, approaching five miles," was my next announcement. However, we were still unable to make visual contact. Leaden skies surrounded us; they produced an enclosed feeling in the drab airspace.

"Target remains on the nose as we approach four miles," I called. We could spot various fishing vessels in the vicinity. We were aware, too, that a passing helicopter was in the area; the machine had no rescue winch, but it provided a companionable presence to the survivors until our arrival. Suddenly, appearing out of the mists, an extraordinary scene began to emerge.

Sitting on the surface of the sea was a helicopter with brightly coloured buoyancy aids sprouting from the side-sponsons. The doors of the machine were wide open and the S61 appeared deserted; the helicopter had a *Marie Celeste* aura as it bobbed up and down gently in the sea swell. The machine seemed somehow defiant as it sat upright in the water. An insidious sign, however, confirmed that the helicopter's fate had been sealed already: issuing from the point just behind the cockpit surged a pall of thick black smoke. Accompanying this smoke were orange tongues, as flames darted around the engine bay area.

Observing this curious drama, at a distance of around half a mile, were two groups of survivors. The men sat patiently in rubber dinghies, distinctly marked in vivid Dayglo colours, as they awaited the arrival of the Coastguard Helicopter.

"Reducing speed and height. Standby to open cargo door." McHat/McCoat was brisk and business-like as the crew went through their well versed pre-winching procedure. The nose of our aircraft reared upwards as the Captain applied cyclic movement to slow our airspeed from one hundred and ten knots. He kept the collective lever fully down to prevent the machine from climbing, and quite rapidly the airspeed reduced below fifty knots, towards twenty knots. At that point, McHat/McCoat levelled the machine again, and we continued to close steadily onto the nearest of the two dinghies ahead.

"Standby for winching," called McHat/McCoat brusquely. By now, Gary had opened the cargo door. Paul was connected to the winch hook, and was placing himself in a sitting position in the doorway. Gary had started the winch operator's patter as he directed us towards the first dinghy:

"Target on the nose range fifteen... your speed is good... right two as you close... continue your descent."

I glanced at McHat/McCoat as he positively applied the demanded corrections. On our right side the ditched S61 still burned intensely.

"Target now range twelve... rate of closure is good... safe height, no lower. Right a further two. Your height is good. Target now range ten. You're climbing slightly; down two."

At this stage the Captain said "Full power please."

I raised my right hand, and eased both speed select levers fully forward.

"Target now on the nose, range eight; no further right. Safe height again... no lower. Target range six."

With the wind directly on our nose, the approach was turning out to be ideal.

"Target range five. Your rate of closure is good. Target range four… target range three… maintain your height… target range two… one… steady. Steady. Steady."

Once McHat/McCoat was happy with the aircraft's position, he called abruptly: "You're clear out." Immediately, Gary operated the winch to lift Paul from his sitting position. The winch operator then assisted Paul to manoeuvre so that he faced inwards. Paul was then helped to move clear of the surrounding superstructure, as Gary began to lower him down towards the survivors.

Meanwhile, Gary kept up a running commentary of activities below the helicopter, by then out of the pilots' sight.

"*Winchman now approaching the survivors,*" said Gary. "*The dinghy's canopy has been taken down. Paul is just entering the dinghy. Maintain your position.*"

McHat/McCoat kept a steady hover above the scene.

"The winchman is now unbuckling his harness."

With these words, McHat/McCoat and I glanced at each other momentarily. We both knew the implication: a member of our crew had been physically detached from the aircraft. The crewman had himself, in effect, become one of the survivors.

"Winchman now assisting two survivors into the double strop. Steady… steady. Two survivors shortly about to be winched in. Right one… your height is good… steady."

Just ahead, and to our left, the occupants of the other dinghy could be seen as they apprehensively supervised our activities. The down-draught from our rotors was blown away from their craft by the prevailing wind; fortunately we caused them no interference.

"Winching in two survivors."

These words from the winch operator brought stark focus to the reality of the situation; the procedures so far had had the familiarity of a training flight. The fact that this was 'for real' was further emphasised when we felt the S61 lurch slightly as the weight of two men was taken up. I monitored the helicopter's torque gauge carefully.

"Torque now sixty-five to seventy percent," I said. We were quite comfortable with that figure; there was plenty of power margin. However, McHat/McCoat and I were simultaneously thinking ahead. With twenty-one survivors to be taken on board, we may have insufficient power. This would be shown by excessive torque readings. If the torque reading passed beyond one hundred percent, the gear-box would be over-stressed; ultimately it could disintegrate.

"With this number of survivors, we're going to be pushed for power towards the end," said McHat/McCoat. "We might have to make the aircraft lighter by dumping fuel. Can you work out our minimum acceptable fuel level, please?"

While I made the calculations, Gary continued his commentary: *"Two survivors are now being winched clear of the dinghy. They're rotating slightly as I continue to winch in. The survivors are now half way to the door."* McHat/McCoat still maintained a steady hover. *"Two survivors approaching the door."*

As Gary said this, I turned briefly, and looked back. The two men advancing to the door wore orange coloured suits; the bright colour accentuated the ashen complexion of their faces. The men hugged the winch hook as they were taken upwards in the double strop. Soon, Gary had manoeuvred the survivors through the doorway, and into the cabin. At this stage, he loosened the strop, before removing it from the men.

"The first two men are now going to the rear of the cabin," Gary continued his patter. *"Lowering the hook for the next survivors."*

I had made the fuel calculation by then, and as the hook was being lowered again, I discussed the implications with McHat/McCoat.

"We'll just have to keep an eye on the torque," he said, "but we'll probably need to dump fuel when we're half-way through the winching operations."

When the Captain had said this, Gary continued: *"The winchman is now grabbing the hook... he's about to secure the next two survivors into the strop... standby for winch in."*

Gary's calm commentary displayed his long experience as a winch operator, and his professional patter painted a clear picture of events beneath the helicopter.

While the process of recovering the survivors proceeded, occasionally I glanced across at the blazing remains of the downed helicopter. It astounded me that a metal structure managed to burn so successfully. The flames had moved back from the engine bay area, towards the cabin itself, and the engines had started to collapse from their supports; they sank down into the devastated area behind the cockpit. Scraps of paper, charred upholstery, and pools of oil floated in the sea around the wreck of the S61.

As the skilful winching operations progressed, the cabin of the Coastguard helicopter began to become crowded as more survivors were brought on board. Already, we had evacuated the personnel from the first dinghy, which floated away slowly. While we continued to winch up survivors from the second craft, I monitored the increasing level of torque as the helicopter became gradually heavier:

"Torque now ninety percent to ninety-five percent," I said.

McHat/McCoat looked impassive as he continued to hold the helicopter in a steady hover, but when I called: "Torque ninety-five percent, occasionally touching ninety-eight percent," he asked,

"How many survivors have we got in the back now, Gary?"

Gary did a quick re-count of numbers, then said: "Fourteen in the back. Five oilmen, two pilots, and Paul remain to be rescued."

"In that case," said the Captain, "we'd better leave, and fly a circuit so we can dump fuel."

As Gary brought the winch hook back to its stowage position, he waved briefly to his colleague in the dinghy below. Having ensured the security of the winch, Gary closed the cargo door. McHat/McCoat then eased the cyclic stick forward to gain airspeed. As we flew away from the dinghy, Gary mentioned the anxious looks on the faces left behind.

"It's OK," said the Captain, "Paul will explain to them what we're doing."

McHat/McCoat climbed the machine to one thousand feet as he began the circuit. Then he said to me: "We're well clear of the survivors now. Operate the dump switch, please." On the lower console by my hand was a guarded switch. I lifted the guard clear, and flicked forward the switch beneath. Looking in the rear-view mirror, I soon detected a fine spray under the aircraft as fuel was released from the tanks. McHat/McCoat and I carefully monitored the fuel gauges; as soon as the required fuel level was indicated, I turned off the dump switch, and returned the guard.

The Captain then proceeded to manoeuvre the S61 back towards the remaining survivors in the second dinghy, and Gary resumed his patter as we approached the craft.

"Target on the nose range fifteen... your rate of closure is good.. safe height, no lower... "

Soon, the helicopter came to a hover over the dinghy once more. Quite quickly, we were aware of the lower torque readings.

"Torque now seventy-five to eighty percent," I called.

"That sounds better," commented McHat/McCoat.

"The winchman has hold of the hook now... he's attaching two more survivors... standby for winch in."

Gary's commentary progressed again as McHat/McCoat continued to hold a hover. Shortly, we were aware of the helicopter's slight lurch as the winch took up the weight of the next two men.

As the two survivors were winched up, I called out the new torque reading.

"Torque now seventy-eight, occasionally touching just over eighty percent," I called.

This reading was comfortable; McHat/McCoat looked happy. However, with the next two men, the torque increased significantly.

"Confirm four left to be winched up?" McHat/McCoat asked.

"That's correct," replied Gary briefly. He was lowering the winch hook once more and within moments he was saying:

"The winchman has the hook... he's putting the strop round the survivors... standby for winch in... "

When the S61 gave its familiar lurch as the winch took the strain, I noticed a worried frown briefly cross the Captain's face when I called: *"Torque now ninety percent, occasionally touching ninety-five percent."*

Despite this, Gary's commentary continued.

"Two survivors now being lifted clear of the dinghy... steady... steady... survivors approaching the door. One of them is the co-pilot."

I glanced back and noticed the dark blue colour of the co-pilot's flying suit. As Gary assisted the men into the crowded cabin, I continued to call the torque reading:

"Torque remains at ninety percent, occasionally reaching ninety-five percent," I said.

"We can't dump any more fuel," said McHat/McCoat. "Or we won't have enough. We'll just have to see how it goes with these last two."

With this, the winch operator started to lower the winch hook for the final time.

"The winch hook is travelling down... the winchman has grasped the hook... he's fitting the strop around the last survivor. He's begun to attach himself to the strop... standby for winch in..."

McHat/McCoat maintained the hover. His impassive expression, however, appeared disturbed; I could see the signs of strain on our Captain.

"Winching in... now... " called Gary.

As Gary said this, and as we felt the winch take up the weight of the men, the torque suddenly went to maximum.

"One hundred percent torque...!" I cried.

"Stop winching! Stop winching!" yelled the Captain.

Immediately, we felt a slight jerk as Gary released his winch operator's switch. The helicopter's rotor blades continued to beat noisily while we maintained a hover. The last two survivors were held just clear of the surface of the sea, moving neither up nor down. We were held in a nightmarish pause, as if gripped within a grotesque time warp. Not a word was spoken; the crew maintained an anguished silence. The delay became long-drawn out, and awkward. A sense of mortification began to creep into the atmosphere; how could we possibly face the abandonment of these two men at this last minute?

Finally, I broke the spell. "There's been a slight change in wind direction. I suggest you try easing the nose ten degrees left."

McHat/McCoat said nothing, but grunted gloomily as he followed the suggestion.

"Torque now ninety-eight percent," I called.

McHat/McCoat grunted again, and briefly glanced at the cockpit gauge; this vital piece of information had to be confirmed with his own eyes. The Captain then nodded briefly.

"Clear to re-commence winching," he said eventually.

"Roger... re-commencing winch in... two survivors on the hook... the dinghy is being blown away from us... you are clear to move forward and down."

As McHat/McCoat followed these instructions, I continued to monitor the torque reading.

"Torque maintaining ninety-eight to ninety-nine percent," I called.

As the S61 moved closer to the sea's surface, the 'ground effect' boosted the efficiency of the rotor blades and our torque reading began to reduce even more. "Torque now ninety-seven to ninety-eight percent," I said.

"Last two survivors just approaching the door... " As I glanced back at the welcome figure of Paul, now re-united with his crew, I was suddenly startled by the sight of his hook companion. The Captain of the downed helicopter, a portly man in his early thirties, wore no survival suit. The last of the survivors to be winched up, the Captain was the only person in shirt-sleeve order. He reminded me of Captain Bligh as he grimly (and correctly) clutched the log-book of his doomed craft.

"Survivors entering the cabin... unhooking them... taking the winch up to its stowage."

Swiftly, Gary completed the last of the drills. Soon we heard confirmation that our mission had been successful; the final words were crucial: *"Closing the door... you're clear – up and away."*

Without further prompting, McHat/McCoat immediately eased forward the S61s cyclic stick. He maintained our low altitude as the airspeed began to build up, taking advantage of the ground effect. Quite rapidly, however, the airspeed was past twenty knots, then fifty knots, and McHat/McCoat was able to ease the machine upwards. Soon, we had reached one thousand feet, and the required one hundred and ten knots.

When I looked back into the cabin, the over-crowding looked drastic. Men sat on the floor, draped around equipment, or crouched wherever a space could be found. The niceties of offering our passengers a seat, or even strapping them in, were impossible to observe. Folk looked anxious still, but overall the atmosphere was one of immense relief.

Soon, the familiar features of the Shetland coastline began to loom out of the mist. Helli Ness, Moussa, and No Ness felt like home territory as we flew past, and the well-known sight of Boddam Bay eventually signalled our proximity to Sumburgh Airport.

"Rescue 117, request clearance to land," I called Air Traffic Control when we approached the village of Toab.

"Roger, Rescue 117, you are clear to land."

We continued our finals turn onto the runway heading, and soon we were flying over the airfield perimeter. As the runway itself appeared beneath us, McHat/McCoat smoothly eased down the S61. He completed a gentle landing, before taxying the machine towards the main terminal.

As the survivors were shepherded away from the helicopter into the main terminal building, most of them looked up at the crew. Some nodded briefly. Several gave thumbs-up signs; a few even managed a smile as they mouthed the words 'thank you'.

McHat/McCoat then taxied the S61 away from the main terminal, crossed the duty runway, and soon we spotted Peter as he marshalled us back to the Company hangar.

"I'll leave you to close down the machine while I get on with the paperwork," McHat/McCoat said to me. He left his seat stiffly and walked back to the 'airstair' door.

The helicopter close-down procedure took some five minutes. Firstly, with both engines still 'burning and turning', a special wash device was held up in turn to the engines. When Peter looked at me, I gave a thumbs-up sign, which was the signal for him to open the tap of the wash rig. I then timed two minutes, during which period the pervasive effects of salt corrosion were washed away. The process was then repeated for the second engine. When this had been done, I brought the speed select levers back to 'ground idle' and timed a further minute. During the procedure, I noticed Ruben observing the helicopter while he spoke on the telephone.

Ruben was still on the phone when I passed the radio room, having completed the shut-down. He briefly returned my wave. In the offices beyond, I noticed that McHat/McCoat remained in his flying suit while he dealt with paperwork.

"I wonder when the hat will go back on," I thought to myself.

In the chief engineer's office, the vexed Irishman was arguing with someone on the telephone.

"This bloody company is led from the bottom up," he yelled. "If it wasn't for us, the whole kit and caboodle would fall apart at the seams with the garbage down there who call themselves managers..."

In the coffee bar, I noticed that Paul and Gary had already begun to 'do the honours'; the mundane life rudely interrupted by the scramble alarm just an hour and a half ago, had been resumed so rapidly. It was as if nothing had really happened during our absence.

As I made towards the coffee bar, Joan entered directly ahead of me. The atmosphere was still smoky, although there were no engineers in the room; they were busy dealing with the helicopter after-flight procedures. Joan looked around grouchily. Her unspoken words were: "The bloody aircrew are back, just to get in the way again." Paul and Gary were discussing the details of the recent rescue. They stood by the hot water urn, and I felt a sense of respect as I walked towards them. Their modest bravery, generally under-appreciated and played down in this oddball set-up, had just saved so many lives.

Joan watched me as I approached the other two men. Her tired face creased when she frowned slightly. The two crewmen maintained their discussions about the recent winching operations. Unhurried now, they reached for mugs and for the coffee-makings as they talked. Joan continued to observe casually; it had been a long day for her and she was about to go home. Paul and Gary's conversation had become quite technical as they debriefed the flight.

"I was wondering at first whether to use a high-line," said Gary. "But we seemed to manage fine without one."

"I agree," said Paul. "It's not often you need a high-line in conditions like that."

As Joan listened to the crew's conversation, she seemed disinterested in the technicalities. She looked at her watch and frowned again. It was definitely time for her to go home. The crew remained absorbed in their flying matters; it seemed such a chasm between the airborne scene, and the humdrum hangar life.

Eventually, Joan could wait no longer and grew impatient. After a moment she coughed curtly and abruptly interrupted the aircrew discussion.

"Mind ye'r big feet, you lot," she said, taking the conversation smartly down to ground level. "I've only just finished cleaning them floors!"

CHAPTER 11

Coastguard Duties

ONE YEAR LATER

At Stornoway, in the Outer Hebrides, the austere Lews Castle looked over the town with a grave air. Ostensibly dominated by the 'Wee Free' religious faction, Stornoway was nevertheless tormented by graffiti which defaced many of the town's public buildings. The graffiti words suggested that the local population was less than convinced by the harangues of the exacting 'Wee Frees'.

The movement of fishing vessels in and out of the harbour gave some life to Stornoway, as did the constant cry of gulls. In general, however, there was an isolated, and somewhat seedy aura about this frayed-at-the-edges metropolis.

Within the town, an unexpected facet was evident from time to time: a significant population of Asian immigrants ran local stores and restaurants. The bulk of folk, however, appeared to be related to a 'McLeod'. The religious influence could be observed by the plethora of churches which graced the many side streets. The incumbent ministers sternly berated those who failed to observe Sundays with due gravity. Televisions had to be switched off, with screens turned to a wall; the ferries did not operate; newspapers were a definite no-no. Any form of partying or jollification was proclaimed anti-social, an aspect which did not rest easily, however, with the often seen inebriation about town.

A few miles out of Stornoway, to the east, was a small airfield used by a number of agencies, including the Coastguard. The Coastguard had contracted my Company to operate a S61 helicopter, similar to that at Sumburgh, for search and rescue duties. The machine had to be kept at constant readiness, day and night.

Sunday training flights were usually arranged to overfly Ullapool, on the edge of Loch Broom in Wester Ross. The purchase of Sunday newspapers by the helicopter crews enabled them to circumvent the constraints of Stornoway's religious inhibitions. These were probably the only Sunday newspapers to contaminate the whole of the Western Isles.

In June 1989, I was sent for a few days of duty as co-pilot with the Stornoway Coastguard unit. As at the Shetland base, the Stornoway unit was positioned close to the sea shore, and the opportunity of solitary strolls along deserted sands sometimes eased the long hours of waiting on 'standby'. The rescues at Stornoway were normally at sea, involving fishing and other vessels, but occasionally the unit covered mountain rescue incidents.

"What do you think of our wee town, then?" I was asked one day by Jenny, just newly employed as the unit secretary.

"Not bad. Not bad," I replied cagily.

"Oh come now," Jenny looked at me directly. "Everyone thinks it's a terrible place, but it's no' so bad really. Those dances in the Hotel are really great. You ought to come along tonight." For a moment, I wondered if this was an invitation.

"Yes, perhaps," I replied. "I'm sure it will be fun."

"You ask Geoff there. He's been to lots of the dances," said Jenny. Geoff's progress along the passageway was halted as he over-heard the remark.

"My name being mentioned?" he asked, poking his head around the door.

"We were just discussing the dances at the Hotel," said Jenny.

Geoff grimaced before replying: "The last *ceilidh* I went to there resulted in a punch-up. There were drunken bodies lying around all over the place."

"Come, come," said Jenny fingering her necklace. "I'm sure that's an exaggeration."

"The band were supplied with non-stop whisky," persisted Geoff. "Eventually, the trombone player got mixed up with his neighbour's bagpipes, and the drummer fell off his stool."

"Well I'm sure it added to the quality of the music," interjected the pretty Jenny.

"Not exactly," said Geoff. "The bagpipe player began to get upset, so he decided to play a different tune to the rest of the band."

"Ochhh," said Jenny as she glanced at me. "I'll bet that was ow'er Jimmy McLeod. He gets kind of excited from time to time, I must admit."

"You can say that again," replied Geoff, as he moved casually from the doorway into the room itself. "What upset him most was that no-one noticed when he played the wrong tune."

"Och," repeated Jenny, as she stood up. "It's easily done," she added benevolently.

"Mind you," said Geoff, as he wandered towards the window, "the Band leader didn't exactly help matters."

"Mmm," said the lovely Jenny. "Let me think now. That was probably wee Willy McLeod. He has this minor problem, I'm afraid." As Jenny gave us a knowing look, Geoff and I glanced at each other uneasily. Jenny reached into a filing cabinet, and took a file to her desk. "But I don't think we ought to go into that just now," added Jenny coyly. "By the way," she said, tactfully changing the subject. "I'm sure I read something about you two recently."

"Fame at last?" asked Geoff.

"Maybe... " said Jenny. "I can't quite remember... " She pulled a face, and looked out of the window for a moment. "Ach, yes. I know where it was. In one of those albums next door. I'll show you."

As the three of us walked into the crew room next door, Jenny led the way. The television had been left switched on, and the announcer was sombre as he described the dramatic events in China. The student-led pro-democracy movement had provoked mass demonstrations during the visit of the Soviet leader, Mikhail Gorbachev, last month. Soon after Gorbachev's departure, a brutal crack-down was ordered by the Chinese authorities. "It has been estimated," said the announcer gravely, "that more than two thousand unarmed protesters have been massacred by army troops in Beijing's Tiananmen Square."

We watched the announcement sadly.

"That's just awful," said Jenny.

At length, we moved across to one corner of the room, where some outsized albums lay on a table top. Jenny checked the dates written on the covers, then picked a particular album.

"This is the one, I'm fairly sure," Jenny said as she opened the pages. The album contained a miscellany of photographs, press cuttings, and letters, laid out in date order. Jenny paged back to the beginning of 1988, then stopped.

"Here you are," she said. "This is it."

In the middle of the page was a press cutting with the headline: 'French trawler sinks after crew rescued'. Just beside the cutting was a letter written from 'Edinbourg'. The letter said:

> Dear Sir,
>
> May I send you my sincere thanks, both in an official capacity and on a personal level, for the part you played in the rescue operation involving the sailors from the French trawler *St Patrick* on Sunday, 14 February 1988.
>
> In doing so, you and your team have demonstrated your selfless courage and devotion to duty.
>
> I stand in your debt.

The letter was signed by the French Consul-General.

"Yes, that was quite a day," I said. "The rescue happened just off Orkney."

Jenny moved across to the television set, and switched it off.

"I can't bear listening to any more of that," she said. "It's just too depressing." Jenny then walked back to the album, and again scrutinised the letter and the press cutting. After a while, she looked up and surveyed us both in turn. We felt modestly self-conscious under the gaze of this slip-of-a-lass. At length, she sighed slightly and just said quietly: "Tell me what happened."

CHAPTER 12

The Saint Patrick

Geoff and I glanced at Jenny as she continued to study the album page. We remained quiet, but our expressions asked: "Are you sure?"

"Yes," she went on gently, as if speaking to herself. "I'm going to be up-dating these albums routinely. It would be nice to hear a first-hand account."

Geoff looked at me as if to say: "Over to you, my lad." I shrugged briefly, then said in a reflective manner: "Okay. But I'll have to think about this for a while..." Jenny looked at me with her head on one side. Having looked in vain for some seconds as I did not go on, she returned her gaze to the album.

I studied the letter and press cuttings for a few more moments, then continued: "The story starts for me, I suppose, a couple of days before the flight itself, when I was sent here for a short spell of duty." After a pause, Geoff nodded when I said: "Geoff was based here full-time." We scrutinised the album again. "Yes... that's right," I said slowly, as we examined the Consul-General's letter. "St Valentine's Day in 1988 happened to fall on a Sunday."

When I reported for duty on that Sunday, I was greeted by John, the assigned Search and Rescue Captain.

"It's a good day for a training flight," grinned John. "Let's go over to the mountains around Wester Ross, and further north. We should get some useful practice in mountain flying techniques." After a moment he continued: "We might just have to arrange our flight to pass near Ullapool. And we might *just* need to check out the newspaper shop there," he added with a wink.

As was normal procedure, it was my job as co-pilot to walk ahead of the rest of the crew to start the S61 'turning and burning'. The helicopter was parked outside the ex-World War Two hangar, facing towards the seashore, when I went through the familiar pre-start drills. There was no Ruben-equivalent at Stornoway to observe my start procedures, just the duty engineer who stood near the ground power unit as he clutched a fire extinguisher. I was supervised as well by a conglomeration of gulls along the shoreline.

Soon John walked out to the aircraft, along with Geoff as the winch operator, and Mick as the winchman. Our Captain, John, was an outwardly placid and affable person, although in fact he was highly strung. The calm surface was a facade; underneath lay a nervous character. Some years in the future, John had to leave search and rescue duties promptly after a flying accident for which he was held to blame. Certain crew members found it hard to rub along with John, although Geoff and I agreed we had no difficulty that day. Indeed, it was a valuable education for me as a pilot, and I appreciated learning from his many years of experience as a search and rescue man.

"Run through the before take-off checks, please," John asked me.

I produced the check-list card, and read out the procedures. In particular, we ensured the machine had a full fuel load; we wanted good reserves to allow us to fly directly to any emergency situation if required. Having completed the checks, I made a 'blind call' on the aircraft radio; Air Traffic Control was not manned that Sunday. "Golf Bravo Delta India India, lifting Stornoway airfield in two minutes, departing low level to the south," I called.

John then glanced at me. "You can do the flying," he said. "It'll be good experience for you to get used to 'Beady Eyes'."

'Beady Eyes' was the nickname for this particular aircraft, with its hull letters of G-BDII. I took control of the aircraft, and Geoff stood by the front cargo door as he looked around for obstructions.

"It's all clear above and behind," announced Geoff eventually. "You're clear to lift." As I raised the collective lever, we slickly lifted into the hover, and turned away from the hangar. We then flew low over the airfield's grass expanse, gaining airspeed before taking up a southerly heading.

As we flew away from the airfield, we followed the craggy eastern shoreline of the Isle of Lewis. On our right side, the territory was mainly flat, and beyond Amish Moor we could make out the area of Callanish, with its famous standing stones. We passed the entrance to Loch Erisort, and soon the terrain on our right became hilly as we flew past the dividing boundary between the Isle of Lewis and the Isle of Harris.

"They're the Shiants coming up ahead," said John as we saw a cluster of small islands to the east of Tarbert. "Sometimes you come across impressive seal colonies there."

Beyond the Shiant Islands, we could see the spectacular outline of the Isle of Skye. We peered down, searching for the seal colonies as we over-flew the Shiants, then maintained a southerly direction as we crossed the Minch.

"Keep your eyes skinned as we fly over the Minch, guys," Geoff said. "There's an outside chance of spying a whale. It's a bit like the Falkland Sound here," he added.

However, we saw no whales that day, and as we approached Skye, John said to me: "Fly down the east side of Loch Snizort ahead, and then aim for the Cuillins." The scenery which favoured the Isle of Skye was easy to appreciate from the cockpit of a helicopter. The weather was generally fine, and splashes of sunlight accentuated the area's intrinsic beauty.

"Bonnie Prince Charlie took refuge here after the Battle of Culloden," Geoff reminded us of history as we flew down the length of the Island. On our left, we could see Portree, the chief port which was wrapped around the security of its inlet. Beyond Portree, as we approached the Cuillin Hills, John said: "From time to time we're called out to rescue climbers who get into difficulty on these hills." The steep contours of the hills, topped by distinctive ridge-lines, clearly held inherent dangers.

"Time to get the Sunday papers, I think, " John said, eventually. As I turned onto a northerly heading away from the Cuillins, the Captain said: "Let's go just to the left of the high ground as we fly up the western coastline of Scotland." We went past various lochs, including Kishorn and Torridon, and the land-locked Loch Maree.

Geoff called out conspicuous hilltops as he followed our route on his map. "That's Slioch over there, beyond Loch Maree," he said. "It's one of the two hundred and eighty-four impressive-looking Munros around here."

I glanced at Geoff. "What's the height of Slioch, Geoff?" I asked.

Geoff studied his chart again, then replied: "According to this map, Slioch is three thousand, two hundred and fifteen feet."

Eventually, we could see Loch Broom coming into view ahead, with Ullapool on the far shore. As we circled the town, John pointed out our landing site, and read out the pre-landing checks. We confirmed the wind direction by observing smoke from a local bonfire, and as we made an approach to the selected field, I ensured that we headed into the wind.

At length, we made contact with *terra firma*, then Mick left the aircraft to walk over to the paper shop.

"Look at this lot," said Geoff, as numerous people rapidly appeared, intrigued by the sudden arrival of a helicopter. "Shall we show those kids inside the helicopter?"

"It's a nice idea," said the Captain. "But it would take up too much time, I fear."

Mick soon emerged from the newspaper shop, laden with Sunday newspapers for the privileged few from Stornoway who were aware of this eccentric facility. He climbed the steps of the 'airstair' door, and placed the newspapers within the security of the aircraft's rear hold. Mick then slammed shut the 'airstair' door, and strapped himself into a seat. Geoff stood by the front cargo door, and waved back at the company of local spectators as he called: "It's all clear above and behind. You're okay to lift."

John waved as well to the fascinated crowd when I lifted the machine into a hover, and lowered the nose to gain airspeed. "It makes you feel like a film star," he said.

I took up a northerly heading as we flew away from Ullapool, and we soon saw the Coigach hills ahead. Keeping to the shoreline, we approached Achiltibue, separated from the famous Summer Isles by Badentarbat Bay. "My friends Trish and Peter are here on a fishing trip," I commented as we over-flew the area.

"Perhaps that's them down there," suggested Geoff as he returned the hand-waves of a family walking along the seashore. He naturally had no idea that it was probably at around this moment that calamity would strike the French trawler *Saint Patrick*. The vessel was about to run aground on the North Shoal, a notorious rock off Orkney, imperilling its fifteen crew members.

As we flew beyond Achiltibuie, we spotted the distinctive outline of Stac Pollaidh, a hill favoured by rock climbers seeking extra challenge. "We sometimes get involved with tricky rescues from there," John indicated. (His words would become a disastrous reality nine years in the future, when the Stornoway Coastguard helicopter was called out to rescue a seriously injured climber. The climber had fallen onto a ledge beneath the summit of Stac Pollaidh, which made rescue by helicopter extra challenging. The machine had to fly perilously close to the rock-face. As the S61 inched its way sideways, ever closer to the rock face, it was suddenly hit by a freak gust. The helicopter was blown so close to the rocks, that the main rotor tips struck the rock surface. The machine immediately started to vibrate fiercely, and simultaneously began a violent descent towards the peaty soil below. The pilot had just sufficient control left to allow him to cushion the landing, thus saving the crew. The injured climber was rescued later by other means).

"We'll fly a bit further north," said John as we flew away from Stac Pollaidh, "then we can delve into the hills for our training exercise."

At length, our route took us past Reay Forest, and in the distance we could make out the northern shoreline of Scotland, marked by Cape Wrath at the western point. As we approached Loch Inchard, with Kinlochbervie on the far side, John asked me to take up a south-easterly direction. "This'll do nicely," he said. "If we're recalled for an emergency, the heading back to Stornoway from here is pretty much due west."

Just north of our flight path was the dramatic outline of the Foinaven Hills. We passed a number of small lochs, and soon the ground ahead was rising. "You've got to watch out here," said John. "We're effectively being sucked into a dead-end. A mis-judgement of the winds could lead us into difficulty." As we climbed gradually to follow the contours, a small loch became visible at the end of the valley. "We'll have to turn around the loch, then make an escape from the dead-end," said John. "The important thing is to ensure we're in up-drafting air."

"One of the tricky jobs is to work out the wind direction, bearing in mind local influences from this hilly terrain," continued John. We tried to confirm the direction of the wind by looking at the effect of the breeze on nearby trees and shrubs, and even the grass. At length, we approached the small loch, and I reduced our speed slightly before starting a turn in the direction John and I had agreed. The helicopter was buffeted by turbulent air as we re-traced our flight path along the valley, away from the loch.

Eventually, as we approached the mouth of the valley, John said: "For our next exercise, let's go and have a look at that peak to the north. We can practice high level hovering techniques there."

"That peak is called Ganu Mòr, according to my map," said Geoff. "It's just below three thousand feet, so it doesn't qualify as a Munro."

I made a sweeping turn to the north, which gave us the opportunity to gain height before we approached the hill-top. "Just aim for that high point ahead," said John, "and come to a hover there." As I aimed for the spot, I gradually reduced our forward airspeed, intending to enter the hover just as we reached the hill-top. It was a useful exercise in co-ordination. While I concentrated on the flying, John turned round briefly and said to Geoff: "Time for an operations normal call, I believe?"

"Standby," said Geoff. "I'll just try to raise the Coastguard now." Every fifteen minutes or so, we used a special Coastguard frequency to inform them of our on-going safety. I continued to gradually reduce airspeed as Geoff made the radio call. The helicopter was affected by more turbulence from the hills, and I tried to prevent the airspeed from decreasing too rapidly.

As I persisted with my efforts to reach the Ganu Mòr peak, the local winds continued to give problems. We still had several hundred meters to run when there was a sudden murmur from Geoff. He had a concentrated look when I glanced at him: Geoff was listening to something intently. At length, he said in a slightly ruffled voice:

"Standby guys, there's an urgent message from the Coastguard coming through."

There was a short pause as we digested the implications of this, then John said to me decisively: "Overshoot, please. Maintain this heading for now." I lowered the nose of the helicopter, and simultaneously raised the collective lever to initiate our overshoot away from Ganu Mòr. The hill-top soon rushed beneath the helicopter during the overshoot procedure, and I flew at three thousand feet, a height which gave good radio reception.

While we awaited further details from Geoff, John and I quickly checked the fuel remaining, and calculated an on-task time. We reckoned to have over two and a half hours of available fuel.

"Okay, gents," Geoff said eventually. "There's a fishing vessel called *Saint Patrick* in trouble to the west of Orkney. The Coastguard want us to end our training exercise immediately, and proceed to a position nine miles west of Brough Head."

At this point, there was an interruption to the account. Jenny coughed dryly, and we looked out of the crew room window when an Islander aircraft passed overhead noisily. I gazed at the flat expanse of the airfield, and as the commotion from the Islander subsided, a moment of hush occurred in the crew-room. During the lull, we began to sense a mood of increasing expectation. The tenor of the story, like the atmosphere within the helicopter on the day itself, had started to reflect the curious mix of emotions when an emergency situation was suddenly confronted. The information passed to crews was often sketchy and inadequate; until arrival at the scene, a full assessment was unlikely.

Jenny said nothing, nevertheless she appeared eager for me to continue the account. Her expression, was one of impatience. *"Go on,"* insinuated Jenny's unspoken instructions, *"I'm dying to hear what happened next..."*

CHAPTER 13

Air/Sea Rescue

Immediately after the Coastguard message was relayed by Geoff, I noticed a sudden tension from our Captain.

"I'll take control now, thanks," he said edgily. After a pause, he continued: "I think our present fuel state should work out quite well for this task. But just double-check the figures, please." Geoff handed me a map at this point, and I calculated a flight time of just over thirty minutes to reach the required location.

Meanwhile, we saw the coastline ahead, and John began a slow descent as we left the area of high ground. We obtained clearance from the Air Traffic Control unit to fly directly to the scene, and I made efforts to adjust our radar picture. Soon, the radar showed a distinctive line which signified the northern coast of Scotland; beyond, the radar painted a picture which highlighted the idiosyncratic outline of the Orkney Islands. In between, we could make out a number of radar returns, but one in particular appeared close to our aiming point. "That could well be them there," I said, pointing at the small radar screen.

"Yeah, I agree," concurred John. He maintained a descent towards the sea, where we could spot shifting cloud shadows across the surface. Overall, though, the weather conditions remained generally good, and we had clear visibility. In the cabin, Mick was making ready various items of equipment. He tightened straps, and checked the seals on his suit as he anticipated being winched down to the surface of the sea.

As we crossed the coastline with Strathy Point on our right side, we continued to confer about the radar return. We were anxious, as far as possible, to ensure that we flew directly to the right spot. Soon, when we levelled just above the sea's surface, John said: "Read out the pre-winching checks now, please."

"Hoist Master to 'Crew' ... Ts and Ps... fuel contents... " I quickly read out the scheduled items. Then I returned my concentration to the radar picture. At the same time, I frequently glanced out of the cockpit, hoping for a visual sighting as early as possible. A collection of vessels in the distance appeared to coincide with the speculated radar return.

"Approaching ten miles from the scene," I called. "There appear to be a number of vessels clustered together." The aircrew focused their attention on looking in front at that stage. As I continued to count-down the radar ranges, a clearer visual picture gradually began to emerge. A fishing trawler seemed to be the centre of attraction. The vessel was a large one, with a white-painted bridge area; the box-like design stood out distinctly from the rest of the ship's structure. To the stern was a sturdy mast for hauling nets; close to the mast, a small crane jutted out. The whole vessel rested in the sea at an awkward, nose-down angle; plainly, the ship was sinking.

To one side of the sinking vessel, the bright colours of a life-raft stood out flamboyantly. In the vicinity, several other vessels moved about, including two other fishing trawlers, similar in size to the crippled one.

"Okay, gents," said our Captain as we drew close to the scene. "I'm going to slowly orbit the area while we make an assessment." John had reduced our airspeed to around fifty knots at this point, which felt comfortable as he entered a turn to the right. Geoff had opened the cargo door already; he was secured by the special winch-operator's harness. Geoff was able to lean out of the doorway precipitously in order to observe beneath.

While we made a sweeping orbit of the scene, the aircrew discussed their plan of action. "I can see a number of survivors in the dinghy," Geoff said. "But bearing in mind the size of ship, I can't believe that's the whole crew. I think as a first step we should check for any personnel still on board the sinking vessel."

The aircrew discussed this briefly, after which John rolled out of the turn when the helicopter faced into the wind. At that point, he reduced airspeed even further before saying: "Both speed selects fully forward now, please." John then started to bring the S61 to a hover just short of the *Saint Patrick.* As he was doing so, I called out the torque readings; they indicated that we had plenty of available power.

The Captain then flew the helicopter in a high hover-taxi method, while he crept towards the sinking vessel. I continued to call out the torque readings from time to time and all the aircrew searched intently for any signs of activity on the *Saint Patrick.* The nose of the doomed ship sank ever lower into the sea; water was evidently flooding into the bow of the vessel. Beneath the water-line, invisible to the eye, we could imagine the incision caused by the ship's collision with the North Shoal rock.

"I can't see anything moving on board at all," said Geoff at length.

"Nor can I," agreed the Captain. We made a final search, but after some moments he continued: "Okay, I don't think this inspection should become too prolonged. So what we'll do now is move across to the dinghy, and winch-up all the survivors there."

John then began to fly the S61 towards the life-raft. As he manoeuvred across, he said: "We can ask the survivors in the dinghy if they're aware of anybody left on the sinking vessel." After a moment, he added: "How's your French, Geoff?"

"*Magnifique,*" replied Geoff. There was a pause, then he reverted to a form of *Franglais* for his winch-operator's patter: "*Forward ten as you approach the survivors. Down* quatre *as you close... right* deux, *our rate of closure is good... down* deux, *and right a further one.*" I glanced across at the sinking vessel; fortunately it remained well clear of the dinghy. *"You have a further* cinque *to run,"* continued Geoff, *"the target is on the nose... safe height no lower... your rate of closure is good... range* quatre... trois... deux... un... *steady, steady, steady...* "

Mick was already in position by the door, and soon Geoff winched him up from his sitting position. Geoff then helped the winchman to turn around, facing towards the side of the helicopter. As soon as Mick was ready, he gave a thumbs-up sign. Geoff operated his switch at that point to lower the winchman towards the dinghy. At the same time, Geoff resumed his commentary to the pilots: *"The dinghy canopy has been removed... the winchman is being lowered towards the dinghy... forward one... the winchman is approaching the dinghy. Your position is now good... steady... steady."* I quickly looked at the S61s temperatures and pressures at that moment; I confirmed that all systems were functioning correctly before we started to winch-in survivors.

"The winchman is now placing the double strop over the first survivor," continued Geoff. *"Steady... steady... the winchman has given me a thumbs-up... standby for winch-in."* I glanced across at John as he concentrated on the winch operator's patter. We felt the familiar lurch of the helicopter as the winch took the combined weight of the two men. *"Winching in...now. The winchman has the first survivor in the double strop... right one... steady... steady. The winchman is approaching the door... he's turning the survivor. The survivor now has his back to the door... we're placing him in the cabin... winchman is now removing the double strop from the survivor. Standby a minute. I'm just going to have a word with Mick."*

As I looked back, the survivor was being directed to the rear of the cabin area. He was an older man with a rough beard, and his harassed appearance made him seem uneasy, and shifty. He glanced around nervously; his eyes were sunken and his complexion was pallid. The survivor apprehensively scratched his head as he examined the inside of the helicopter.

Meanwhile, Geoff and Mick were holding a conference by the cargo door. Mick indicated that there were six more survivors in the dinghy. He had talked briefly with the men, one of whom spoke reasonable English. Mick had been told by the survivors in the dinghy that, as far as they were aware, no personnel remained on board the *Saint Patrick,* however eight men had been picked up by the *Saint Patrick's* sister ship *Otterbank.*

"Roger," said the Captain when he heard this news. "We'll pick up the rest of the survivors from this dinghy. When we've completed that, we'll move across to the *Otterbank* to uplift the eight men there."

"Copied," replied Geoff. *"Now commencing winch-out... the winchman is descending again to the dinghy... steady... steady... "* I continued to call out the torque readings during the winching

operations. However, with the relatively few numbers to be rescued, the readings remained well within safe limits. *"The winchman is placing the next survivor in the double strop... he's securing the strap... standby for winch-in... "*

While the winch operations proceeded, I regularly checked our remaining fuel. I maintained on-going calculations to ensure sufficient reserves to allow us to remain on task, followed by a flight to a diversion airfield. "The nearest diversion from here is Kirkwall, although we could still reach Sumburgh or Wick if necessary," I told the Captain.

"Understood," replied John. "When you get a chance, have a word with the Coastguard, please. Ask if they have any preference for where we should take the survivors."

While Geoff proceeded with his commentary, I re-checked the switch selections on the aircraft radio box before speaking to the Coastguard. I wanted to ensure no interruption to the Captain's concentration during the winch-operator's patter.

Eventually, at a suitable moment, I said to the Captain: "I've spoken to the Coastguard. They'd like us to take the survivors to Kirkwall, if possible. The survivors will be checked over in the Balfour Hospital there, and then looked after by the Missions to Seamen. Furthermore, the local Missions rep is fixing up lunch in a Kirkwall hotel for the aircrew." John maintained his concentration on the flying when I said this, although I noticed him raise one eyebrow in a gesture of surprise at the latter part of the message.

At length, we heard: *"The winchman has the last survivor in the double strop... shortly winching-in."* Geoff sounded relaxed as his professional patter ensued. The first phase of our rescue operation would be concluded shortly. *"Winchman and last survivor are approaching the door... turning them... helping them into the cabin... "*

"Well done Geoff," said the Captain at that point. "You can keep the cargo door open. When the survivors in the back are secure, I'll move the short distance across to the *Otterbank*. Hopefully, it won't take long to pick up the eight survivors there."

"Copied, Captain," said Geoff. "Some of *notre amis* in the cabin look a bit rumbled. I'll just unplug my headset for a mo while I help Mick to sort it out. We should be ready shortly."

I glanced back, and noticed that Mick and Geoff were struggling to make themselves understood. They attempted to persuade our recalcitrant passengers to strap into the available seats. The Frenchmen appeared more interested in wandering about the cabin restlessly as they made vigorous hand gesticulations.

"Mais non... merde... nous sommes pee'ssed off... merde... " even above the noise of the helicopter, we picked up the drift of strident Gallic opinions.

Eventually, however, Geoff moved forward, and plugged in his headset again. "Okay guys," he spoke rather breathlessly. *"Entente cordiale* has taken a mild battering, but you're clear to move now." John grinned as he nodded in response. He then began to fly slowly towards the *Otterbank,* at which point I used one of the marine FM frequencies on our radio to attempt to speak to the crew of the *Otterbank.*

After a while, a strongly accented voice said on the radio: *"'Elicopteur... 'zis is 'ze Otterbank... you come 'ere, huh?"*

"Affirmative, *Otterbank,*" I replied. "We'll be with you in two minutes to uplift eight survivors."

"Okay, 'elicopteur... we get 'zem ready."

Geoff leant out of the cargo door as we approached the *Otterbank.* He gave an assessment of the vessel as we approached, including comment on aerials and other hazards. Then he said: "The deck area on the prow appears to be the clearest place for winching. I'll give you directions to there."

"Okay," replied the Captain. "Ready for your directions."

"Forward ten, and down two as we approach the vessel," said Geoff. *"Safe height, no lower... the vessel is steaming slightly out of wind ... turn right... forward eight... your height is still good... forward five, four, three, two, one... steady, steady."*

As we came to a hover above the prow of the *Otterbank*, we maintained a safe height from the aerials surrounding the bridge area. From the bridge itself, we were observed by a number of enthralled crew members. Reflections from some of the glass windows on the bridge gave the pilots an unusual, if distorted, impression of events beneath the helicopter.

"Survivors are appearing on deck in dribs and drabs," Geoff's commentary continued. *"I'm going to winch down Mick shortly... steady... steady. Back one. Mick is now ready... back a further one... winching Mick down to the deck... he's about to touch the deck... your position is good again... steady... steady."*

I continued to call out the torque readings. The figures stayed within safe limits, helped by a good breeze which was supplemented by the vessel's forward progress.

"I think we should be okay for power today," commented the Captain.

"The winchman is putting the double strop around the first survivor... left one... I have a thumbs-up from the winchman... starting to winch in... steady... steady... "

Before long, Mick appeared by the cargo door with the survivor. As he did so, I looked back into the cabin and gestured to the passengers already on board to remain seated. Fortunately, they appeared to realise that co-operation with the aircrew would be their best policy; the passengers sat down. Soon they were joined by the new arrival, who moved towards the rear of the cabin. En-route, the new man shook hands with all the other passengers, which delayed his progress, but eventually he found a place in the back of the cabin.

As the rescue of the remaining survivors proceeded, we began to sense a gradual change of atmosphere within the cabin. With the arrival of each newcomer, his fellow survivors began to smile and clap. This was soon followed by a ritual of vigorous hand-shaking. "They'll burst into song at any moment," commented Geoff as we discussed the almost carnival-like spirit which was developing.

"Two survivors remain to be winched in," Geoff said at length. As he conducted the last winch-ins, marking the final phase of the rescue operation, we made further hand signals to the latest arrivals in the cabin. By that stage, there were no more seats available and each new arrival therefore had to be encouraged to find a secure part of the aircraft structure to hold.

At length, the last survivor was attached to the winch. By the time he was assisted through the helicopter's door, the cabin had become quite cramped. The passengers, though, appeared to take it in good heart; the crowded scene somehow added to the festive atmosphere. The men conversed and joked with each other, excited by the unscheduled nature of their surroundings. The noise of the helicopter failed to act as a deterrent to their animated conversations, still embellished by graphic hand gestures.

Eventually, when the aircrew were satisfied that the passenger arrangements were safe, Geoff concluded his commentary:

"Stowing the winch... closing the door... you're clear above and behind... you're clear up and away."

These words were quickly followed by the S61 gaining speed as the Captain lowered the nose of the machine. As the helicopter picked up speed, John turned onto a heading just south of east, and began to gain altitude. Before long, he was levelling the S61 at one thousand feet.

"Thank you, gentlemen," the Captain said at length. "That operation seemed to go quite well." John appeared to give a quiet sigh of relief.

The coastline of Orkney was visible already, and soon Geoff was pointing out an eccentric-looking rock at the base of Rora Head. "There's the Old Man of Hoy," said Geoff, as he peered below. Beyond the Isle of Hoy, we saw the sheltered expanse of Scapa Flow.

"Over seventy German warships were scuttled there just after the end of World War One," John reminded us, as he signalled towards the stretch of water.

Shortly, I put out a radio message: "Kirkwall this is the Coastguard helicopter, requesting landing clearance," I called as we made out the small airfield to the south-east of Kirkwall Town.

"Roger, Coastguard helicopter," came a lilting accent in reply. "You're clear to land."

Our Captain turned towards the airfield, and soon he reduced forward airspeed before making a smooth touchdown. After landing, he promptly appeared to become more relaxed. He kept the helicopter rolling forward after the touchdown, as he began to taxi the machine towards the Airport Terminal.

"We'll close down 'Beady Eyes' before letting the passengers off," said John, as he manoeuvred the helicopter.

He was perhaps unprepared for the outbreak of Gallic enthusiasm about to hit us. As soon as the S61 reached its parking spot, the exuberant survivors stood up and cheered. Our two crewmen became swamped by the spontaneous agitation of passengers as the survivors tried to move about in the confined space. The two pilots attempted to complete the shut-down procedures hurriedly, but the passionate Frenchmen seemed unabashed. Each survivor insisted on moving forward in turn to vigorously shake our hands. In spite of the atmosphere of euphoria, we sensed that in reality many of them were nervous and uneasy.

Finally, when the engines had been closed down, and the rotor brake applied, Geoff managed to reach the airstair door to open it. Slowly, and with their elation apparently becoming more subdued, the survivors left the helicopter one by one to be met by representatives from the Missions to Seamen (later re-named The Mission to Seafarers) and other officials. As they were led into the Terminal Building, the survivors looked back and waved.

Meanwhile, the aircrew concluded their after-flight activities. They secured the S61, and supervised refuelling operations. The engineering turn-round procedures were performed by the pilots: we opened hatches to inspect the engines, and to check oil and hydraulic levels. In addition, we examined the rotor blades for signs of damage, and the crewmen carefully scrutinised the winch.

While managing these tasks, we became aware that the Missions to Seamen's representative had left the survivors, and had moved away from the Terminal Building to see us. A tall man, with a distinctive beard, he looked on with interest. At first, he stood to one side, some distance from the helicopter, anxious not to interfere with the aircrew activities.

Eventually, however, when we had nearly completed the turn-round procedures, the Missions to Seamen's representative cleared his throat. John and I looked up, and walked over to where he stood.

Geoff and Mick left their chores to join us. The representative glanced at us hesitantly, and briefly smiled.

"Gentlemen, I would like to thank you most earnestly," he said.

The aircrew looked pleased, and nodded an acknowledgement. After some rescues they received no thanks at all; indeed, on some occasions, they even received abuse. That day, however, was different. We sensed a genuine, and warm attitude from the Missions man. Nevertheless, he seemed a little tense as he coughed slightly, and glanced at us again. Then he said with sincerity: "I'm sure that seafarers the world over would like to express how much they appreciate and admire the service you provide in emergency situations like today's. You've done a fantastic job. We salute the skill and bravery of you and your colleagues."

When I reached this stage in my account, I looked once more at the album and charts laid out on the crew room table. I glanced at Jenny, and noticed that she was nodding with a serious air. I felt that she was about to say something.

However, at that moment we heard the ring of the telephone in her office. Jenny looked at Geoff, and at me, briefly. She raised her eyebrows slightly, but in the end she said nothing. Jenny just stood up, and hurried to answer the telephone.

CHAPTER 14

Some Light Relief

Geoff and I moved away from the album when Jenny went to her office.

"Hello," we overheard Jenny as she spoke on the telephone. "Hi Frank. Yes… Okay… I'll believe that when it happens… "

While Jenny took the telephone message, Geoff offered to make some coffee. "I felt quite nostalgic being reminded about that episode last year," said Geoff as we walked towards the coffee bar. "Thinking back, it makes you feel kind of strange though, doesn't it?" He shook his head in amusement. "I thought we were going to have a party on board the helicopter at one point... those Frenchmen were something else..." He reached for the coffee mugs.

"It was an odd atmosphere really," I added. "Despite the outward shows of joy, I think they were actually quite disturbed."

"Yeah, I'm sure that's right," said Geoff. "I guess they realised how lucky they were no-one was injured. They were also lucky with the weather. Admittedly, that begs the question as to why they hit the rock in the first place, but that's another matter."

After a pause, Geoff's tone altered when he said: "You've got to laugh, though, when the stereotypical images come true." Geoff spooned coffee into the mugs. "Which reminds me," he added at length. "Have you heard the one about the three slaters?"

"Go on."

"This," said Geoff with a mock air, "is a sad tale of culinary *ennui*."

"Fine," I said.

"Well, when it came to his lunch-time," continued Geoff, "the first slater, an Englishman, looked at his sandwiches with disgust and said, 'Oh no, not cheese again. If I have cheese once more, I think I'll jump off this roof'."

Jenny was still on the telephone. Geoff glanced towards her office when we heard her voice become animated.

"When the second slater, a Scotsman, opened his pack of sandwiches, he saw with anguish that they were filled with ham. 'Oh no,' said the Scotsman. 'If my wife gives me ham one more time, I think I'll jump off the roof too.' Then it was the turn of the third slater, an Irishman. 'Begorra,' said the Irishman, scratching his head during the sandwich inspection process. 'Would you look at that now? Bloody jam again!'"

Once more, we noticed the raised tone of Jenny's voice. Geoff looked towards her office briefly, and then proceeded.

"The following day," continued Geoff, "when it came to lunch-time, the three slaters were appalled to discover that their sandwich contents were the same as usual. 'That's it,' said the Englishman, 'I'm jumping off this roof right now'." Geoff feigned a grimace. "He was closely, and tragically followed by his companions.".

Geoff paused for a few seconds while he stirred the coffee.

"At the men's combined funeral service, their three wives tried to console each other.

'I can't understand it,' said the Englishman's wife. 'If I had only known, I would have given him something else.'

'Same here,' agreed the Scotsman's wife."

Geoff looked at me briefly, as if to say, 'are you ready for this? Here comes the punch-line.'

"The Irishman's wife felt distraught when her companions spoke. At length she looked in dismay at the others and said: 'It's a complete mystery to me too... Paddy always made his own sandwiches!'"

"I've got a racist joke as well," Jenny had just joined us after her telephone call. Geoff and I looked at her, but Jenny evidently had no desire to tell us about her conversation. "Only I'm not convinced that I can remember it properly."

There was a noise outside at that moment, and as we gazed through the crew-room windows, we noticed that the engineers had started to tow the Coastguard S61 out of the hangar.

"Do they know something we don't?" asked Geoff. The helicopter rotor blades had tip-socks fitted to limit 'sailing', but the blades nevertheless moved up and down quite vigorously in the breezy conditions.

"I've got a mildly religious joke, though," said Jenny after a while.

"That's dangerous for this part of the world," quipped Geoff.

"Ah, but this one features Loch Ness," replied Jenny.

After a minute, she continued: "There was this atheist rowing across the Loch..."

Geoff and I glanced at her vaguely but she persisted.

"... when he suddenly found himself thrust twenty feet into the air, staring into the ugly chasm of a vast mouth."

Geoff raised a sceptical eyebrow. Jenny was undeterred.

"'Lord, save me!' screamed the terrified rower. Quite rapidly, the clouds parted, the heavens appeared, and a booming voice called out: 'But you don't believe in me.'"

Jenny paused for a second, took a sip from her mug of coffee, then continued: "The rower looked around him in amazement. His situation was hard to believe."

Geoff shook his head slightly.

"Then the rower gazed up to heaven as he cried: 'Give me a break! I didn't believe in the Loch Ness monster until two minutes ago'."

The engineers by the Coastguard S61 were starting a ground power unit. Soon, the monotonous tone from the machine wailed through the air, and when we looked out of the window we noticed a plume of black smoke rise from the yellow-painted generator as it fired up.

"Well that's dealt with racism and religion," said Geoff eventually. "Are there any other taboos while we're at it?"

"There's always *l'amour*," offered Jenny. Following a short pause, she frowned slightly as she added : "Which gives me an idea." Jenny frowned again as Geoff and I glanced at her. She then moved back to the table with the albums. "Yes, I thought so," said Jenny after a few moments. "Come and look at this."

Geoff and I left the coffee bar area, and felt intrigued as we walked across to inspect the albums again. "It's here, just below the items about the *Saint Patrick* rescue," said Jenny, as Geoff and I joined her. A small press cutting from the local newspaper, dated February 1988, had been placed in one corner of the album. The heading said: 'Pregnant woman saved by Coastguard helicopter.'

Geoff and I looked at each other. "That was us again," we said. Jenny stared at us for a second. "The rescue bit, I mean," confirmed Geoff.

Jenny examined the press cutting once more.

"It seems that was a good couple of days you had."

"It was most peculiar actually," said Geoff. He moved closer to the album, and we continued to scrutinise the press cutting for a few moments, then Geoff went on: "Having been stood down after the *Saint Patrick* rescue, the same crew held duty again the following afternoon. We were scrambled shortly after starting the duty period."

"What was even more peculiar," I added, "was the sequence of events during the rescue itself."

"In fact," said Geoff decisively, "the whole episode was a minor miracle really."

CHAPTER 15

Called Out Again

FEBRUARY 1988

When I drove to Stornoway Airfield at lunch-time on that Monday in February 1988, the weather was more akin to a normal Scottish winter's day; the conditions had been unseasonably kind to us during the *Saint Patrick* rescue the day before. The bleak Monday landscape, however, held the whole region in a damp, gloomy mood. During the drive, a few other cars crept around, but generally the roads seemed deserted as many folk just stayed indoors, hibernating from the February glum. Even at the day's zenith, the atmosphere was melancholy, the surroundings felt dark. Already, haphazard splashes of light could be seen from scattered homes. The occasional brightened window clashed with ambient dreich, struggling to dispel the drab environment.

After parking by the Company hangar, I walked upstairs to the operations set-up, and I was soon joined by the other crew members. "Thanks once more for yesterday's effort, guys," said John, our Captain again. We studied the weather forecasts, air traffic notices, and other aviation relevance before starting individual checks and assignments, and formally relieving the current duty crew. "A general cloudbase of 500 to 1000 feet, with local visibilities of 4 to 6 kilometres, reducing to 2 kilometres or less in some areas, is the Met man's prediction for the Western Isles today," said John with a grimace.

While the Captain checked documents, and signed the technical log, I entered the aircraft cockpit. As part of the co-pilot's tasks, I had to test certain equipment, and I had to pre-set various switches, ready for a quick start in the event of a call-out. Meanwhile, the crewmen examined the winch, performed functional tests, and checked medical and other equipment.

While I went through my duties, from time to time I glanced at the other crew members. As we followed the necessary routines, it struck me what a high standard was expected of each individual. All members of the crew displayed a thorough discipline; every person by nature and training was methodical, professional, and reliable.

After some time, having completed their numerous checks, the crew made sure that paper-work was up-to-date, and signed logs when required. The aircrew then went upstairs again, and eventually they congregated in the coffee bar. The crew chatted informally about aspects of yesterday's *Saint Patrick* rescue. "It was quite fortunate that one of the survivors spoke reasonable English," commented Mick.

At length, during a lull in the conversation, I reminded my colleagues that it was lunch-time. "Anyone for a sandwich?" I asked.

"Not for me, thanks," said John. "I'm on a diet," he added ominously as he sat down in an armchair.

"I'll make a pot of tea, then," I suggested.

"Good plan," said Geoff and Mick, as they moved towards the frayed armchairs, which had been placed handily in front of the television.

"Shall we watch a bit of telly?" asked John. The others frowned in a discouraging manner, and sat down resignedly.

"It's such rubbish on the box nowadays," growled Mick, as he leant across to pick up a magazine. Geoff sat quietly, looking slightly bored. However, his expression suddenly changed. Geoff immediately volunteered to answer the telephone when we heard it ring.

"I'll get it," announced Geoff. He quickly rose from his chair, and dashed through to the operations room. His speedy reaction had been prompted by the special ring of the Coastguard telephone.

"Hello... yes... " Geoff sounded quite terse. While he spoke, the other members of the crew were alert as they listened-in to his conversation. After a moment he called: "John!" and I noticed our Captain's slightly worried expression as he stood up and moved hastily through to the operations room. We heard him grunt a few brusque responses as he took the call: "Yeah… no problem… we can do that –" then, shortly afterwards, with raised voice: "Get moving guys, we've got a job already. I'll brief you when we're in the aircraft." Simultaneously, we heard the screech of the alarm as John operated the scramble switch.

At that moment, the whole atmosphere took on a drastic change. The dreary feelings induced by the prospect of hours of inactivity were promptly swept aside, and our mood of listless apathy was suddenly replaced by an electric excitement. Despite over-hearing some of John's telephone conversation, we had gleaned little background information. This added to our sense of curiosity and apprehension.

As the aircrew and their support team were galvanised into action, I quickly abandoned my tea-making activity. Firstly, I rushed to collect my flying suit and struggled as I tried to don it in an instant: *"… don't mess me about… stupid suit –"* Then I moved rapidly towards the stairs. I hurried down the steps, and ran along a corridor which led into the hangar area. When I entered the hangar itself, I noticed that the engineers had already opened the large doors which stretched across the side of the old hangar. The Coastguard S61 was being towed to a specific spot outside. As the machine reached the spot, I sprinted towards the helicopter's airstair door.

The external checks around the S61 had been done earlier as part of my signing-on responsibilities. However, the duty engineer was double-checking various items on the outside of the machine. While he did that, I paced up the steps of the airstair door, and dashed forward to the cockpit. My lifejacket had been placed in a convenient manner over the seat. It was a slick manoeuvre to button up the lifejacket as I settled into the seat. My headset had been carefully placed on the cockpit coaming. Quickly, I put the headset over my ears. Then I nimbly went through the pre-start checks: *… batteries on… start master on… fuel valves on…* The routine was extra-rapid by having set-up the machine earlier.

Soon, I was ready to start the first engine. As I went through the start drill, the engine swiftly wound up, and when it had stabilised, I gave another signal to the duty engineer. My signal was promptly returned, and I was then enabled to release the rotor brake. *"Easy does it... easy does it... "* It was so tempting to be over-hasty.

When the rotors were turning, I gave a further sign to the engineer, who then cleared me to start the second engine. Just as I initiated the start cycle for the second engine, John came forward to the cockpit, and sat down in the right-hand seat. He glanced at me, and monitored the start-up procedure while he strapped in. When he was ready, he simply said: "I have control, thank you. I'll have the before take-off checks now." Having extracted the check-list card from its special stowage, I started to read through the obligatory items. While I was doing this, the two winchmen climbed aboard. Geoff briskly moved through the cabin towards the cockpit, and plugged in his head-set to speak to the pilots. Mick slammed shut the airstair door, before strapping himself into a seat in the cabin.

As I reached the last item on the check list, Geoff said breathlessly: "Just confirm we're going to Benbecula, Captain."

"We're going to South Uist, beyond Benbecula," replied the Captain. "Once we're airborne, Geoff, I'd like you to get more details from the Coastguard. All I really know so far is that there's an urgent medical case down there, and the local doctor has requested our assistance."

After the Captain had said this, Geoff began to search for the required maps. Meanwhile, I called on the radio: "Stornoway Tower, Coastguard helicopter request clearance for immediate departure to the south at low level."

"Roger, Coastguard helicopter, you are clear to lift from your present position. There's no conflicting traffic."

John then said, "Give me full power please." I eased forward both speed select levers, and John progressively raised the collective lever. Rapidly, but smoothly, he lifted the machine into a hover, briefly checked that all systems functioned correctly, then further raised the collective lever to gain height and airspeed.

"Coastguard helicopter, maintaining five hundred feet and below, following the coastline on a southerly heading," I called Air Traffic Control as we flew away from the airfield. By tracking the coastline, our navigation was simplified, and we ensured clearance from high ground. As we hugged the coastal territory, I followed our route on the local area map which Geoff had handed me. When we spotted various features, I called out the names. Soon, we approached the Sound of Shiant, but we could hardly make out the Shiant Islands in the poor visibility.

"This weather's really terrible compared to yesterday," said our Captain at that point. As we strained to see ahead in the misty conditions, he added: "We'll just stick to the general line of the coast, though. It'll be our best policy." Shortly after he had said this, we lost visual contact with the shoreline at the spot where a large bay marked the entrance to Loch Seaforth. The aircraft radar, however, was invaluable as it continued to paint the further coastal outline towards North Uist.

"Visual with that lighthouse ahead," called the Captain after some moments. We approached the small island of Scalpay, with its lighthouse at Eilean Glas. For the time being, John managed to maintain our airspeed at one hundred and ten knots; we were eager to reach the casualty as quickly as possible. Nevertheless, if the visibility reduced drastically, he would fly at a lower airspeed for safety, even though our anticipated flight time of thirty minutes or so would be extended as a consequence.

"Okay, guys," Geoff was speaking. "I've got a message from the Coastguard when you're ready." While the pilots monitored the main radio, Geoff had been using a separate radio box to speak to the Coastguard. He was anxious not to disturb the pilots' concentration while they navigated in the difficult conditions.

"Yes, go ahead with the message, Geoff," said John.

"The Coastguard are still talking with the authorities at South Uist," said Geoff. "However, I can confirm that we've been called out to help a woman with medical complications. The Coastguard understand the woman is pregnant and they're checking on the anticipated imminence of the birth, and assessing the chances of a delivery on board the helicopter."

As Geoff was giving this message, the forward visibility had begun to reduce even further. Apart from occasional glimpses, we could no longer see the coastline. We relied implicitly on the aircraft radar.

"Thanks, Geoff," said our Captain tersely. "I'm going to have to reduce forward airspeed," he added. At the same time, he descended the helicopter below two hundred feet, which allowed us to maintain visual contact with the sea.

"We'll be approaching Renish Point shortly," I said. The southern tip of the Isle of Harris was confirmed by the radar picture. Beyond Renish Point, the Sound of Harris provided an expanse of water before the land-mass of North Uist.

"If things carry on like this, I think we'll be forced to make a radar approach to Benbecula airfield," eventually John said with a gloomy expression. "Then we'll have to wait there while they drive the patient to the airfield by ambulance." The Captain's first responsibility was to ensure a safe flight. Nevertheless, we were acutely aware of the need to reach the patient as swiftly as possible. These conflicting aims would test the aircrew to the limit this day.

"Have a word with Benbecula, please," John said to me as we crossed the Sound of Harris. "See what their current weather's like, and tell them about our intentions." While I spoke to Benbecula Air Traffic Control, I noticed that John was struggling to maintain visual contact with the sea. He re-set the bug on his radio altimeter to below one hundred feet; this prevented distraction from the audio warning which was triggered when our height reached the bug's pre-set level. John then descended further to keep the sea in sight.

At length, the outer territories of North Uist loomed closer on the radar picture. As we continued to follow the line of the coast, we caught fleeting glimpses of land. In general, however, we relied on the aircraft radar and our ability to see the surface of the sea. These were our only tenuous links with *terra firma;* if they became even more tenuous, our next step would be to obtain clearance from Air Traffic Control to climb immediately to the published safety altitude. We would then continue to fly under 'Instrument Flight Rules' to a suitable diversion airfield.

To avoid distracting the Captain, I arranged the radio switches to allow me to speak discreetly to Benbecula airfield. After some while, I said: "I've spoken to Benbecula Air Traffic Control. Their weather is pretty poor, I'm afraid, with patchy mist and low cloud."

"Roger," replied the Captain. "I can still just about maintain visual contact with the sea. However, if the visibility gets any worse, and we're forced to climb, we've plenty of fuel for a couple of radar approaches to Benbecula. If we don't get in there, we'll have to return to Stornoway."

While the Captain persisted with his efforts to keep the sea in sight, Geoff said after a minute or two: "I've just had another word with the Coastguard, guys. The medics are taking the patient to a school playing field slightly north of the village where the lady lives. I've got the grid reference for the pick-up point when you're ready." Quickly, Geoff read out the details of the grid reference, and I marked the spot on my map. Then Geoff continued: "The police will have a van at the pick-up point. The vehicle will have a flashing blue light and headlights on to help us locate them. There'll also be an ambulance at the site."

We followed a straight stretch of coast at that stage, but it was still difficult to see the shoreline. "Don't be tempted to turn right here," I warned the Captain. "The ground rises quite rapidly. This mist is hiding the hills of North Lee and South Lee."

"That's understood," said John. "I'll remain on this southerly heading." He flew at an airspeed of ninety knots by then, occasionally even less when it proved necessary in the marginal conditions. The Captain continued to fly low, adjusting his height in order to maintain contact with the sea.

"We'll shortly be flying due east of Benbecula," I said after a while.

"Roger," replied the Captain. Then he spoken in a measured way as he added: "If we lose visual contact with the sea, our escape route will be to turn hard left away from the coast. When cleared by Benbecula, we'll then start a climb to safety altitude." After a pause, he continued: "However, once we've turned inland towards the pick-up point, we'll have to adopt different tactics. Once inland, our escape route will involve climbing in whichever direction is the most suitable to take us away from high ground. Can you ask Benbecula if they're currently aware of any other air traffic in the vicinity, please?"

While I spoke to Benbecula, I noticed the worried frown on the Captain's brow. He concentrated intensely as he followed the coastline, still only erratically visible in the patchy mists. He persevered with flying at extra low level, and at reduced airspeed, as he fought to maintain sight of the sea. Again, I arranged the radio switches to allow discreet speech with Benbecula airfield.

"I've spoken to Benbecula," I said at length. "They're not aware of any other air traffic in the area at this time."

"Good," replied the Captain, briefly, as he remained absorbed with his task.

By that stage, we approached the end territories of South Uist. "That's Loch Eynort on the right," I said. "There's a stretch of coast for eight kilometres or so coming up, then there's the entrance to Loch Boisdale. We need to turn right at that entrance, to follow the Loch inland." As we flew towards Loch Boisdale, I warned John of rising ground ahead as we approached the small Island of Stuley.

"Thanks," said the Captain. As the Island of Stuley loomed out of the mist, he climbed slightly to fly over the obstruction. When clear, he said: "Give me the pre-landing checks now, please."

"Undercarriage down... altimeters set... parking brake off... " I hastily read out the items on the check-list card, as far as possible trying not to interfere with the Captain's acute concentration.

Having completed the pre-landing checks, I said: "About two kilometres ahead, there's another small island, then we should be clear of obstructions until the entrance to Loch Boisdale."

At length, having passed the small island, we became aware that the coast was curving to the right. "This is the point which marks the entrance to Loch Boisdale," I said at that stage. "If you now follow the coastline inland, we should end up on a westerly heading." The Captain grunted slightly as he complied with my directions.

"There's high ground on the right," I warned the Captain. Then I soon continued: "Shortly we'll spot two small islands. Just north of the second island is the start of a road. I want you to follow that road." While I was giving the detailed instructions to the Captain, I held the map in quite a high position against the cockpit coaming in front of me. This allowed me to move my eyes rapidly from the map inside the cockpit, to the visual picture outside.

We had planned our route over low-lying territory; the high ground remained north and south of our track. As he followed my instructions, the Captain suddenly called: "Visual with the road." By this stage he had reduced our airspeed and height even further; he now flew the helicopter virtually in a high hover.

"Well done John," I said. "This road should take us on a heading slightly north of west towards a T-junction about five or six kilometres ahead. I estimate that the pick-up point is just north of that T-junction."

As the Captain followed the line of the road, we saw some headlights emerging out of the mist.

"That's just a delivery van," I said after a moment, as we watched the vehicle slow down, the driver alarmed no doubt by the unexpected proximity of the helicopter. "We've still got over four kilometres to run to the pick up point,"

The Captain persisted with flying in a high hover technique and the bleak territory passed by slowly. Nevertheless, it seemed quite soon when he suddenly called out: "I think I can see the pick-up area ahead now." As I peered in front, the faint flash of a blue light could be seen intermittently. In addition, there appeared to be a number of vehicle headlights marking the spot.

"That looks like it," I said. "That area seems to coincide pretty well with the grid reference." Quickly, I ran through the finals checks: *"Undercarriage confirmed down… radar to standby…"*

As we drew closer to the scene, the Captain said, "Okay, I'm going to land just north of the vehicles, in that far corner of the field. The ground looks quite flat, and the area appears to be clear of obstructions."

The Captain's words caused an unspoken sense of relief. The difficult conditions had caused our flight to take some fifteen minutes longer than expected. In spite of that, however, the achievement of our immediate objective had been confirmed: the pick-up point had been identified. Rescue was now a reality.

CHAPTER 16

A Life & Death Struggle

The Captain sounded more relaxed as he continued to make his assessment of the landing area. "There's a low hedge I can see, but no trees in the close proximity." As he persevered with the high hover technique towards the selected spot, we had an opportunity to evaluate the scene below.

An ambulance was parked near the entrance to the school playing field. One door at the rear of the ambulance was open, and a few figures appeared to be moving about in the vicinity. Near the ambulance was a private car, and a short distance from these vehicles, a police van had been positioned. The van had its headlights on, and a flashing blue light on the roof was reflected by the swirling mists. A few bystanders huddled near the vehicles as they observed the goings-on.

"Okay Captain, your position is good," Geoff began his winch operator's patter as we approached the landing site. "The ground below looks safe. You're clear down ten... eight... five... " As Geoff continued the final part of his talk-down, we eventually felt the helicopter's wheels make light contact with the grass. "Still looking good... the wheels are holding... we don't appear to be sinking into the mud... " The Captain cautiously lowered the S61's collective lever further. However, he was ready to lift into the hover again if the ten ton weight of the machine proved excessive for the field's surface. "This looks fine, John," said Geoff at length, as he leant out of the cargo door to inspect the wheels. "We don't appear to be sinking."

The Captain carefully lowered the helicopter's collective lever fully, and once he was satisfied with safety, he called: "You're clear out." It was the signal for Mick to open the airstair door, after which he walked quickly down the steps. Mick appeared to struggle slightly in his heavy duty flying suit as he then went towards the waiting ambulance.

Meanwhile, Geoff was busy in the cabin as he prepared for the patient's arrival. He made adjustments to the specially designed stretcher, and cleared the area by the cargo door, where the stretcher was secured.

"I could nip out now to give a hand," I suggested to the Captain.

"I should hang on a minute," he replied. "I suspect there are quite a few people about; they may not want the pilots getting in the way."

As I looked back into the cabin, Geoff gave me a thumbs-up sign as he said: "The cabin's prepared now, guys. So I'll go over to the ambulance, and see what's happening." Geoff then unplugged his headset, and walked through the cabin towards the airstair door.

"We could think about our departure from here, while they're doing that," said John.

I held the map in the centre area of the cockpit, and we studied the aviation chart to work out our flight path. After a while, I said: "If we fly out straight ahead, it looks reasonably clear according to the map. There's a golf course beyond this village, and then the coastline itself beyond the golf course. However, I think our safest option might be to fly back along the route we used to get here."

The Captain scrutinised the map closely for a few more moments, before saying: "Hidden in the mists there could be some electricity wires and other obstructions near this village. I agree, I think our safest option will be to fly back the way we came in. We know its proven, and once we meet the sea, we can obtain clearance from Benbecula to climb to safety altitude. We'll then return to Stornoway at high level." The Captain pondered for a short while before continuing: "We'll have a word with the medics, but if they're happy for the patient to be flown to Stornoway at high level, it would be better from our point of view. If there's no real requirement, there seems little point in groping our way back low level in this murky weather."

While the Captain and I had these discussions, the two crewmen could be seen talking to folk near the ambulance. After some minutes, Geoff returned to the helicopter. The pilots looked back at him as he walked through the cabin, and then plugged-in his head set. "Okay, guys," said Geoff at length. "Here's the plan." He glanced at us both before continuing: "The doctor has agreed that the patient can walk to the helicopter; he reckons it will be more comfortable for her than being manhandled on a stretcher. Once she's on board, though, the Doc wants her to lie down on the aircraft's stretcher for the flight to Stornoway. The Doc and nurse will accompany her during the flight."

Shortly after Geoff had said this, we noticed the patient being assisted from the rear of the ambulance. She walked slowly, and was supported by the doctor and the nurse, holding her under each arm. Mick acted as the rear party, and followed the others towards the airstair door. I noticed that he carried the doctor's medical bag. From the rear of the ambulance, two other folk appeared after a minute, and observed the group as they approached the helicopter. When the patient reached the steps of the airstair door, the nurse moved ahead, and the doctor helped the casualty from behind as she walked up the stairs.

Geoff went to the rear of the cabin and acted as welcome party. As she entered the cabin, the patient seemed flustered and bewildered by the noisy helicopter; Geoff offered her ear-protectors. While they walked slowly through the cabin, Geoff offered hearing-protectors to the nurse and doctor as well. Soon the medical staff assisted their patient to lie down on the aircraft's stretcher, and the doctor briefly rummaged inside his medical bag. Meanwhile, Mick slammed shut the airstair door, and gave a thumbs-up sign to the pilots.

While the doctor and nurse settled their patient onto the stretcher, Geoff half-closed the cargo door, to reduce the draught. He then assisted the medics to ensure the patient was safely strapped to the stretcher, before guiding the nurse and doctor to seats.

"Okay, guys," Geoff said to the pilots quite soon. "Everyone is secure in the back. Standby..." Geoff opened the cargo door again, and leant out, "... all clear above and behind, as far as I can see. You're clear to depart."

The Captain then lifted the S61 into a low hover, turned the machine through one hundred and eighty degrees, and gradually flew away from the pick-up point as we maintained an easterly heading, following the line of the road. I called out the various features as we progressed: "We'll soon overfly the small village of Lochboisdale. The road will finish at the far end of the village. Shortly after that, we'll see two small islands on our starboard side… " The Captain flew the helicopter low and slow as he followed my directions.

At length, having passed the two islands, we flew over the entrance to Loch Boisdale. The open sea, and clearance from high ground lay ahead. "Have a word with Benbecula, please," the Captain asked me at that point. "See if we have permission to climb."

Benbecula personnel were aware of our presence already. The airfield's duty Air Traffic Controller promptly agreed to our request. John then raised the collective lever, and initiated a climb towards safety altitude.

As we approached the required height, Geoff swiftly asked: "Is it okay if the medics leave their seats now, John? They want to check the patient."

"Yup. No problem," replied the Captain. "They can do that now."

The Captain had begun to ease down the collective lever to level the aircraft at the top of climb. We flew in thick cloud by that time; he had to rely entirely on the aircraft instruments for orientation. Nevertheless, as we had anticipated, the flight was considerably less stressful without the need to maintain visual contact with the sea. In addition, the flying conditions were smoother at the higher altitude, and we began to feel more at ease.

While we progressed the flight northwards, I spoke to Air Traffic Control at Stornoway. I passed an estimated arrival time, and asked for an update of the local weather conditions. "Standby," said the Air Traffic Controller. "I'll call you back with the weather."

Shortly after this radio call, we became aware of unexpected activity in the cabin. There was a sudden commotion as folk began to bustle about. I turned round hastily, and John too glanced back before returning his concentration to the instrument flying. After a moment, he asked in an anxious tone: "Everything okay in the back, Geoff?"

Geoff, however, seemed preoccupied. We heard only a brief: "Standby... " before Geoff's headset was unplugged. I looked back again, and was aware of hectic movement as the medical staff, together with Geoff and Mick, appeared to deal with the patient.

"What's going on?" the Captain asked me.

"I'm not sure... " Once more I looked back, wondering if there was anything the pilots could do to help.

"Shit... " said John after a moment. At that instant, a thought had occurred to him: "She's not giving birth is she?" The two pilots glanced at each other ominously. The medical team continued to work frantically as they attended to their patient. Above the noise of the helicopter, the doctor shouted an instruction. Geoff rapidly moved to the medical bag, and handed a syringe together with a small phial to the nurse. The nurse began to fill the syringe; she looked flustered as the vibrations from the helicopter caused her some difficulty. Eventually, however, she handed the syringe to the doctor.

At that stage, my attention was diverted away from the casualty. Stornoway Air Traffic Control had called me with a message. I wrote down various details, including information about the airfield's weather. "It sounds as if the weather at Stonoway's improved a bit," I said.

"Okay, that's good. We'll confirm what it's like when we get closer," replied the Captain. "But if possible, we'll fly the patient directly to the hospital."

Just then we heard Geoff as he re-connected his head-set. He said nothing at first and appeared distressed as he looked at the pilots in an awkward manner. Eventually, sounding a little breathless, he said:

"Sorry about that, guys. Bit of a panic stations back here for a mo."
"We wondered if the baby had..."

"No, no..." said Geoff, as he moved his head from side to side in a deliberate fashion. He lowered his eyes and went on: "No, in fact it was a greater drama than that." I watched his expression for a second. He was clearly moved as he said slowly: "our patient..." he grimaced, "Our patient died, actually."

The Captain turned hurriedly and stared at the crewman.

"Shit..." he hissed through clenched teeth.

Geoff nodded steadily as he continued.

"It was touch and go, but the Doc and nurse have managed to resuscitate her."

"Is she stable now, or could she suffer a relapse?" asked the Captain tersely.

"They've given her an injection. It should stabilise her," replied Geoff.

There was a moment of quiet between the crew at this point. The Captain continued to concentrate on the instrument flying. Geoff looked back at the patient while the doctor and nurse monitored her progress. Mick stood near the medical team, ready to offer help. I looked at my board, and re-checked the weather details which I had just written down. We all felt shocked, and disinclined to speak.

"Coastguard helicopter, this is Stornoway," the Controller abruptly interrupted the quiet spell in the cockpit.

"Go ahead," I replied.

"Roger. We have you on radar, you are clear to descend initially to fifteen hundred feet."

"Copied," I said. "Shortly commencing descent." Quickly, I produced the check-list card, and read out the pre-descent checks. "*... Altimeters set... radalt bugs at one thousand feet... check fuel contents...* " The Captain eased down the collective lever to initiate descent once the checks had been completed.

We continued to glance occasionally at the casualty and her attendants, but they all appeared to remain calm. Apparently, the medication had worked. Soon, we received clearance from Air Traffic Control to descend further. "Approaching ten miles from the airfield, continue your descent." Quite rapidly, as the aircraft descended further, we passed through the cloudbase and were able then to see the surface of the sea.

"The visibility here is definitely better than further south," commented the Captain. He continued to reduce height steadily as we approached Stornoway, and when we were some five miles from the airfield, the Eye Peninsular to the east was faintly visible. "I'm happy to fly the patient directly to the hospital in these weather conditions," said the Captain.

Quickly, I told Air Traffic Control of our intentions. "Roger, you're clear to proceed directly to the hospital," replied the Controller. The Captain adjusted our heading slightly, and flew towards the entrance to Stornoway harbour; I had already performed the pre-landing checks when he said: "Visual with the hospital landing site." He slowed the machine, and made a further heading adjustment when the wind direction could be determined from the wind-sock.

"You're clear below," called Geoff as he leant out of the cargo door, and guided the Captain for landing. "Down five... four... three... two... one... just touching... " The landing site was on grass again, and Geoff checked the aircraft wheels before calling: "The ground seems firm. The wheels are holding."

I glanced back after the landing, and was surprised to see that the casualty was sitting up. The stretcher's straps had been loosened by the doctor and the nurse; the patient was looking around her with a bewildered expression. Mick had moved back to open the airstair door, and Geoff helped the medical team. The team were gently aiding the patient to her feet.

Slowly, the group then shuffled through the cabin towards the airstair door. Mick had already walked down the steps, and he spoke to some paramedics and nurses who stood near the helicopter with a wheeled stretcher. The group helped the patient down the steps, before assisting her onto the stretcher. Soon, the patient was being pushed away from the helicopter, towards the hospital building.

At that point Geoff returned to the S61. He walked up the steps of the airstair door, made his way forward towards the cockpit and plugged-in his headset. He glanced at both the pilots for a moment; he still seemed somewhat preoccupied by the exceptional events. At length, he sighed and said in a subdued way: "Well... bloody hell, that must be something for the record books, guys." He hesitated for a moment before continuing. "A patient walks onto the aircraft... dies during the flight... and walks off again after landing!"

The Captain looked at Geoff briefly. Then he shook his head. There was an unusual atmosphere in the cockpit; we all sensed that, somehow, we had been part of a higher plan. As we looked across, we noticed that the patient and her attendants were just disappearing into the hospital.

"Shit," said the Captain eventually, repeating once more his favoured word for the day. "*Definitely* one for the record books," he concluded.

CHAPTER 17

Religious Convictions

JUNE 1989

"Jenny? Ah, there you are." Alan, the Chief Pilot at Stornoway peered around the crew room door. Jenny, along with Geoff and with me, continued to look intently at the album laid on the table top. The press cuttings about the *Saint Patrick* and South Uist incidents still held our rapt attention. While we had been reminiscing, Alan had been ensconced in his office along with Vince, the other duty crewman on that morning in June 1989. Alan walked over to where we studied the press cuttings. A very experienced search and rescue man, Alan's directness occasionally upset some folk.

"What have you got there, then?" asked Alan.

"We were reminiscing about a couple of rescues we did at the beginning of last year," I said.

"Oh, yeah," said Alan as he looked at the album. "I remember that letter from the French Consul-General. You guys did a good job..." He scanned through the cuttings, briefly. "...and you did well with that South Uist rescue too."

After a pause he turned to Jenny.

"Anyway, Jenny... I need you to type a couple of letters please."

Jenny stood up, and began to move towards her office.

"As for us, chaps..." he said, nodding to the aircrew, "we've got an unusual flight lined up for later this morning. We'll be flying over to Iona for a special task which has been agreed by the Coastguard. We'll route via Oban to pick up a team from the fire brigade and then take them to Iona for a practise fire drill at the Abbey."

He paused before adding, cryptically, "It'll mean we'll be working past the normal duty hand-over time, I'm afraid, but that's just too bad."

"It's a nice day for flying," shrugged Vince as Alan left the crew room to go back to his office. Vince crossed the room and switched on the television.

"... Following the massacres in Tiananmen Square," the presenter remained sombre as he read out more details about the dramatic events in China, *"further information is coming in concerning executions and the imposition of martial law. We are receiving reports also about the expulsion of foreign correspondents..."*

Geoff and I closed up the large albums and began to search through the drawers in a special chest containing various aviation maps and charts.

"We could have a look at the Iona map, while we're at it," I said.

"It should be here, in this group of charts..." said Geoff.

After a minute or two of searching, we pulled out the relevant map. "What's this Iona Abbey about, anyway?" he asked.

"Saint Columba and all that, I suppose," I replied. "And there's an active religious community still there, I believe." We unrolled the chart, and placed it carefully over the top of the map chest.

"I don't go along with all this religious stuff," muttered Geoff as we studied the chart.

"You'd better not let the 'Wee Frees' hear you say that."

"They're too busy squabbling amongst themselves to worry about the likes of me," grumbled Geoff. We continued to study the map, then Geoff briefly glanced at me. "You're not one of these religious freaks yourself, are you?" he asked me with a suspicious air.

"I do my best," I said somewhat defensively. We went on looking at the map, searching for danger areas, bird sanctuaries and other marked hazards.

"Waste of time this religious business, if you ask me," said Geoff eventually. "I mean, what's the point of it all, anyway?"

"Well, what's the point of life?" I asked. "Where's it all leading?"

Geoff thought about this for a moment, then he said: "But religion causes so much strife. Look at Northern Ireland, and the Middle East.

And there are so many crack-pots around, and weird religious sects. Even when you do go to church, it's an endless round of the same old stuff; all they seem to do is preach to the converted. There's also a lot of hierarchical pomposity which is off-putting. Best stay well out of it, if you want my opinion."

"That's the easy option, I guess," I shrugged.

"What about all the troubles in Jerusalem recently?" queried Geoff, after a minute. "The very centre of Christianity and other faiths, and look at the grief and struggles that go on there."

"You're right; it's sad they can't get their act together."

"Bloody hell," said Geoff. "It's more than sad. It's disastrous. What would Jesus have to say about it all?"

"I don't suppose he'd be too impressed."

"Impressed? Pah!" Geoff appeared to have become quite heated. "Murder and misery, all in the name of religion. I should think Jesus might regret inflicting religion on the world."

"I think religion was around long before Jesus' time," I said. "Anyway, surely it was 'religion' *per se* that led to His crucifixion."

"Humph!" Geoff growled with a perplexed expression. "So where does that leave us? Are we saying that God and religion aren't the same thing?"

We looked across at Vince at that point. He continued to be absorbed as he watched the television. Ominous snippets of information about the problems in China were released by the presenter as the news came in. Between the news flashes, the serious situation was being discussed by a panel of experts. At length, I glanced back at Geoff as I said in a subdued voice: "I think you may have hit the nail on the head actually, Geoff."

Geoff and I then moved away from the map chest, and stood behind Vince's chair. We became silent, and there was an air of pessimism as the three of us watched the television. The crew room felt stuffy; the weather conditions on that early summer's day were unusually good. There was bright sunshine bearing into the room as I went to open some windows.

"Gee whizz!" said Vince, as another item of astonishing news was announced. "For sure, June 1989 will go down in the annals of history." As I opened the windows, the fresh breeze immediately began to ventilate the room. The others seemed too engrossed with the television to notice, but a smell of sea air had seeped into the crew room quite rapidly.

I gazed out of the window for a moment, towards the shoreline. Gulls swooped with intuitive agility, a scene of continuous movement against the clear skies, their haunting cries wafting towards us. The heat from the sun felt welcoming and my spirits were given a refreshing fillip. As I drank in the scene, I felt a curious surge of emotion. It was hard to pin down; perhaps it was the eager anticipation of the unusual flight which we were about to carry out, or perhaps, following Geoff's conversation, it was the appreciation of nature's mysterious and wonderful free gifts.

Whatever the reason, I was at that moment struck by a powerful sense that Geoff, however inadvertently, had touched upon a thorny truth: God was the certainty, *not* religion. Then my sentiments suddenly changed. The sense of elation was abruptly replaced by a sense of failure. I had a feeling of mortification – of inadequacy; the non-believers missed out, yet they were so hard to convince. I stared at my colleagues for a second.

"I'm just going down to the aircraft to check we've got the right maps," the others looked up briefly as I said this. They appeared slightly surprised; their expressions said: 'Of course we've got the right maps'. However, at that moment, I felt the need for a little space to sort out my thoughts; the maps provided a good excuse. The two crewmen reverted their gaze to the television without comment as I left the room.

During my walk along the corridor, Jenny smiled at me briefly as she busily typed away. In the next office, Alan had adopted a rather secretive tone while he spoke on the telephone. The sound of his voice faded gradually when I walked downstairs, and towards the hangar.

"Hello, Bob," I said to one of the engineers, as I entered the hangar. Bob was performing a routine task on the Coastguard helicopter, which had just been towed in from outside. "I'd like to check the maps on board, if that's okay with you."

"Sure, no problem," replied Bob. "You're going on a pre-planned flight soon, I believe," he added.

"Yeah, we're off to Iona for a practise fire drill at the Abbey."

"At least it'll be something different, I suppose, " commented Bob gruffly.

I nodded and grinned at Bob when I walked up the steps of the airstair door. As I went through the cabin towards the cockpit, I was careful not to interfere with the equipment which crew members had prepared in an individual way, ready for a quick get-away. In the cockpit itself, the life-jackets had been laid judiciously on the pilots' seats as usual, and the pilots' headsets rested on top of the cockpit coaming.

"While you're there, just release the rotor brake for a sec, would you please?" Bob's voice called out.

"Okay. Standby," I shouted back. I gripped the rotor brake lever, and eased it back. After some seconds, I was aware that the main rotor blades were turning slowly as the engineers pushed them around.

"That'll do. Rotor brake back on, now please," called Bob.

As I re-applied the rotor brake, there was a sudden noise from behind. "You dropped this." It was Sandy, Bob's assistant, who spoke.

"Thanks, Sandy," I said, returning the card to my pocket. "Would you like me to stay here to operate the rotor brake, if you've got more to do?"

"That would be helpful. Thanks, pal," said Sandy in his distinctive local accent. He then walked back outside to join Bob.

"Rotor brake off now, please," shouted Bob. I eased back the lever. Soon, the rotor blades began their slow progression once more as they were pushed by the engineers. I sat down in the co-pilot's seat at that stage, attempting not to disturb the carefully placed life-jacket. I used my right hand to operate the rotor brake, and glanced in the rear-view mirror just outside the aircraft side window. Sandy stood on a special ladder arrangement, close to the tail-rotor. When required, he turned the tail-rotor, which in turn moved the main rotors.

While I sat passively, ready to perform my mundane rotor brake duties, I began to appreciate the welcome moment of 'space'. My mind instinctively appeared to wind down. Mysteriously, however, I suddenly found myself reflecting on an incident which had occurred some ten years ago. Quite swiftly – and bizarrely – I began to pick up an uncomfortable feeling. A startling sense of giddiness grew in my head; I recalled the events so vividly. At the time, I was a helicopter pilot serving with the Royal Air Force's Number 18 Squadron, based at Gütersloh in northern Germany.

IT HAD STARTED AS A GOOD DAY REALLY. I had just returned to Gütersloh after a training flight over the plains of Westphalia, near Münster. Together with my crewman, Frank, I had walked from the Wessex helicopter to the engineering line hut, where I would sign the aircraft log. I had nattered casually with Frank, an Irishman who was a good friend. He had a practical, down-to-earth attitude, and Frank was renowned for his kindness to children; the younger generation would warm to him instinctively.

"I'll just sign the log, Frank," I had said. "See you in the ops room shortly."

As I signed the aircraft log, I chatted with the engineers. There was good humoured banter; everyone seemed in a convivial mood. Of course, we had no idea that anything was wrong at that stage, indeed that disaster was probably occurring at that very moment. All seemed quite normal to us just then; the flying tasks for the day progressed according to plan.

Having completed the log signing ritual, I left the line hut to walk over to the Operations Room. I was perhaps half way through my journey, when I first had an inkling that something was wrong. It was a combination of small things: a raised voice; sudden movement; an uncomfortable atmosphere. Within moments, the duty Operations Officer appeared. His harassed look caught me off guard.

"We need you two immediately," called the Operations Officer. Frank turned round sharply as he was about to enter the aircrew changing room. I stared at the Operations Officer, and increased my pace towards the Operations Room. As I entered the room, I sensed an unusual hush. A few Officers stood around with anxious, expectant expressions. The Operations Officer himself had just picked up the telephone. Frank joined me as I waited; we overheard his telephone conversation with a sense of growing apprehension.

"Okay... yes... I've got one crew here on immediate standby. I can get you another within twenty-five minutes, and two more crews within forty-five minutes. As soon as the Doc arrives here, this crew will fly him to the scene straight away... "

When the Operations Officer had finished his call, he looked at us blankly for a second. Then his eyes seemed to suddenly focus. He had to be swift; more arrangements had to be made, more urgent telephone calls were required.

"I'll come straight to the point, gents," he said. "A Harrier aircraft has just crashed after take-off. We need you to fly the doctor to the scene, which is about five miles on the Gütersloh runway's extended centre-line." At that moment, as the telephone rang, the Officer grabbed the receiver violently.

Frank and I glanced at each other, then quickly went into action mode. Frank dashed outside to ensure that refuelling procedures were hastened. I signed the Authorisation Book in the Operations Room before running back to the line hut. Briskly, I informed the Duty Engineer what was happening. As I did this, I noticed that the Station Senior Medical Officer was just arriving. I quickly left the line hut, and went outside to meet the doctor. A tall man with a somewhat diffident air, his pale face and serious expression momentarily struck a chord within me.

There was little time for sentimentality just then, however. The doctor shrugged briefly as I offered to carry his medical pack, and I soon noticed that he carried something else. Tucked under one arm, the doctor carried some extra-strong plastic bags.

Frank was rapidly checking over the Wessex as I accompanied the doctor towards the aircraft, and assisted him into the cabin.

"Okay Skipper," Frank had called out to me then. "We're all set to go." Quickly, I climbed up the steps on the side of the Wessex, and clambered into the cockpit. Frank stood outside, fire bottle at the ready in case of problems during the start procedures. Soon, I had the engines started, and the rotors were turning.

As Frank returned to the cabin and secured himself to the special crewman's harness, I spoke to Air Traffic Control. The Duty Controller sounded agitated as he cleared us to fly directly to the scene. Within moments, I had ground-taxied clear of other aircraft, and lifted the Wessex into a hover as Frank gave directions. I then lowered the nose of the helicopter, and rapidly picked up airspeed as we turned onto a westerly heading.

The flat local terrain felt familiar as we flew away from the airfield. For a short while, it was easy to be deluded into thinking that our mission was merely the accustomed routine. Quite soon, however, just a few miles ahead, a harsh reminder of the reality of our distasteful duty gradually became evident. We spotted a pall of black smoke rising from behind some trees. I flew the machine at maximum airspeed towards this signal; the rest of the surrounding countryside still looked normal and innocuous at that stage. However, as we drew closer to the scene, other odious signs of a startling destructiveness – far from normal and innocuous – soon came into view.

A recent crater, scorched and irregular, had been gouged from a field. Across a wide area, torn particles of metal were haphazardly dispersed. Pathetic remnants of aircraft lay scattered at random. A rubber tyre looked undamaged as it rested in isolation. Razor-sharp scraps of aluminium had been flung across the terrain. Showers of fuel and other liquids had caused discolouration of the ground in arbitrary patches; black smoke from some of the patches spiralled into the air.

Caught in a nearby tree, violently ripped from its fuselage, lay a section of wing. The wing had been lassoed by a sturdy rope already. A group of German fireman stood one behind the other, gripping the lasso. Their immaculate uniforms somehow looked out of place as the firemen heaved at the rope, attempting to dislodge the wing. As the firemen struggled, local police were still arriving; they leapt out of their cars to assist colleagues cordon off the area.

As we approached our chosen site, quite near the firemen, Frank talked me down for our landing. When it was safe, Frank gave a thumbs-up sign to the doctor. As he stepped out of the Wessex, the doctor looked around nervously, trying to assimilate the scene as quickly as possible. However, there was no reception party for him that day; the doctor's concentrated look revealed the loneliness he must have felt just then. He walked away from the helicopter in a deliberate manner, scrupulously examining the surface of the ground as he went.

While the doctor proceeded with his offensive task, Frank and I glanced at him occasionally. Frank stood beside the helicopter; we kept the machine running, ready for a rapid departure if required. The doctor held a plastic bag resolutely in one hand; quite soon, a putrid collection began to appear inside the bag. We instinctively looked away; somehow we felt intruders. The doctor's chore was obscene and pitiable; it was also solitary.

The doctor eventually began to wander further away from the helicopter, so from time to time, we checked on his whereabouts. As I did so one particular time, I suddenly caught my breath. Frank, too, appeared to have noticed something, simultaneously. A little distance behind the helicopter, leaning almost casually against the side of a ditch, we had sighted a torso. The torn vestiges of a green flying suit hung from it in bedraggled tatters. The splintered remains of a canopy lay nearby. Beyond that, the muddied carcass of an unused ejection seat was perched against a fragmented bush.

Frank said nothing at first, but as we stared at the torso with a sense of disbelief, I noticed that Frank, a devout Catholic, quietly crossed himself. At that instant, our unspoken thoughts probably coincided. No priest was in sight; the respects had to be improvised, and remote.

The commotion produced by the helicopter rotors created an unwelcome hiatus; the harsh site of fatality, however coarse, deserved a greater reverence. As we waited, the tense atmosphere seemed to become more poignant. The German policemen hurried in their duties as they placed extensive cordons around the site. Perhaps they felt glad to have some positive function.

Then Frank glanced up at me and said: "We don't even know yet who the pilot was, let alone his religious persuasion." Frank demurred; he glanced at me once more. His eyes had started to brim. "Perhaps he was a man of faith, whoever he was. It's too late now, anyway... or is it?" Frank remained silent for a few more disconcerting seconds. "Buddhism... Judaism... Christianity... Confucianism," Frank spoke softly, as if to himself. "Surely it's God that matters, not the religion." The painful scenario was heart-rending. We felt helpless, and puny; the sense of distress was over-powering.

The firemen were gradually making headway as they tugged at the section of wing. The doctor had started to move slowly towards the direction of the torso. His back was turned to us; his head was lowered, his face hidden. At length, Frank looked at me once more. He shook his head abruptly; it appeared to be an act of private frustration. We both felt a confusion of grief and impotence. "Whatever his religion," Frank said eventually, "may God..." he was clearly moved, and faltered as he spoke "... rest his soul."

THE TAP ON MY ARM FELT QUITE SHARP. "That's it, pal. We've finished, thanks." I was suddenly conscious of Sandy's voice behind me. I had re-applied the rotor brake some minutes ago, following Bob's sporadic instructions. A lull in proceedings had followed; the tranquil interval had sanctioned my vivid flash-back.

"By the way... " Sandy began to say something. He quickly stopped, though, caught in mid-sentence. I had turned around at that second to glance at Sandy, and to acknowledge his thanks. However, when I turned, I spotted Geoff as he entered the cabin and as he began to walk forward to the cockpit area.

"You were right," Geoff said airily while he waved some maps. "A couple of the charts have been amended recently. These are up-to-date, so I'll exchange them for the old ones on board." Geoff started to rummage around the map container, searching for the out-of-date editions.

"Here's one of the affected charts," said Geoff as he pulled out a specific copy. "It covers the area adjacent to Iona."

"Interesting spot, Iona," commented Sandy while he gazed at the map. "I've never been there, like. But I believe the place has a powerful atmosphere."

"We were discussing it earlier," said Geoff, as he investigated other charts in the container. "I guess it depends on whether or not you're impressed by all this religious malarky."

"There are quite a few important historical characters buried there, I believe," remarked Sandy, as he continued to study the map. "Scottish Kings and that."

"I guess they took religion more seriously in those days," said Geoff. "They were a devout lot."

"In this part of the world," said Sandy glancing at us, "some folk are still trying to be devout. And you have to admit," continued Sandy, "they've got a point, like. After all, everyone's got to die some time. You never know what's around the next corner."

"Don't you start," retorted Geoff, as he pulled another map from the container. "You guys will have me converted soon."

"We're in a line of work where things can turn pear-shaped rather quickly," I pointed out. "One time, I had the misfortune to witness the tragic after-effects of a flying accident."

When I had said this, Geoff adopted a thoughtful expression. He shook his head in a solemn fashion. Then he said in a subdued way: "I had the same experience myself, not so long ago." After a pause, Geoff simply said: "It was just horrific."

The three of us fell silent for a moment or two. We heard a telephone shrill in one of the far offices, and we noticed that the call was answered quite swiftly.

After a few moments, though, Sandy suddenly appeared to brighten. He coughed quietly before saying in a cheerful manner: "Well, if you two are going to talk yourselves into a cycle of doom and gloom, like, there's only one thing for it," Sandy gazed at us in turn. He handed the Iona map back to Geoff as he went on: "As far as I can see, both of you'd better buck up your religious ideas, like. And to help you along," Sandy frowned as he coughed again, "both of you'd better make a bee-line for the nearest priest when you get to Iona."

CHAPTER 18

Bloody Bay

"You can fly us to Iona..." Alan glanced at me as he made this declaration, "and I'll do the navigation." He adjusted the map on his knee. "This should be a rather interesting flight. When you're ready, we'll head off towards the Shiants, initially." He made a call to Air Traffic Control at Stornoway.

"You're clear to depart to the south, low level," the Controller said.

As I lifted 'Beady Eyes' into a hover, it felt abnormally hot in the cockpit. The glass of the aircraft instruments reflected the sunlight in spasmodic dazzles. Alan put on some sunglasses.

"Okay in the back?" Alan turned round and looked at Geoff and Vince briefly.

"You're clear above and behind," replied Geoff as he leant out of the cargo door. He then closed the door firmly while I lowered the nose of the S61 to pick up airspeed. The grass beneath the helicopter quickly became a blur as we proceeded with the take-off.

"If you overfly the largest of the Shiant Islands," said Geoff, "there's a good chance that we might spot some seal colonies today." As we flew away from Stornoway, the familiar coastline of the Isle of Lewis glittered curiously in the brilliant light of that day's sunshine. The crew all felt in high spirits; the unusual flight had stimulated an atmosphere of excitement.

"Just slow down a bit here," said Alan as we approached the Shiants. The aircrew peered below, searching for the seals. The colonies were well camouflaged, but we soon saw the dishevelled creatures start to shift uncomfortably on their rocky beds. A few seals began to flounder towards the sea; they glanced at each other suspiciously as they slid into the water. Shortly afterwards, the seals' heads with their bulbous, worried eyes would appear out of the sea as the beasts stared all around.

Soon, we left the Shiants behind as we proceeded down the Little Minch, towards the Isle of Skye. "Aim for Waternish Point, and then Dunvegan Head beyond that," said Alan. The northern coast of the Isle of Skye, with its various lochs, looked battered and weather-beaten as we approached. A ferry steamed purposefully across the water. "On its way to Tarbert, probably," commented Alan. As we passed Dunvegan Head, and the small Loch of Pooltiel, Geoff pointed out the high ground of Healabhal Mhor, and Healabhal Bheag.

"Those peaks are not as striking as the Cuillins," said Geoff. "But nevertheless walkers get into difficulty there from time to time." We looked across, searching for folk, but the hills were too far away for us to spot any walkers. The peaty colours of the Isle of Skye were highlighted by the brilliant sunshine, and the clear day's visibility allowed us a fascinating overview of the area. Soon, we approached Idrigill Point and as we flew over a series of small islands, Geoff commented: "Those rock structures near the base of Idrigill Point are known as Macleod's Maidens."

We then flew past the entrance to Loch Bracadale, and shortly the spectacular rise of the Cuillin Hills dominated the skyline to our north. "The heights on my map are written in meters," complained Alan. "Do the Cuillins qualify as a Munro, Geoff?" he asked.

"The highest point is nearly three thousand two hundred feet, according to my chart," replied Geoff. "So presumably they do qualify."

We gazed at the Cuillins for a few moments, then Alan referred to his map once more as he said to me: "I suggest you take up a southerly direction now, and head towards Rhum." I made an adjustment to the aircraft heading, and soon we flew down the eastern shore of the Island of Rhum. "That's Kinloch Castle at the end of Loch Scresort," commented Alan. "And the high point just to the south is Askival."

The rounded outline of Rhum, with its smaller neighbours of Canna, Eigg, and Muck, looked somehow noble and intriguing as we flew low level over the Sound of Rhum. I glanced at the radio altimeter to check my height; on calm days the sea's surface could be deceptive. In the past there had been occasions when pilots unwittingly flew into water, lured down by the glassy surface of the sea.

Beyond the Isle of Muck, I maintained my southerly heading as I flew towards a lighthouse at the base of the Point of Ardnamurchan, on the mainland of Scotland. On our right side were the Islands of Coll and Tiree; they appeared flat and featureless compared to the dramatic high grounds elsewhere. Soon, I was turning the helicopter gradually to the left as we aimed to fly along the Sound of Mull. With the northern point of the Island of Mull on our right side, Alan said: "We should see Tobermory soon, just around this Bloody Bay."

"What bloody bay?" asked Geoff.

"The Bloody Bay around this bloody corner," responded Alan.

Stretched along the strand of Bloody Bay was a golf course, and at one end of the Bay stood a lighthouse. I reduced airspeed at that stage so that we could peer at the startling frontage of Tobermory, just beyond the lighthouse. The various houses located by the water's edge had been painted in flamboyant style; the bright yellow, blue, orange, and other colours contrasted sharply with the dark green of the trees in the background. The reflections of the vivid hues, shimmering in the waters of the small bay, were as graphic as the buildings themselves. Fishing vessels, sailing craft, and other small boats moved around the bay, pottering at a leisurely pace.

At length, I increased our airspeed to one hundred and ten knots once more as we passed Calve Island, and continued our flight down the Sound of Mull. The shorelines on both sides of the Sound of Mull were marked by minor roads, twisting continuously to follow the water's edge. Clusters of dwellings broke up the uninhabited wilderness from time to time, but in general the scarcity of movement added to the air of desertion.

"There's an old castle at Aros Mains on the right side coming up soon," said Alan, "and a small airstrip south of that, just on the coast at Pennygown." Beyond that, we noticed a ferry crossing the waters between the Island of Mull and the mainland. I slowed the helicopter again, and Alan opened his side window to return the hand-waves of passengers on the ferry.

As we continued towards the south-east corner of the Island of Mull, we flew past several more bays, then Alan said: "We're approaching a narrow gauge railway shortly, just south of Craignure Bay." We soon spotted this unlikely transport system, connecting Craignure Bay with its neighbouring Duart Bay. Overlooking Duart Bay itself we sighted two castles. "That's Torosay Castle to the north," Alan pointed out. "A Victorian edifice, I believe. Just south, over there, is the ancient Duart Castle."

Shortly, however, we had to leave the two castles behind as we flew across the Firth of Lorn towards Oban. On our left side was the slim outline of the Island of Lismore, and as we approached Oban, Alan pointed to another castle. "That's Dunstaffnage Castle to the north," he said. "It's famous for once having housed Scotland's Stone of Destiny," he added.

By that stage, we had completed the before landing checks, and I had slowed the helicopter to allow Geoff to open the cargo door. "There's a clear area to the south of Oban Bay," said Geoff. Then he quickly added: "I think I can see the landing site now. Turn onto a south-westerly heading towards the Sound of Kerrera; I reckon I can see a couple of fire engines."

As I made the turn, Alan interjected: "Oh yes. I can see them now."

I continued to fly towards the fire engines, which had been parked in one corner of a large field. After a while, I said: "Ready for your directions now, Geoff." He gave me a thumbs-up sign, then Geoff took up his winch operator's patter: *"Forward thirty... your rate of descent is good... that's a good approach path... we're clear of obstructions... forward twenty-five... maintain this heading... "*

At length, we flew to a position near the two fire engines, and I brought the S61 to a hover. Geoff then concluded his talk-down: *"Your position is good... steady... steady... down five... four... three... two... one... the wheels are just touching... "* As I lowered the collective lever for the final stages of the landing, Geoff said: *"The wheels seem firm; they're not sinking into the ground."*

Alan then said: "Well done, guys. We'll close down the machine here; it'll make it easier for the firemen to load their gear on board if we're not 'burning and turning'." At that point, I brought back the speed select levers to the ground idle position, and started my stop-watch to time one minute. A group of firemen stood by their vehicles; one pointed in our direction as they watched the helicopter. When the minute had elapsed, I brought back the speed select levers further; the noise from the engines ceased immediately. As the rotor revolutions gauge reached forty percent, I applied the rotor brake.

"I'll go and have a word with these firemen," said Alan as he climbed out of the cockpit. Meanwhile, I completed the remaining shut-down drills, then unstrapped and left my cockpit seat.

"We may as well go outside too," I said, stretching my arms after the flight. Vince walked down the airstair door, followed by Geoff and myself. We checked around the helicopter, searching for traces of oil leaks or other faults. I inspected the aircraft wheels for signs of damage. "It's quite flat here," I said. "We should be fine without wheel chocks." We moved towards the group of firemen then, ready to assist with the lifting of their gear. The firemen were unloading the specialist equipment from their vehicles.

"Don't I know you?" I turned round swiftly, and looked at the Station Fire Officer who had just spoken.

"Yes... hello... I'm sure I recognise you," I replied.

"Weren't you at Royal Air Force Leuchars?" he asked.

"Yes," I responded. "It must be nearly fifteen years ago now, but I used to be a pilot with number Forty Three Squadron."

"They flew Phantoms in those days, didn't they?"

"That's right," I said. After a moment, I added nostalgically: "The Phantom was a troublesome aircraft, but nevertheless they were good times." The Station Fire Officer nodded slowly. Then he glanced at me again.

"Weren't you part of a formation team of Phantoms one year? If my memory is correct, you flew in a display for one of the Battle of Britain Open Days at Leuchars."

"You've got a good memory."

"Never forget a face," grinned the Station Fire Officer. "I was based at Leuchars myself in those days," he added. "Then I was posted to this job near Glasgow a few years ago." At that point, the Station Fire Officer went to instruct some of his colleagues. "Excuse me a minute," he said. "Perhaps catch up with you later."

Geoff and I then walked back to the helicopter, ready to receive the firemen's specialist gear. "I think they're best left to do the unloading by themselves," said Geoff. "We'll probably just get in the way at this stage." After a pause, Geoff continued: "What was that all about by the by?"

"It's a small world," I commented ruefully. "That guy knew me at Leuchars."

"So I overheard," said Geoff. "What was the bit about the formation display?"

"It seems such a different life now," I said. "I'd almost forgotten about that display."

"Well you'd better tell me what happened before you do forget," retorted Geoff. I sat down on one of the steps of the airstair door just then, and we gazed across at the firemen, busy with their unloading duties. We felt warm and relaxed in the ambient sunshine. "Go on, tell me all," said Geoff impatiently. He had picked a long grass, and sucked at one end. "They'll be tied up for quite a while yet, and I'm dying to hear about this formation business." I glanced at Geoff; already the memory of the day was returning quite strongly.

THERE HAD BEEN SUCH A CARNIVAL ATMOSPHERE at Leuchars that day. It was mid-September, 1974; Battle of Britain remembrance time across the country.

"We'll take off in a stream of four Phantoms," the Commanding Officer had briefed. "It will simulate a scramble, and enthral the crowds." The Wing Commander looked at us with an amused expression. Later cashiered from the Service, this CO's weak points fortunately did not include a lack of flying skills; the Wing Commander was an excellent pilot. "We'll have to start up and taxi out in plenty of time," the CO added. "Everything takes much longer with crowds of people to contend with."

The four Phantoms had been part of a static display during the morning, and when the time for start up approached, the pilots and navigators were driven to their aircraft in a special aircrew bus. The crews bantered amongst themselves nervously during the short journey. When the bus reached the aircraft parking area, the crews stepped out nonchalantly. They glanced around with casual expressions, which belied their true sense of excitement. The Phantoms had been cordoned off safely, and police monitored the crowds as they jostled for position near the cordon. The eight aircrew strolled proudly to their allotted Phantoms, and performed external checks before climbing up the aircraft steps. It was a further opportunity to bask in short-lived glory.

The ground-crew had put on special overalls for the occasion; they too seemed nervous and excited as they assisted the aircrew strap into their cockpits. Eventually, my headset was handed to me, and I secured the clip by my side which connected vital functions: oxygen to my face mask; air to my anti-g suit; electric power to my headset. I then gave a thumbs-up sign to the member of groundcrew, who made a final check that the ejection seat pins had been removed before he stepped down.

"Hear me Okay, Dave?" I adjusted my rubber face mask while I spoke with my navigator in the rear seat.

"Yeah fine, thanks," he replied. "Can you see that blond beauty in the crowd over there?" I gazed across, momentarily intrigued, but soon busied myself with the cockpit procedures; there was no time to waste. A young bachelor, Dave was an extremely keen aviator; a minor eyesight problem had regrettably precluded him from becoming a pilot.

"Ready for the start up, Dave?" I asked.

"Sure," replied Dave curtly. "All set." I then looked at the CO's aircraft, ready to give the pre-briefed signal. All four Phantoms would start up together. Soon the Wing Commander glanced at the waiting Phantoms. The pilots each gave a thumbs-up sign, and the formation leader then spoke to Air Traffic Control for start clearance.

"Standby, Chequers," retorted the Controller. "I'll give you start clearance shortly."

In my aircraft mirror, I noticed Dave studying the crowds. In some respects, the flight would hold special difficulties for him, and for the other navigators. The navigators' role would be purely passive, calling out information which would help the pilots. If they talked too much, it could interfere with the pilots' concentration. On the other hand, useful information passed prudently from time to time was most beneficial.

"Chequers leader from Air Traffic," the Controller suddenly spoke.

"Go ahead," responded the leader.

"Roger, you will be clear to start in two minutes."

The timing for the Air Display was crucial; Air Traffic Control's task was not easy. If the events were poorly co-ordinated, long intervals would occur; the crowds would grow restless. On the other hand, the safe running of the Air Display was the over-riding priority.

Soon, the two minutes had been precisely counted down, and the formation leader boldly held his hand in the air as the signal for the four Phantoms to start engines. The crowd began to jostle excitedly. I briefly glanced at them as I pressed the button to activate the first engine's start sequence. The sudden surge of noise caused a number of folk to quickly place hands over ears; several parents helped their youngsters.

Fortunately, the engine instruments during the start cycle showed everything to be in order. The engine revolutions were in the right band; the engine temperature was normal; all seemed to be correct. Soon, I held up a finger again, and the ground-crew promptly cleared me to start the second engine.

Once the second engine had stabilised, I gave a further sign to the start crew. Quickly, the external power unit was removed, the ground-crew member had a final check around the aircraft, and then stood in front, ready to act as marshaller. When all four marshallers were in position, the Wing Commander called for clearance to taxi out.

The Controller soon gave taxi clearance, and the lead Phantom then slowly moved forward, the aircraft nose edging towards the enthusiastic crowd. Several onlookers waved vigorously to the aircrew. Some members of the crowd had notebooks, and seemed to make careful jottings about the details of the four Phantoms. On our tail plane, for example, adjacent to the Squadron emblem of the Fighting Cock, the tail letter 'J' would have been noted. A little further forward, the aircraft registration 'XT 874', stencilled in small letters, would have been annotated in the aircraft spotters' books.

Once the leader was moving safely along the taxiway, Roger, the pilot of the second aircraft eased forward in turn. I looked at the crowd; most folk held their positions with determination as the noisy Phantoms started to move. People evidently had implicit trust in the Phantom's braking system.

Soon, as the number three in the formation, it was our turn to move. I glanced in the aircraft mirror, and Dave gave me a thumbs-up sign. Dave's signal appeared to be a little exaggerated. Even the blond beauty in the crowd may have noticed his sign; "Funny old thing," I thought to myself wryly. As we taxied slowly forward, I quickly checked the function of the nose wheel steering; it seemed to be working normally. In just the right position on the taxiway, I pressed the small button again to activate the nose wheel steering; I then pushed the rudder pedals to operate the steering system.

We moved at a leisurely pace, maintaining a constant distance from the aircraft ahead. As we progressed steadily along the taxiway, Dave and I got a closer feel for the enthusiasm of the thousands of onlookers. We kept our canopies open, which made it easier to return the sea of hand-waves. As we moved, Dave quickly read out the before take-off checks. Dave was rather hurried; he was keen not to miss out on the hand-waving opportunities.

Soon we approached the take-off point, and we saw that the leader and his navigator were beginning to lower their aircraft canopies. Our crowd waving opportunities were about to come to an abrupt end. "We'll lower our canopies now," I said to Dave. As the individual perspex tops clamped down, we swiftly seemed to enter another world. The confines of our cockpits felt familiar, and business-like; the wave-a-crowd exercise was a mere fleeting fantasy.

Air Traffic Control had cleared the formation already to proceed with the briefed take-off technique: the four aircraft would take off as individuals, with a separation of ten seconds between them. The Wing Commander would then do a sweeping turn to the south of the airfield, allowing the others to join up in close formation. The crowds of onlookers thus would have a grand stand view of the four aircraft as the Phantoms joined up in close formation.

I glanced in my aircraft mirror at that point, and confirmed that the fourth aircraft, piloted by John, was following in the correct place. Then I looked across at the leader. Already the Wing Commander had started his take-off run. The lead Phantom rapidly picked up airspeed as it began to move away from the start of the runway; quite soon, the rate of acceleration increased dramatically as the aircraft reheats lit.

Meanwhile, Roger was taxiing his aircraft onto the runway, ready to follow the leader at exactly the right spacing. I continued to move towards the runway, maintaining a careful distance from the aircraft in front. At the instant we spotted Roger open the throttles of his Phantom, Dave curtly called: "Counting NOW... ten... nine... eight..." – I slightly quickened our pace to turn onto the runway, and again glanced in my mirror. John remained in place – "... seven... six... five... four... " Dave spoke in a clear-cut manner as he continued the countdown. Ahead, I noticed that the leader was just getting airborne, and was about to begin his turn to the south of the airfield. Out of the corner of my eye, I was aware of the massive crowds watching. I was well positioned on the runway by then, ready for the final part of Dave's count-down.

"... three... two... one... NOW." Immediately, I advanced the engine throttles to full cold power. There was a surge of acceleration, and an increase in noise as the giant Rolls Royce engines began to wind up. We felt a punch in our backs as the aircraft started to move rapidly down the runway. The airspeed indicator advanced briskly. After some moments, I eased the twin throttles outboard. There was a fractional pause, then a furious roar as the engine reheats lit. We felt a further surge of acceleration from the power of the reheat system as the aircraft was propelled down the runway faster and faster. I concentrated on looking ahead; the runway edges appeared hazily in my peripheral vision.

Soon, I eased back on the aircraft stick to raise the nose-wheel off the ground. With my right hand holding the stick, I maintained the backward pressure. I made continuous minor stick adjustments to hold the nose-wheel at the correct height above the tarmac surface. Then, monitoring the airspeed indicator, I made a further backward pressure on the stick to ensure the main wheels lifted away cleanly from the runway.

As our aircraft gained height, I looked ahead to keep the other two Phantoms in sight. Promptly, I eased back the throttles to cancel the reheat system, and to prevent the airspeed from increasing too briskly. As Dave read out the after take off checks, I slickly raised the undercarriage and flaps, and turned the aircraft towards the other machines. The rate of closure on the other two required careful judgement. If we were too slow, it appeared sloppy. If we were too quick, there was the embarrassing danger of overtaking the leader.

Roger was closing neatly onto the leader. Soon, he would take up position next to the leader's right wing: echelon starboard. Our place was next to the leader's left wing – echelon port – and John would fill the space behind the leader to complete the box-shaped formation. I glanced anxiously at our airspeed indicator for guidance. We had been pre-briefed on the leader's airspeed.

"Airspeed approaching 350 knots," Dave provided a useful commentary at this stage. He called out our airspeed at regular intervals, which allowed me to concentrate on looking outside the cockpit. Roger was nearly in position already. Beneath us, I fleetingly noticed the paper mill at Guardbridge. I maintained a fairly high airspeed, keen to close as rapidly as possible.

Suddenly, I realised that the lead aircraft and his number two were looming up too swiftly. "Airspeed 380 knots," Dave called out with a note of alarm. Immediately, I brought back both throttles to the idle position. The engine instruments reacted instantly as the Rolls Royce engines wound back towards idle. We sensed the rate of closure beginning to reduce, but still the other two machines appeared to be rushing towards us. I felt an uncomfortable irritation on the back of my neck.

"Airspeed now 340 knots, reducing," called Dave, still with tension in his voice. The number two Phantom made final adjustments as he took up position next to the Wing Commander. The lead aircraft slowly began to roll out of his turn as he adopted an easterly heading. This gave me a further period of grace; our rate of closure seemed to be more controlled. "Airspeed 310 knots," called Dave, sounding marginally more at ease.

The lead Phantom and his number two were by now in a neat close formation position. I had just a short distance to go before joining them. Quite soon, as nimbly as I dared, I eased our machine the last few feet into the echelon port station. The leader glanced across at me. My full concentration was on his aircraft; I followed every movement as rapidly, and as flowingly as possible. My peripheral vision confirmed that John was closing into place to complete our box formation.

"Turning left now," the Wing Commander called tersely. On our right, beyond the formation, I was aware of the town of St Andrews in the background. As the leader began his turn towards the airfield, I also noticed the grey colouring of the sea. Gradually, the lead aircraft tightened his turn, and I sensed that my anti-g suit was inflating. It was important that I stayed as relaxed as possible. I left one of the twin throttles in a constant position, and made regular small adjustments with the other throttle; this was a good technique to avoid throttle over-control.

"Pulling up now," the leader's voice was brusque. My anti-g suit inflated further as I followed the lead Phantom's manoeuvres. We were not cleared for low level aerobatics; that was the job of the Red Arrows. Nevertheless, the series of steep turns and wing-overs, practised regularly for several days beforehand, were designed to look impressive from the ground. The thousands of spectators saw the four Phantoms swoop and dive, climb and circle, as the leader maintained position in the vicinity of the airfield. Occasionally, as we proceeded with our gyrations, I was aware of the vast crowds of people beneath. We were not allowed to infringe the 'crowd line', but I still picked up periodic glimpses of the multitude of folk watching.

As expected, Dave remained quiet during the display itself. If anything sufficiently urgent cropped up, he would speak. Otherwise he was silent; Dave realised that I needed one hundred percent concentration. Unnecessary talk could have been a hazardous interruption.

At one stage, the leader induced a minor amount of negative 'g'. As I pushed forward on the stick, in spite of the lowered visor in front of my face, a particle of dust from the cockpit floor flew into one of my eyes. I gave a slight gasp, and Dave sensed a small wobble away from our formation position.

"Okay... ?" Dave enquired anxiously. I blinked the affected eye furiously; it began to water. I was longing to remove my left hand from the throttles, and attempt to wipe the eye, but I dared not. My other eye was fortunately unaffected; I was able to maintain our formation position. I continued to blink the affected eye, and eventually, fortuitously, I was aware that the dust particle had been washed away. "Fine now... " I had no opportunity for explanations just then.

At length, as our planned programme drew to a conclusion, the leader called for a formation change: "Echelon starboard... go." The aircraft were just rolling out of a turn; once more I was aware of the grey-coloured sea below us. Following the Wing Commander's instruction, I eased back the throttles, and moved behind the lead aircraft, and the number two aircraft. The number four Phantom also moved as we adjusted the box-shaped formation.

Soon, the four Phantoms were flying abreast, slightly swept back from each other. The aircraft juggled dextrously as they adjusted to the echelon starboard formation pattern. We were lining up for the final 'break' into the circuit. Gradually, we became aware that the leader was increasing speed, and progressively reducing height. At that stage, my concentration was on the number two aircraft. The number two Phantom still watched the leader; number four followed me.

As the four aircraft approached the centre point of the runway, the leader called: "Standby... breaking... NOW." At once, the Wing Commander applied a high angle of bank away from the formation.

The remaining three aircraft maintained station, but after two seconds, the second aircraft also applied bank. "Thousand-and-one... thousand-and-two... NOW." Dave's voice was sharp during the count-down. Immediately, I moved the stick positively to the left. I turned my head hard round in order to maintain visual contact with the other aircraft. My anti-g suit inflated firmly as I applied 4 'g'.

In front, the other two Phantoms were level at one thousand feet, our pre-briefed height in the circuit. I monitored my altimeter, and asked Dave to read out the pre-landing checks. "Undercarriage down... flaps down... check QFE set... " I made regular adjustments to our height as Dave rapidly read out the checks. With the four aircraft strung out in line astern, it was easy for the formation to look ragged.

Soon, I was turning the Phantom towards the runway for the start of the 'finals' leg. I double-checked that the wheels and flaps were lowered, and worked to ensure that I maintained an even spacing from the other two aircraft in front. Our height gradually reduced as we approached the runway, and I began to ease the throttles back to peg the airspeed at the correct touch-down speed. Ahead, I could see the tail parachutes of the other two F4s as the aircraft moved along the runway after landing.

Quite swiftly, the airfield boundary began to career beneath the aircraft; we got progressively lower as I continued to manoeuvre the aircraft positively towards the touch-down point. There was a minor bump as the mainwheels touched down, closely followed by the nose wheel. I delayed slightly, then operated a switch to release the tail parachute. We felt an immediate deceleration; gradually, I applied the wheel brakes to further slow the aircraft.

"Well done," as we approached the end of the runway, at last Dave felt able to make comment; we both began to wind down after the intense concentration. "That seemed to go pretty well."

"Thanks," I replied. "Although I thought the join-up after take-off was a bit fraught at one point."

"We got there in the end," said the tactful Dave. "And I guess it looked quite slick from the ground."

Both our canopies were open by this stage, and soon we began to taxi past the crowds. Some folk clapped as we went by, others waved exuberantly. Dave was in his element again, and I glanced in my mirror from time to time to watch him return the vigorous hand-waves. When we approached our parking spot, I followed the directions of the ground-crew, and operated the nose wheel steering during the manoeuvres. As I looked at the ground-crew member for the final positioning, I suddenly noticed that the blond bombshell was still in her place. Quickly, I looked in my mirror, and briefly caught sight of Dave gazing at her.

On the agreed signal, all four Phantoms closed down their engines simultaneously. Eventually, when all the shut-down checks had been completed, the aircrew were able to leave their cockpits. As I climbed out of the Phantom, I stood for a moment on the aircraft seat while I inserted the ejection seat safety pins. When I had placed the pins securely, I glanced up at the watching crowd. The hand-waves had died down by then, apart from one; I suddenly noticed that my wife was waving vigorously. Lizzie, nine months old in that summer of 1974, was on Sue's shoulders, and watched me as I waved back. Sue told me later that she had not liked to appear earlier, in case I was put off.

Then I looked at Dave, climbing stiffly out of his cockpit. After placing his ejection seat pins, Dave paused for a moment, and gazed at the crowd. He began waving again, and my eyes soon caught sight of the blond bombshell as she shyly returned Dave's special hand-wave.

"I think there's someone there who'd like your signature, Dave," I said. We slowly stepped down from our cockpits.

"She can have my signature right now," retorted Dave, and made as if to wander towards his fan club. The eagle eye of the Wing Commander, however, swiftly discouraged Dave, who decided to join the rest of the pilots and navigators as they walked over to the aircrew bus. The crews chatted with each other as they made their way towards the bus; they appeared rather self-conscious in front of the crowds. I looked back, and waved once more to Sue and Lizzie.

As the aircrew walked onto the bus, they continued to discuss the recent flight with animated enthusiasm. There were several outbursts of laughter. Soon we sat down, and I glanced at my colleagues. I could not help noticing that all the aircrew seemed to look quite pleased with themselves.

"I'm not surprised," said Alan who, together with Vince, had wandered across to listen. "It's not often we get moments of glory, is it?"

"It must have been a fantastic experience, though, being part of a formation like that," said Geoff. We noticed that the firemen were lugging a heavy generator towards the helicopter. We stood up, and walked up the steps of the airstair door into the helicopter, ready to receive the firemen's gear.

Soon, the generator was heaved into the cabin, and the aircrew used straps to secure the bulky equipment onto the floor area by the cargo door. The aircrew then followed as the firemen walked outside once more, ready to collect the next item. As we traipsed down the airstair door's steps, the Station Fire Officer suddenly turned around.

"You've been hearing about the Leuchars Battle of Britain display, have you?" the Fire Officer asked my colleagues.

"It was his moment of glory," commented Geoff, glancing at me.

We stood outside the helicopter just then, by the airstair door. I faced the group, and said: "And now look at me. Carting heavy firemen's gear... in a muddy field... in the middle of nowhere." I paused and rolled my eyes upwards. "Wonderful."

The Station Fire Officer began to grin.

"Don't knock it," he said. "At least it's employment." He hesitated as we continued to stand by the airstair door. A hardy type with a kindly expression, he glanced at the aircrew. His firemen had started to walk across for the next load, and the Fire Officer, keen to get on with the Iona mission, needed to help them.

"Anyway..." he said eventually, as he raised his eyes up to the sky, "moments of glory are best left to Him up there." He sighed, hastily checked his watch and added: "As for us... we must be off to Iona."

CHAPTER 19

Flying the Waves

OCTOBER, 2000

"Give her some money."

There was an embarrassed silence.

"I've already given her stacks of money," I moaned. My wife looked at me with an appealing expression.

"You won't miss a bit more then, will you?" she asked in a soothing tone of voice. I looked at her grouchily, and we fell silent again.

"The wretched girl will drive us all to bankruptcy if we carry on like this," eventually I re-opened the conversation.

"Come, come," said Sue as she gazed dreamily out of our kitchen window. In the garden just outside the window, *Blenheim Orange* apple trees were laden; the appetising fruits faced a race against time as they struggled to ripen ahead of the frosts. Beyond the trees, high banks of *Rosa Gloire de Rosamund* displayed some spectacular rose hip berries. All around there were signs of autumn colours as yellowing leaves vied with their recalcitrant neighbours, still a vivid green. "Don't be so gloomy," continued Sue. "Anyway, she's not a 'wretched girl'. She's our gorgeous daughter."

"That may well be the case," I replied. "But some time or other she's in severe danger of actually – shock horror – having to find a job."

"Well you're only young once," said my wife cheerfully. "And let's face it," she added, "Lizzie needed this trip to Australia to recover from the Nepal experience."

Lizzie had telephoned earlier, her voice bubbling with enthusiasm about her Australian adventures. Eventually, however, we had moved on to more general discussions. The pecuniary requests having been diplomatically conveyed, Lizzie prudently decided to encourage a swift change of subject. "By the way," she asked airily. "Have you heard the news?"

"No. What news?" I replied tersely.

"Oh. You know… "

"What? That we won all those Gold medals in the Sydney Olympic Games?"

"No. I didn't mean that."

"What then? That Arthur Scargill has just become a grandfather?"

"No, no, no. I meant about old Slobber.. Slobby… Slapper… "

"Do you mean Slobodan Milosevic, by any chance?"

"That's the one," said Lizzie. "Your *bête noir* in Kosovo last year."

"I'm surprised you even hear about that sort of thing in your part of the world."

"The bush telegraph is pretty good really, you know," retorted Lizzie.

The recent announcement of the rapid downfall of Slobodan Milosevic of Yugoslavia had stunned the world. Hundreds of thousands of demonstrators had thronged the streets in Belgrade following the refusal of Milosevic to concede electoral defeat. Eventually, however, the initial harsh response of the police and army had faltered. "The police themselves began to change sides," commented Lizzie, not noted for her interest in current affairs; perhaps the world tour was opening her eyes.

"That Russian fellow, Ivy... Ivory… I've-'ad-enough… "

"Ivanov, do you mean?"

"That's the fellow. Well, he finally fixed it, didn't he?"

"He certainly did," I replied convincingly. The Russian Foreign Minister had been assured eventually that Milosevic would step aside in favour of the democratically elected opposition leader, Vojislav Kostinuca. At last there was an end to the Communist dictatorship which had gripped Yugoslavia for so many years, firstly under Tito, then under Milosevic.

A welcome spin-off from these events had been the immediate release of two British policemen, arrested along with two Canadians by the Milosevic regime. The Britons had been working in the border area between Montenegro and Kosovo, as they assisted with the training of local police.

"I know that border area quite well," I told my wife. "When I was there last year, we flew emergency rations to the isolated farms and communities in the mountain regions around there. It was an extraordinary set-up, really. We were lucky not to get arrested ourselves."

"That would be kind of problematic considering you were flying in a helicopter at the time," responded Sue, practical as ever.

"It was incredible, though, thinking back," I briefly shook my head before continuing. "We weren't able to land the helicopters, so we ended up literally kicking boxes of rations out of the aircraft door."

"You performed an important task on your swan song," commented Sue. We fell silent again for a while. I glanced at my wife; her face looked distressed, her eyes had started to brim. She was still unhappy about Lizzie's recent departure to the other side of the world for several months.

"Come on," I said at length. "Let's get some fresh air." Sue nodded slowly as I stood up, and went to get our Wellington boots, quite necessary after recent rains. Soon we set off for the familiar walk to Dameye. As we strolled past the redwoods, we had an instinctive feeling of affinity. The trees had such a familiarity after so many years; the timbers almost appeared to greet their friends.

"I daren't count the number of times we've been here," commented Sue. "Do you remember when we first discovered this walk?" Sue had an amused smile as she said: "The children were so little then; they hadn't a clue when you tried to describe North Sea flying."

"At that stage in my training," I chuckled, "I hadn't much of a clue myself!"

Sue moved her head slowly, in a nostalgic way. "I don't know," she said. "It seems just five minutes ago that she was on my shoulders as a tiny tot, watching your flying display at Leuchars."

We gazed at Bennachie as we walked slowly along the muddied track; gathering rain showers were about to enshroud the hill-tops. Near the redwood trees, we looked at a collection of rough brambles, and noticed that some of the blackberries were ripened. The field beyond the redwoods had been harvested recently; we glanced through the thicket at round bales of hay. Reared pheasants raced between the bales, squabbling noisily. Within the thicket itself, dilapidated stalks of rose-bay willow-herb were packed next to haphazard clumps of mountain ash.

"We always managed to find comfort on this walk after traumatic events," continued Sue after some moments. "During the Falklands crisis, for instance, or after the Piper Alpha disaster; and when you'd had a stressful flight, or been involved with search and rescue missions. A Dameye walk never failed to provide solace."

The autumn chill was accentuated just then as we were affected by an approaching rain shower. Bennachie had become barely visible. We shivered slightly, and pulled on our coats tightly. Stray gusts of wind ahead of the rain shower began to unsettle the surrounding shrubs; ferns swayed in alarm, and tall birch trees seemed to totter ominously above their roots.

"You're right about the time rushing by," I said with a sentimental air. "I can clearly remember that moment after the flying display, when I looked up and saw Lizzie perched on your shoulders."

"And now look at what she's up to," Sue added quietly.

After a pause, I said: "That was an interesting 'good luck' card we gave Lizzie just before she left. Can you remember the words we wrote inside the card?"

"Of course I can," replied Sue. At that juncture, we stooped to avoid some overhanging branches. The spindly offshoots agitated with indignation in the squally conditions. As we brushed by, my wife continued. "The words came from an old Celtic prayer." Sue's voice sounded moved as she went on:

"May the road rise with you,
May the wind be always at your back.
May the sun shine warm upon your face,
And the rain fall soft upon your fields;
And until we meet again
May God keep you in the hollow of His hand."

We approached the crossing of Clyan's Burn just then; Dameye itself was a short distance beyond. We had spotted the swans already, paddling at the far end of the small loch.

At length, I asked Sue: "Do you recall where I first saw those words?" We listened to the wind's discordant wavering as we continued to tramp through muddy puddles. Sue fell quiet as she contemplated my question. Then she glanced at me and asked: "Wasn't it when you were at Iona?"

I nodded slowly as I went through the events in my mind. "I was given a small card by one of the priests there," I said eventually. "He was really kind that day, and offered to show the aircrew around the Abbey while the firemen went through their drills. 'The Abbey burnt down in the 15th century,' said the priest. 'So it's about time we had another fire drill.' Just as we were leaving, the priest handed us the cards. 'A souvenir from Iona', he said. The Celtic prayer was written inside the cards."

The swans had paddled up to us quite quickly. This time we were well prepared to feed them with bread. The surface of the Dameye loch erupted into untidy ripples as the swans splashed about expectantly.

We began to break off bite-sized lumps of bread, and throw them at the water's surface. The swans continued to paddle eagerly in the vicinity. At length, I said: "It was interesting when we got airborne from Iona. Shortly after take-off, we spotted a tourist cruiser heading for Staffa, the small island north of Iona." As the swans pecked at the bread, their graceful necks darted around anxiously. On the far side of the loch, some ducks flapped across the water.

"Wasn't Staffa Island the inspiration for Mendelssohn's *Hebridean Overture*?" asked Sue.

"Yes, that's right," I said. Then I went on: "I think the Master of the tourist cruiser must have been explaining that to his passengers just when he spotted the helicopter."

"Why, what did he do?"

"He spoke to us on the radio. His voice had a note of alarm when he called up on the special marine frequency. He sounded quite concerned; he radioed to ask if there was a problem."

"You presumably put his mind at rest?"

"Oh yes, it was all quite friendly, really. As we departed to take the firemen back to Oban, I called the Master on the radio again to say farewell, and *bon voyage*. 'Good luck sailing the waves', I said to him."

"And what was his reply?" asked Sue as she fed the last crumbs of bread to the swans.

I paused for a few moments while we watched the consumption of the final pieces of bread. Even though their food had disappeared, the swans continued to paddle in the area, their dark eyes watching us hopefully. Sue and I clutched at our coats resolutely as the squall blustered around us, the disorderly air currents interrupting the usual quiet setting of Dameye. The unwelcome hiatus had flustered the pheasants in the field behind us; the harassed birds squawked with outrage as they scampered amongst the bales.

Eventually, I said to Sue: "We saw some of his passengers waving to us as we flew towards the overhead of the vessel. Then we noticed that the Master, too, was observing us from the bridge of his craft. When we overflew the ship, the Master opened his bridge door, and stepped outside to wave farewell. With one hand, the Master held his cap high; in the other hand, he held a radio microphone as he called:

'Goodbye... and good luck flying the waves'."